Women and Families

𝔹

FAMILY, SEXUALITY AND SOCIAL RELATIONS IN PAST TIMES

GENERAL EDITORS:
Peter Laslett and Michael Anderson

Western Sexuality: Practice and Precept in Past and Present Times**
Edited by Philippe Ariès and André Béjin

The Explanation of Ideology: Family Structures and Social Systems**
Emmanuel Todd

The Causes of Progress: Culture, Authority and Change
Emmanuel Todd

An Ordered Society: Gender and Class in Early Modern England**
Susan Dwyer Amussen

Sexuality and Social Control, Scotland, 1660–1780
Rosalind Mitchison and Leah Leneman

A History of Contraception: From Antiquity to the Present**
Angus McLaren

The Children of the Poor: Representations of Childhood since the Seventeenth Century
Hugh Cunningham

A History of Youth**
Michael Mitterauer

Marriage and the English Reformation
Eric Josef Carlson

Medieval Prostitution*
Jacques Rossiaud

Wet Nursing: A History*
Valerie Fildes

Porneia: On Desire and the Body in Antiquity**
Aline Rousselle

Highley, 1550–1880: The Development of a Community*
Gwyneth Nair

The English Noble Household, 1250–1600*
Kate Mertes

Country House Life: Family and Servants, 1815–1914
Jessica Gerard

Women and Families: An Oral History, 1940–1970
Elizabeth Roberts

A Woman's Place: An Oral History of Working-Class Women, 1890–1940**
Elizabeth Roberts

FORTHCOMING

Londoners: The Family and Kinship in Early Modern London
Vivien Brodsky

Pre-Marital Sex in Rural England
Gwyneth Nair and Derek Sayer

* out of print   ** available in paperback

Women and Families

An Oral History,
1940–1970

Elizabeth Roberts

BLACKWELL
Oxford UK & Cambridge USA

The right of Elizabeth Mauchline Roberts to be identified as author of this work has been
asserted in accordance with the Copyright, Designs and Patents Act 1988.

First published 1995

Reprinted 1996

Blackwell Publishers Ltd
108 Cowley Road
Oxford OX4 1JF, UK

Blackwell Publishers Inc.
238 Main Street
Cambridge, Massachusetts 02142, USA

British Library Cataloguing in Publication Data
A CIP catalogue record for this book is available from the British Library

Library of Congress Cataloging in Publication Data
Roberts, Elizabeth.
Women and families: an oral history, 1940-1970/Elizabeth Roberts.
p. cm. - (Family, sexuality, and social relations in past times)
Includes bibliographical references and index.
ISBN 0-631-19612-9 - ISBN 0-631-19613-7 (pbk)
1. Working-class women - England - History - 20th century.
2. Working-class families - England - History - 20th century.
I. Title. II. Series.
HQ1599.E5R624   1995
305.4'0942 - dc20
94-20715 CIP

Typeset in 11 on 13pt Garamond 3
by Pure Tech Corporation, Pondicherry, India.
Printed and bound in Great Britain by T. J. Press Ltd, Padstow, Cornwall

This book is printed on acid-free paper

For my parents, *and* Hugh, David, Eleanor, Kate and Jeremy

Contents

Plates

Tables

Acknowledgements

I owe the deepest debt of gratitude to Dr Lucinda McCray Beier (now of Illinois State University) who worked as my Research Assistant in the years 1987–9. Half the interviews were carried out by her, and I benefited enormously from her perceptions and her keen analysis of the data. She also undertook the task of critically reading the book in draft. Without her the book would not have been written.

I am also very indebted to colleagues who read parts of the manuscript and provided many helpful comments. My thanks to Dr Lynn Abrams of Lancaster University; Dr Joanna Bornat of the Open University; Dr Lynn Hayes, Lancaster University; Dr Kereen Reiger, La Trobe University, Melbourne; Dr Penny Summerfield, Lancaster University, and Melanie Tebbut, Tameside College of Technology. Professor Michael Anderson was particularly helpful in the later stages of preparing the manuscript. Needless to say, the final responsibility for any errors or misinterpretations is mine.

My special thanks go to my husband, Hugh, who did so much to produce the several 'final' versions of the typescript.

Grateful acknowledgement is due to the Economic and Social Research Council who funded the original research project in 1987–9: 'Familial and Social Change and Continuity in Working-class Families, 1940–1970'.

This book could not, of course, have been possible without the co-operation of our respondents. We received abundant help, hospitality and kindness from them. Not all have been quoted, but everyone, through his or her evidence, contributed to our thinking about the project. It seems inadequate simply to offer them our sincerest thanks in return.

1

The Context

It is a truism that individuals contribute to and in turn are affected by the times in which they live; the exact relationship, however, between the general and the particular is almost impossible to unravel. The social historian, in a single study, has to concentrate on the one rather than the other aspect of history. As this is a book based chiefly on oral evidence, it is primarily concerned with the local and the personal. It would be unwise to draw from it too many conclusions about a wider society, but it is hoped that it will raise questions in other historians' minds about the complex and contradictory thirty-year period, 1940–70. It was clearly a time of fundamental social, cultural, demographic and economic changes, all of which profoundly affected the family, and especially the lives of women. As will be seen, these changes meant that in such vital matters as family size, occupation, type of home and possessions, ordinary people had more, but not unlimited, choice than ever before. And yet, as in all historical periods, there were also continuities. It is the interconnections and interrelationships between general changes, individual choices and working-class traditions which made this study both challenging and rewarding.

A *Woman's Place* was first published in 1984. It is an oral history of working-class women in the period 1890–1940.[1] This volume is, to some extent, a sequel to that book, but it also stands on its own account. Its chief focus remains the lives of women but, as the title indicates, there is consideration of families too. Clearly, women themselves, as well as contemporary experts and politicians, perceived their lives as being inextricably interconnected with, and influenced by, both possible future children and those already alive.[2]

The Oral Evidence

This book is one result of a study of working-class family and social life in the period 1940–70.[3] It is largely based on interviews carried out with ninety-eight men and women in the years 1988–90. Summaries of the respondents appear in tables 1.1 and 1.2. The appendix 'About the Respondents' contains biographical information about those respondents who are directly quoted in the text. Much has been written about the use of oral

Table 1.1 Summary of respondents

| Date of birth | Town to which their evidence relates | | |
	Barrow	Lancaster	Preston
1910–19	2 men	1 man	nil
	2 women	1 woman	1 woman
1920–9	5 men	6 men	4 men
	4 women	5 women	4 women
1930–9	6 men	5 men	4 men
	6 women	6 women	6 women
1940–9	4 men	4 men	6 men
	4 women	7 women	4 women
1950–9	nil	nil	1 woman
Totals	17 men	16 men	14 men
	16 women	19 women	16 women

Overall total: 47 men and 51 women = 98 respondents

Table 1.2 Occupations of respondents' fathers, male respondents and husbands of respondents

A *Respondents' fathers' occupations*[a]

Unskilled	Skilled	Self-employ.	Profes-sional[b]	Clerical/finance	Commercial	Mgmt
57	20	10	2	3	4	1

B *Male respondents' and respondents' husbands' occupations in 1970*[c]

Unskilled	Skilled	Self-employ.	Profes-sional	Clerical/finance	Commercial	Mgmt
21	27	2	9	3	4	1

Notes
[a] One respondent was illegitimate and did not know her father's occupation.
[b] Professional includes chemists, police, nurses (male), teachers.
[c] Clearly, not all women respondents were married and not all men had finished their education.

evidence.[4] It is not intended to discuss here its potential or its limitations. It is perhaps permissible to observe that all history contains bias, there are omissions, distortions and ambiguities in all primary historical sources, whether they be written or oral. There is also bias in the historian, because he or she has to select material and construct arguments, processes which are inevitably affected by her own experiences and preconceptions as well as by conscious choice.

The project began with the researchers adopting no particular theoretical standpoint but with assumptions inherited from the previous study which was recorded in *A Woman's Place*. These included an expectation of finding women in a central and important position in the home and family, controlling the family budget, being responsible for the children and their upbringing and contributing to the financial well-being of the family by their household magagement skills and possibly also through their own wages. It was also anticipated that the extended family and neighbourhood would offer practical help and social support. As will be seen, the empirical evidence for the period 1940–70 did not always accord with these assumptions.

Location of the Survey

The study was carried out in the three northern towns of Barrow-in-Furness, Lancaster and Preston. Barrow was a town of heavy engineering, shipbuilding and iron and steel-making. In the post-war period there were attempts to introduce newer lighter industries; these never played a dominant role in the town's economy but they were successful during this period. Lancaster continued to have a very mixed economy with linoleum and oil-cloth works, some cotton and artificial fibre mills, a furniture and fine joinery works and a great variety of small shops and businesses. The nature of its economy began to change at the end of the 1950s with the transference of the major part of its linoleum works and workers to Kirkcaldy in Scotland and the closure of the furniture factory. There had always been a large service sector in the town with several large hospitals. This sector was greatly enhanced in the early 1960s with the arrival of a College of Education and a University. Preston enjoyed a brief boom in the cotton trade in the post-war period but the industry was entering a time of terminal decline; indeed, this trend had been irreversible since at least the 1920s.[5] Engineering played a more and more important part in the town's economy and there were various new light industries too. The structure of male employment in the three towns is shown in tables 1.3, 1.4 and 1.5. Details of women's employment are given in chapter 7 (tables 7.2–7.5).

Table 1.3 Main male occupations in 1931 (%)

	Barrow	Lancaster	Preston
Textile workers	X[a]	4	10
Metal workers	33	6	11
Unskilled/labourers	17	24	9
Transport	9	9	13
Commercial/financial	7	11	12
Clerks/draughtsmen	6	5	5
Woodworkers	5	5	4
Workers in chemicals	X	3	X
Builders/bricklayers	3	5	5
Professionals	X	4	2
Personal service	X	X	3

Note: [a] X indicates less than 2%.
Source: 1931 Census.

Table 1.4 Main male occupations in 1951 (%)

	Barrow	Lancaster	Preston
Textile workers	X[a]	5	4
Metal workers/engineering	31	12	20
Unskilled	14	13	12
Transport	9	9	12
Building/contracting	7	7	6
Commercial/financial	7	8	8
Professional/technical	5	6	4
Clerks/typists	5	5	6
Woodworkers	4	4	3
Personal service	2	3	3
Coal/gas/chemicals	X	6	X

Note: [a] X indicates less than 2%.
Source: 1951 Census.

Before the study began we were aware that the post-war period was a time when British sociologists were undertaking major contemporary studies of families and communities. A formidable list of experts produced books

Table 1.5 Main male occupations in 1971 (%)

	Barrow	Lancaster	Preston
Textile workers	X[a]	n/a	3
Engineering/allied trades	27	n/a	18
Labourers	11	n/a	12
Transport	7	n/a	10
Professional/technical	7	n/a	4
Clerical workers	7	n/a	6
Sales workers	6	n/a	7
Service/sport/recreation	4	n/a	5
Drivers of cranes	4	n/a	X
Woodworkers	4	n/a	2
Electrical workers	3	n/a	3
Building and contracting	3	n/a	3
Ferrous/foundries/gas	3	n/a	X
Warehousing	X	n/a	4

Notes
[a] X indicates less than 2%.
n/a = not available.
Source: 1971 Census.

which have been extensively quoted by other historians. This study was not undertaken either to prove or disprove the validity of any of that work. It has not been possible to analyse how this area of North Lancashire compares and contrasts with others studied in the 1950s and 1960s. Exact comparisons would in any case be difficult because, in our interviews, we posed a different set of questions, which arose out of differing basic assumptions and areas of interest. Gorer, for instance, in his national survey of English character,[6] was particularly interested in exploring what had happened to English aggression, and worked from the assumption that English people are essentially shy and reserved. He was particularly interested in their moods and sociability. Our investigations had a different perspective.

When comparing our findings with those of other investigations some fascinating similarities and differences emerged and these are noted wherever they occur; further historical work is required before it would be possible to be conclusive about why such variations exist. There are, for instance, somewhat stereotypical views about differences between north and south, and more especially between London and the north, but we found some striking similarities between London working-class life and that in this region. The close relationship between mothers and adult daughters in the East End of London, as described by Young and Wilmott,[7] and the attitudes and concerns of working mothers in Bermondsey, as recorded by Jephcott, Seear and Smith,[8] have clear parallels in this area.

On the other hand, relationships between husbands and wives, as described by Young and Wilmott in *The Symmetrical Family*[9] do not accord with evidence from our respondents, and Firth's account of relationships within extended families in *Families and their Relatives*[10] differs from our observations. Such similarities and differences, where they occur, are noted but not explained, for this study is not intended to be a comparative one nor does it attempt to synthesize the work of others. Indeed, if any justice was to be done to the oral evidence, there would not be space in the book for such an undertaking.

There have already been some very valuable surveys done: Josephine Klein's *Samples from English Culture* is a classic comparative analysis of much of the work done in the 1950s and early 1960s.[11] More recently, Elizabeth Wilson has analysed post-war work from a feminist view-point.[12] More specifically, Finch and Summerfield have made a comparative analysis of writings about companionate marriage.[13]

The Working Class

There are difficulties in defining the term 'working-class' in the post-war era. We decided to categorize respondents as working-class if they fulfilled one or more of the following criteria for the period 1940–70:

1 they lived in a working-class area (i.e., small terraced or council housing);
2 they or their fathers or husbands were skilled, semi-skilled or unskilled workers belonging to social classes III, IV and V according to the Registrar General's classification[14] and were therefore paid a weekly wage rather than a monthly salary. Women were categorized according to their husband's and/or father's classification.[15]
3 their parent or parents had been interviewed in an earlier study and had been working-class, whether judged by income, occupation or housing.[16]

It can be argued that it is not sufficient to discuss class simply in concrete terms. Attitudes are also important and the way in which respondents defined themselves in class terms was examined. Respondents' views on class were very varied and difficult to analyse. Goldthorpe et al., in their book on the affluent worker, concluded that improved living standards did not mean that working-class people either followed or aspired to a middle-class life-style or middle-class norms.[17] Our study left us neither with this conclusion nor indeed any other about class attitudes. Indeed, for justice to be done to this complex issue a separate volume would be required. All that can be usefully said here is that some respondents regarded themselves as middle-class, some were very class-conscious, some displayed resentment of those they perceived as middle-class, some asserted that they were totally unaware of class differences, others claimed to be 'as good as anyone else'. Some who, to an observer, could best be described as working class, claimed middle-class childhoods, presumably equating middle-class with 'respectable'; some thought of class simply in terms of money; some, despite a substantial improvement in their standard of living, said they could never describe themselves as anything but working-class, either because they could not or did not wish to escape their origins. Gorer emphasized the importance of parental status, arguing that this influenced adults' responses to questioning about the class to which they considered they belonged.[18] It should be stressed that respondents were aware that they were taking part in a survey of working-class life and therefore it has to be assumed that they considered themselves to be suitable participants.

The great majority of respondents were categorized by us as 'respectable', to differentiate them from the very small group of 'roughs' who can be characterized by violence, whether to people or to property, frequent drunkenness and petty criminality. However, within the large group of the 'respectable' several different sub-sets can be identified with different life-styles and aspirations. One group can be described as ambitious, and can be further subdivided between those who wished to move up the social ladder and become middle-class, and those who wished to improve their financial standing and social status but remain as members of the working class. In families it is not easy to discern whether these ambitions originated with the wife, the husband, or were the result of shared discussion. No clear pattern emerged, although women on the whole were possibly more interested in improving their housing and ensuring that their children 'did well', while men were more concerned with improving their earnings and status in the world of paid work.

Poverty and Prosperity

In 1951 Seebohm Rowntree, in *Poverty and the Welfare State*, suggested that a poverty line could be drawn at £5 for a family of two parents and three children, but this figure excluded rent.[19] Rowntree estimated that only 1.6 per cent of the total population earned less that £5 per week in 1950. If our survey reflected that of Rowntree's we should have among our 98 respondents only one or two who lived in this degree of poverty in the immediate post-war period, but this was not the case; it is possible to identify eleven families who fell below the poverty line in the late 1940s and early 1950s. However, there also appeared to be an undue representation of the more prosperous elements of the working class (as for example in the proportion of home owners).

There was a group of migrants among our respondents. During this period some migrated from their home town as adults and did not return.[20] In this group were three women, one of whom migrated to further her own career; the other two moved because of their husbands' work. Another group, (excluding those doing military or merchant navy service), had spent a substantial period (more than two years) away from home and then returned.[21]

An 'ambitious' group actively worked for change in their lives. Another group simply received all the benefits which resulted from improving circumstances, without particularly seeking them. In this latter group were respondents who prospered through an inheritance, sometimes quite unexpected, and women who found themselves better off than they had anticipated because their husbands 'did well'. Everyone benefited to some degree from the effects of various governmental policies. Some were provided with a council house, or an income when they were ill or unemployed, or free medical treatment, or free secondary and higher education.

Virtually all the respondents enjoyed greater material prosperity than had their parents, although some experienced temporary vicissitudes, most usually resulting from death or divorce of parents, or the breakdown of the respondent's own marriage. Only one man claimed to be permanently worse off than his parents had been, his relative poverty resulting from the collapse of a previously prosperous family firm.[22]

Some respondents were better off in real terms than their parents, who had been among those interviewed as part of the earlier study.[23] However, they remained relatively poor, although the material standing of their families continued to improve throughout the period. The causes of their poverty were not difficult to discern; they were unskilled and tended to earn low wages. Some had larger families than their incomes could easily support. Virtually none of the respondents were poor because of unemployment or prolonged sickness.

Changing Standards of Living

The improvements in living standards for the great majority of the respondents during the period was striking, and simply reflected that enjoyed by a wider population. In the post-war years the population as a whole saw a greater rise in their standards of living than in any previous period. 'The English people were . . . able to achieve a higher living standard, better housing and diet, more leisure and more material possessions than they had enjoyed before.'[24] Average real earnings in 1950 were only 65 per cent

Table 1.6 Average real weekly earnings
Index 1970 = 100

Year	Earnings
1950	65.3
1955	73.4
1960	83.8
1965	94.6
1970	100

Source: Pollard, *The Development of the English Economy, 1914–80*, p. 322.

of those in 1970 (table 1.6).[25] Not only were real wages rising, but rates of unemployment were low throughout the period. They ranged from just over 1 per cent in 1951 to just under 4 per cent in 1971.[26] Locally the rates were also low, as any sampling of the Medical Officer of Health returns shows. In 1960 the Barrow Medical Officer complained that the town had a higher rate of unemployment than the rest of the country, quoting a rate for January of 3.7 per cent compared to 2.1 per cent for the national average. The comparable figure for July had been: Barrow 2.5 per cent, England and Wales 1.3 per cent. Also in 1960, the Preston Medical Officer reported that, during the year, unemployment had not risen above 1.6 per cent and the year's average was 1.2 per cent.[27]

There was also the security, both financial and psychological, offered by the welfare state, established by the Labour government in the period 1945–50. At the very end of the period, Bruce was still able to identify the five objectives of the welfare state being, first, to guarantee to all a decent standard of living; secondly, to protect everyone against the vicissitudes of life (illness, unemployment etc); thirdly, to help family life thrive and develop; fourthly, to treat health and education as public services; and fifthly, to develop public establishments and amenities, such as housing, for the betterment of personal lives.[28] It should be noted that until the mid-1970s social policies continued to assume the dependence of married women on men.[29] Respondents, depending on their own particular circumstances and aspirations, appreciated three particular aspects of the welfare state: the Health Service, the provision of public housing, and free secondary education. Of particular value to respondents was the National Health Service (1948). Previously many women and children had not enjoyed the benefits of health insurance. The provision of health care and preventative medicine continued to improve. An important indicator of the general improvement in living standards is the steady decline in infant mortality

Table 1.7 Infant mortality rates: five-year averages

Period	England and Wales	Barrow	Lancaster	Preston
1896–1900	156	162	172	235
1940–4	51.6	58.0	55.4	68.6
1945–9	39.2	52.3	38.6	51.6
1950–4	27.8	33.0	41.2	31.8
1955–9	23.3	24.1	25.7	31.4
1960–4	21.1	20.4	25.9	29.4
1965–9	18.5	17.5	20.8	25.0

Source: Medical Officers of Health Annual Returns for Barrow, Lancaster and Preston.

rates, as shown in table 1.7. Preston, as in the earlier studies, had generally higher, though declining, rates than the other two towns, an indication of its relative poverty. It is particularly revealing to compare these rates with those for the beginning of the century. Another tangible indicator of rising living standards was the greatly improved quality of housing enjoyed by almost all the respondents and which is examined in the next chapter.

Rising living standards are also illustrated rather more intangibly but importantly in both the tone and the content of the interviews. One of the overriding concerns of those interviewed in the earlier studies was the way in which their families had dealt with poverty. Many shared in a feeling of great achievement because they and their families had survived considerable deprivations and difficulties. Some of the older respondents in the present study also remembered times of great hardship in their pre-war childhoods and had experienced the epic struggles of their parents against poverty caused by low wages and unemployment.

By 1950, in spite of post-war austerity, the heroic age, in which women as household managers and men as earners had waged war against poverty, was largely past. This struggle had had many casualties, but those who survived often had very strong characters forged in the struggle they had endured. Those who grew up after the war lived in gentler and much more optimistic times. Compared to the respondents in the previous studies from earlier decades, there were in this group fewer rugged individuals with their amazing tales of survival.

As real wages rose so, too, did expectations about the ownership of possessions and the levels of amenities and comfort which were required to sustain an acceptable life-style. The age of consumerism was rapidly arriving. Indeed, it seemed that standards of living and expectations continued to chase each other up a never-ending spiral. Concepts of modernization changed rapidly and can be illustrated in respondents' attitudes to houses. One respondent, born in the late 1940s, referred to her childhood home as unmodernized although it had electricity and a bathroom, the hallmarks of modernity for a previous generation. Another, the same age, recounted her feelings of shame about her home because it did not have a fitted kitchen. She was very reluctant to ask her school-friends home on this account.

As the provision of the basic needs of food, clothing and shelter required a continually declining proportion of their income, families had more choice in how their money should be spent. The ability to buy things and the increasing pressure, from both friends and the advertising industry, to acquire more possessions, tended slowly to eradicate both the need and the desire to make things at home. Bought clothes might replace those created by the home dressmaker; easy-to-cook food sometimes replaced the old dishes which needed time, patience and skill to prepare. There was a loss of creativity in some families, which was not necessarily compensated for in their paid work but which was increasingly sought and found in the wave of DIY. This occupation was particularly attractive to men; in some families, for the first time, men were able to be more creative about the house than women.

There were not only rising expectations about possessions and housing, better services were also expected. Here, as in so much of the evidence, there are ambiguities. Some believed that 'better' services were obtained if one paid for them. Increasingly people paid for services which, earlier in the century, had been provided free by relatives and neighbours. For example, although there were still many older women who knew how to lay out the dead, their services were called upon less and less frequently. It would appear that people preferred to pay the undertaker to replace the neighbourhood layer-out. There was a strong feeling that professional services were better than those provided by well-meaning amateurs. Professional help was particularly sought by mothers of babies and small children. Increasingly, the advice of doctors and health visitors was preferred to that of older women in the family or neighbourhood. No one, however, was prepared to pay for these services: they were seen as part of the provision of the Health Service.

Some of the growing respect for 'experts' must have arisen out of the increasing national emphasis, placed by both government and the media, on the importance of education. The 1944 Education Act introduced free secondary education for all children. There were, of course, grammar schools in all three towns before that date. The national pattern for these schools was for the majority of pupils to be fee-paying while the minority were admitted with free scholarship places. It is only fair to record that from the end of the First World War the education authorities in Barrow had admitted the majority of children to the grammar schools on a scholarship basis. By 1935 in both the boys' and the girls' schools, only thirty-six boys and twenty-eight girls were paying fees. (Each school admitted about ninety pupils each year).[30] In the first decades of the century in Barrow, and until the end of the Second World War in the other towns, many parents had not been able to send their academically qualified children to grammar school because they were too poor to pay the fees. Indeed, in all three towns, some parents were deterred from sending their children to grammar school even if they had a scholarship, either because they could not afford the cost of books and uniform, or because they needed their children to leave as soon as possible because their wages were urgently needed to boost the family income. In the post-war world, with increasing prosperity, parents could afford to send their children to grammar school and possibly on to higher education (for which mandatory local authority grants for maintenance were introduced in 1963 in place of the discretionary grants which had been previously available). It should be stressed that although parents may have been able to afford for their children to go to grammar schools and on to higher education, not all of them decided to do so. Some young people chose this course for themselves, others continued to resent their lost educational opportunities. It should also be remembered that some families were still poor and needed their children's wages.[31]

The increased range of choices open to respondents, as will be seen throughout the book, clearly had an effect on relationships within the extended family and the neighbourhood and indeed on the nuclear family itself.

Cultural Values

The cultural and ethical climate during this period was also changing.[32] Any detailed analysis of such a complex topic is beyond the scope of this book, but working-class life is difficult to understand without a passing reference to some of the ideas which were gaining currency during this time. It is not possible to say why individuals adopt some new ideas and reject others; nor can the route which ideas take, from philosophers, experts and other producers of 'new' concepts to ordinary people, be precisely traced.

It is too simplistic to attribute such changes to the media,[33] although the British population was undoubtedly exposed to more media coverage than ever before, from the press, radio and increasingly television. In 1951 only one household in fifteen had a television, by 1975 nine out of ten households had one. In 1969 it was estimated that a quarter of all spare time was spent watching television.[34]

It is not possible to ascribe changes to the consequences of legislation. It is difficult to establish the precise nature of the relationship between private behaviour and public laws. Did legislation come about as the result of changes in behaviour; did changes in the law encourage people to behave differently; or was changing legislation simply registering changing social mores?

The late 1960s saw the introduction of legislation which has sometimes been described as 'permissive'; the Abortion Act of 1967 legalized abortions within certain limits, the 1969 Divorce Reform Act broadened the grounds for divorce to 'irretrievable breakdown'. We found little evidence to suggest that these measures had a direct impact on our respondents during this period, but these legislative changes can be seen to represent a changing social climate within which the respondents were living; it may be said that there was a move towards decreased state regulation of personal lives.

It is not at all clear if people consciously considered new ways of thinking and behaving; it would seem that much was simply absorbed and assumed. What is clear is the erosion which was taking place of some of the 'traditional' mores which had governed so many aspects of working-class life in previous generations. There had always been some who questioned these standards, and it is reasonable to suppose that their numbers were increased because of some individuals' experiences in the Second World War.[35] After the war the pace of change increased; people thought for themselves more.[36] Respondents in the earlier studies and older people in the present study frequently explained many of their actions by saying, 'It was the thing to do.' Younger people are much more likely to talk of 'doing their own thing'. Respondents continued to be aware, of course, of what other people thought and how they behaved.

Fashion was increasingly important and influential, not only through the media but also via friends, the peer group and local shops. It can be argued that fashion was undermining class differences and creating a more homogeneous society; it was certainly more difficult to assess people's status and occupation by the way they dressed. Set against this trend, however, was the tendency of individuals to decide for themselves whether or not to reject certain norms and to retain others. Weeks wrote of a move 'towards the centrality of individual consent, in place of the imperatives of public morality.'[37] Consequently, it is as difficult to speak of 'working-class morality' as it is to define precisely what the respondents understood by the term 'working class'. These definitions were rather more straightforward in the earlier studies.

Individualism

There were changing ideas about the importance of individual rights. Whether one accepts Durkheim's suggestion that individualism resulted from the division of labour in modern industries, or prefers to trace the development of the doctrine of individual rights in philosophy and law, it is clear that there was an increasingly popular view that the aim of society should be the protection and promotion of the integrity, independence and rights of the individual. It is perhaps obvious to state that it was essential for working-class people to have an adequate standard of living before they could adopt views on the importance of the individual. When times were hard, individualism was less important than collective solidarity, whether in the trade union, the workplace or the neighbourhood. All these groups could help the individual in times of adversity. In 1963 Goldthorpe and Lockwood wrote of the weakening of communal attachments and collective action in the workplace, and contrasted this with 'the greater scope and encouragement for a more individualistic outlook as far as expenditure, use of leisure time and general levels of aspiration are concerned'.[38] Many contemporary observers noted and welcomed the growth of individualism, seeing it as a break with the stifling uniformity of the traditional working-class community. Raymond Williams did not share this enthusiasm, arguing that the move towards individualism threatened working-class solidarity, which he felt was an important virtue of that group when at its best.[39]

Closely associated with this tendency to regard individual rights as paramount, was the increasing privatization of the nuclear family.[40] Klein called this process 'individuation' and defined it thus: 'the elementary family separated off, differentiated out as a distinct and to some extent autonomous social group'.[41] The authors of a study of the 'affluent worker' described privatization as 'a process that is manifested in a pattern of social life which is centred on and indeed largely restricted to the home and the conjugal family'.[42] Links with people and institutions outside the family became weaker. Social activities took place more and more within the home; the rapid replacement of cinema-going with television-watching from the late 1950s onwards is a classic example of this trend. When families went out they increasingly did so in the privacy of the family car. In 1945 there were 1,500,000 cars in Britain: one car to every thirty-two people. By 1970 there were 11,500,000 cars: one to every 4.7 people.[43]

Another increasingly common attitude, which was again connected to the one which stressed the importance of individual rights, was that which questioned, and in some cases rejected, authority, whether in the person of a policeman, a clergyman, a teacher or a foreman.

As ideas about individualism and the privacy of the family spread, and as people became more absorbed in their homes and possessions, it is possible to see a declining interest in trade union affairs, politics and religion, especially when these activities demanded some community involvement. Most of the respondents in wage-earning work belonged to a union, but it was mostly a matter of paying their dues and being as little involved as possible in the running of the union; strikes were not a major part of their working lives. Here the respondents would appear to mirror the national experience. In the period 1971–3, 95 per cent of all British workplaces had no stoppages at all, and in the preceding twenty years most strikes had occurred in the mining, metal and car industries.[44] Politics did not arouse the same passion as in the earlier studies. Although respondents continued to vote, this for very many was their only involvement in the political world; the often passionate involvement of earlier generations had gone.

Fewer respondents went to church as the period progressed. Many who had been regular church-goers in the 1950s no longer went in 1970. The Churches continued to play a role in the rites of passage in respondents' lives. Babies were christened, few marriages took place outside a church building, and there was a religious service to mark the ending of a life. The majority of children continued to attend Sunday school. However, religious considerations played a declining role in everyday life; few seemed to have experienced a crisis of faith or a dispute with the Church – both situations which had been in evidence earlier in the century. Instead, respondents talk about being too busy creating a home to go to church, having other things to do. For many the Churches appear to have become an irrelevance; there was a drift to indifference.

Continuing Traditions

There were, of course, some working-class people who, throughout this period, maintained many of the old standards. On the positive side these were concerned with concepts of sociability and mutual help and support. While welcoming the improvements in living standards, they rejected changes in the moral codes with which they had grown up. Expressed rather more negatively, they demanded a conformity to a commonly held set of rules about behaviour, deviance from which was punished – usually by gossip. Klein described them as suffering from 'cognitive poverty'.[45] Those belonging to this group were more likely to be from poorer, close-knit areas, where changes were discouraged and minor deviance ridiculed. Klein suggested that such communities shared certain characteristics: the members followed similar occupations; there was little migration in or out of the area; there were local inter-marriages; there were opportunities for friends and relatives to help one another; there was little demand for physical mobility and little opportunity for social mobility.[46] What is implied in Klein's analysis, and what should be emphasized, is that the 'traditional' working-class person needed the support of a close-knit working-class environment if he or she was to maintain the 'traditional' norms intact. It is difficult to imagine an individual maintaining these standards in isolation, depending as they did on both the support and the sanctions of the community.

It is dangerous, however, to draw too many conclusions from these various observations. It is not possible to make a clear distinction between those Klein described as 'traditional' and those who could be called 'modern'. Some characteristics were shared by both modern and traditional groups. Nor should the apparent confusion and conflicts about standards of behaviour lead one to assume that people were living in a state of 'anomie' – a term first used by the French sociologist, Émile Durkheim.[47] He argued that 'any state where there are unclear, conflicting or unintegrated norms in which the individual had no morally significant relations with others, or in which there were no limits set to the attainment of pleasure, was a state of anomie.' In 1970 it may have been possible to describe some people as approaching this state but only one respondent might be said to be experiencing it.[48] Nor would it be wise to see social life in this particular geographical area as undergoing a cataclysmic change in the previous decade, the 'swinging sixties' so beloved by the popular press. Social change was much more gradual, although there are indications in some of the oral evidence and in statistical information, such as illegitimacy rates, that the speed of change was quickening at the end of the 1960s.

War and National Service

The period 1940–70 was chosen to follow on from our previous study and also because a thirty-year period seemed to be a sensible span to investigate. Although the period includes the Second World War there is no separate section dealing with it. Clearly, the war profoundly affected the politics of the post-war period, and the subsequent introduction of the welfare state and the National Health Service were of great importance to the respondents.[49] The war itself, however, did not figure prominently in the oral evidence and the reasons for this are not difficult to find. In 1940 only a small minority of our respondents were young adults and therefore likely to be involved in some form of war service. An even smaller group were married women with small children at the time, and they did remember the problems of feeding and clothing their families, given the strict rationing then in force. Some lives were changed by the war: a few of the children who were evacuated had life-changing experiences, some did not. Two men who went away to war changed their work on their return to civilian life and prospered in a way that would not have been possible had they continued in their pre-war jobs.[50] These two men were heavily outnumbered by those who returned to their previous occupations and by those in reserved occupations who never left them. The one woman who was a munitions worker enjoyed the experience but never expected to continue with it after the war. She certainly showed no signs of adopting a 'modern' attitude to women's work, in that she went back to a job in a shop in 1945 and never returned to work after the birth of her child in the 1950s.[51] It would therefore be unwise to generalize about the effects of the war on the lives of our respondents given such sparse and contradictory evidence.

After the war national military service was retained until the end of the 1950s, removing about 750,000 young men from the labour market. This undoubtedly helped create a demand for female labour. Individual respondents mostly enjoyed their two years in the services but, as will be seen in chapter 3, it did not permanently disturb the family life of the great majority of young men who returned home to their parents on completion of their national service.

Continuity and Change

The three decades between 1940 and 1970 were clearly times of both continuity and change. However much attitudes altered, changes in an institution as fundamental as the family were slow-moving. From the evidence in this study it is not possible to agree with the view that there was no one kind of family.[52] It is significant that those who supported this argument were writing in the early 1980s, when undoubtedly the situation was changing at a rapid pace. Our evidence shows that it was still possible to define a typical family unit in 1970. It continued to be one which lived close to relatives, one where adult children still lived at home until marriage[53] and one where the husband was still the chief, and sometimes the only, wage-earner, and where considerable differences in the roles of men and women still remained.

There were, however, changes taking place in the lives of women which ultimately would affect family patterns, although it was certainly not a time when women marched inexorably towards full emancipation. The marked decline in the birth rate, apparent in the inter-war period, was not maintained (see table 1.8). This did not mean that women were once again having large families, as had their grandmothers. The most usual size of family among the respondents was two or three children. As will be seen, women were exercising some choice over how they should plan their lives. They did not, as many of their grandmothers had done, spend a period of

Table 1.8 Legitimate fertility rates in Census years
1901–71

| | Live births per 1,000 married women aged 15–45 | | |
Year	Barrow	Lancaster	Preston
1901	258.0	n/a	241.8
1911	203.9	n/a	182.2
1921	173.6	n/a	166.4
1931	116.5	n/a	119.0
1951	105.4	98.3	118.0
1961	127.5	138.8	145.2
1971	125.7	119.6	165.8

Note: n/a = not available.
Source: Census data.

up to twenty years bearing children. Anderson calculates that, for those women who married after the Second World War, the average age at which they ceased childbearing was twenty-eight.[54] But at the very time that women were being released from one area of caring that had been tradition-ally theirs, they were faced with growing demands for their attention elsewhere in the family. The post-war period saw a considerable increase in the proportion of old people in the community (see table 1.9). Almost all families were faced with additional responsibilities towards their older members. This involved major implications for choices that women might have to make in their lives.

Women were also subjected to many and conflicting demands and pres-sures from the state and the wider society, as well as from within the family. By the mid-twentieth century domestic ideology, which had had such a

Table 1.9 Population aged 65 and over (%)

Year	Barrow	Lancaster	Preston
1891	1.9	4.1	3.4
1901	2.4	3.8	3.5
1911	3.7	4.8	4.1
1921	4.4	6.4	5.0
1931	6.1	7.8	6.4
1951	10.7	11.8	10.2
1961	12.2	13.7	11.8
1971	13.6	15.2	14.6

Source: Census data.

profound effect on the familial and social lives of the middle classes since the beginning of the nineteenth century, had been accepted by many working-class people. Indeed, the oral evidence from both the pre-war and the post-war periods shows support for the ideal, even in families where financial necessity forced women to work outside the home. This ideal prescribed that a woman's place was to be in the home, caring for her husband, children and house. In the post-war world greater prosperity and smaller families made it increasingly possible and pleasant for families to adjust their behaviour to fit the ideology. Traditional notions, which equated cleanliness with respectability, united with ideas about the status a family could attain by keeping the woman of the house within its four walls. These women and their families took pride in the daily dusting and cleaning and the preparation of meals which appeared at exactly the same time each day. It is one of the ironies of history that this domestic ideology reached full flowering among the working class just at the time when many people were being influenced by the rival and conflicting ideology of the importance of married women being employed. This conflict of ideologies resulted in contradictory views about the role of women in society. Compared with the earlier study, fewer women expressed a certainty that what they were doing at any point in their lives was the right thing. 'Women today can no longer be certain what is expected of them.'[55]

During the war women had been urged to do men's work, but they were also expected to be efficient household managers. In the immediate post-war period women were told to return to the home and to relinquish their jobs to men. This was almost immediately followed by a renewed demand for their efforts owing to the labour shortages of the late 1940s. The requirements of the labour market established a set of norms which were in direct contrast to those resulting from domestic ideology. Was a woman's place to be in the home or in the workplace, or in both? What was to be her status as a wife, a mother and a worker? Questions about the role of women had inevitable implications for the home and the family, the theatre in which women had held centre-stage throughout history.

The period covered by this study ended in 1970. In the course of the interviews it became very clear that some of the major changes affecting the lives of women have occurred since that date. With reference to the position of British women since 1945 Jane Lewis wrote:

> Three social trends have been of particular importance: first, the increase in
> the percentage of married women in paid employment; second, the dramatic

increase in the divorce rate especially during the 1970s and 80s; and third, what has been called 'the amazing rise of illegitimacy' which changed in the 1960s and increased again rapidly from the late 1970s.[56]

During this period, and in this area of the country only one of these changes appears to have had a significant impact on the lives of our respondents: the dramatic increase in the number of women in paid work. This is a continuing theme of this study.

This book is about attitudes, behaviour and aspects of everyday life as recalled by witnesses living through a fascinating historical period. In the earlier study it was possible, because of the unanimity of so much of the oral evidence, to write with much greater certainty about general patterns of behaviour and of the elements of predictability in everyday working-class life. In the post-war world ever-expanding choices rendered such certainties and generalities dangerous. When reviewing the evidence the words which come to mind are 'complexity', 'paradox', 'ambiguity' and 'uncertainty'. Referring to these post-war years one respondent once asked, 'What went wrong?' There can be no easy answer to such a question and it could be argued that the question itself may have been inappropriate. Respondents were not in agreement about 'what went wrong' between 1940 and 1970, either in their own lives or for the wider society. By 1970 many of them had acquired one or more of the following: a house they owned, a comfortable income, and secondary and possibly higher education for their children. Previously these had been regarded as symbols of middle-class status and success. The fact that there could be doubts about whether these were good times or bad is one small illustration of the ambiguity of progress.

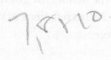

2

Homes and Houses

'Home Sweet Home', 'There's No Place Like Home', 'Home is Where the Heart Is'. These aphorisms could still be found adorning the walls of some homes in the period 1940–70. The image of home is a powerful one, the ideal is cherished but the reality does not accord with the image; nor is the image constant; it changes over time and from individual to individual. Home remained, however, the stage on which the lives of families, and more particularly those of women and children, were played out during this period.

Many families began, and indeed continued through the period to live, in very poor houses; but a striking feature of the oral evidence is the great improvement which took place in housing conditions by 1970. There were changes in the pattern of housing tenure with a marked decline in the number of tenants in private accommodation. Housework routines changed with the increasing use of domestic appliances. Married women at home received less help with the housework from their children and no more help from their husbands than had been the case in previous generations. Paradoxically, some aspects of life and activities in the home continued to be gender-based, whilst on the other hand there was an increase in the time families spent together, either in the family living room or engaged in joint activities.

Change and Continuity in Housing Conditions

Home was more than a building, and yet it is difficult to have a home without a roof and four walls to contain it. Moreover, the size and style of the house within which the home was sited profoundly affected the nature and quality of home life. The thirty-year period 1940–70 saw a transformation in working-class housing. Many tenants became owners, and even more moved into houses which were larger and had more amenities than those previously occupied. Changes had, however, begun earlier. In the inter-war period, and especially in the 1930s, tenants in very poor housing had been rehoused by councils and the more prosperous had bought the typical 1930s 'semi'. which appeared on estates in all three towns. An intermediate group of people had bought small, terraced houses.

Until 1937 Mr Lodge lived in a small house off Ribbleton Lane in Preston, which was typical of so many working-class houses in the late nineteenth and early twentieth centuries:

> It was a two-up and a two-down with a toilet in the backyard. There was no bathroom, one fireplace, no electricity, there was gas lighting downstairs in the front room, there was no gas cooker, there was a gas jet which was coupled by a flexible pipe to a gas ring in the living room for making an early morning cup of tea. The fire range was the main cooking, there was an oven on one side and on the other a tank which you filled with water.[1]

In 1937 the family moved to a near-by house which was newly built out of the materials from a demolished mill. It still had two bedrooms, but it also had a bathroom, electricity, a gas cooker and a hot water supply. It cost £295.

Mr Norton, who was born in 1931, spent his early years in what he described as 'a broken-down stone-built house which fronted on to a back' (it was in fact built behind a shop):

> There was one room and a back kitchen and one bedroom. I'm told I was raised in a drawer. Well I never use the word r-a-t but there were plenty of those about and I'm told that on a couple of occasions they were flicked off my cot, well I should say my drawer really.

His family were rehoused on the Marsh council estate in Lancaster about 1936 and he remembered a rota being made for relatives to come and use the bath while all members of the resident family stuck rigidly to Friday as their bath night.[2]

However, despite the improvements represented by the houses of Mr Lodge and Mr Norton, many people remained in very poor conditions at the beginning of the Second World War. Poor housing was of course a national problem. In 1942 a survey of 5,000 working-class houses in the United Kingdom found that in three-quarters of them water had to be heated specially for washing. Women then did the work with a collection of bowls, 'dollies' and wringers.[3]

It should not be forgotten that, despite all the improvements carried out by individual tenants and owners and by local authorities in the post-war period, some people still remained in appalling housing in 1970. This was particularly true in Preston. The Medical Officer of Health wrote in his report for 1970,

> The . . . population has a morbidity and mortality high above what it should be, high above national norms in every respect. They live in an area of too many slums, large areas of houses with poor amenities, breathing over-contaminated air, drinking water deficient in essential elements and frequently exposed to food which is produced in conditions of poor hygiene.[4]

One of the worst houses in our study was the one in which Mr Boyle spent his childhood in Preston. The family was very poor. Mr Boyle was born in 1937 and lived in the house (apart from times with foster parents) until he was married in 1955:

> Yes, it was a two-up and two-down, no bathroom, outside toilet, no door on it. The kitchen sink was made of stone. Your coal was in the kitchen, a little small kitchen. It just had a small front room. There were no doors on the bedroom, they were took off and chopped up for the fire. We had no electricity. We had one gas lamp in the front room. At night you used to take a candle upstairs. I slept in the back bedroom with my two sisters and my other brother, mam and dad slept in the front bedroom. Then when the other two were born, they moved into the back bedroom and me and my sister moved into the front bedroom with mam and dad.[5]

Very soon after Mr Boyle was married he went to do his National Service. His wife and her new baby lived in appalling circumstances having no fewer than ten different lodgings in two years. Relatives proved to be reluctant to house permanently her and her restless baby who cried incessantly. For a while she lived in her parents-in-law's house:

> There were his mam and dad and brother in the back bedroom. There was his sister in a single bed and then there was me in a double bed with his other sister and little brother. The baby was in a cot at the side of me.[6]

Gross overcrowding continued for some families (albeit a small minority) until the end of the period (and beyond). Mr Kennedy, a Preston docker, and his wife lived in various small terraced houses until 1970. In that year they were expecting their sixth child. 'It was only a three-up, two-down house with no bathroom.' They managed to buy a four-bedroomed house and said simply, 'We were very happy there.'[7]

Families who lived in houses which were overcrowded to some degree tended to regard home rather differently from those who lived more spaciously. Children who not only shared a bedroom but also a bed, as so many did, saw home more as a place to eat and sleep rather than somewhere to spend their leisure hours. Mothers were pleased to get their children from under their feet. Consequently children led substantial parts of their lives outside the home either at school or in the street, but certainly communally. Adults too had a communal life outside the home, men went to the pub or perhaps to the allotment where they could join in with male camaraderie, while women spent a lot of time in the street, ostensibly working, hanging out washing, cleaning the steps, going shopping, but at the same time talking to the neighbours.[8]

Women spent more time than anyone else in the family in the house. It was their space, their working place for varying but often substantial parts of their lives. Therefore changes in housing were likely to affect women substantially.

Owner-occupation and Council Housing

The period 1940–70 was a time of major changes both in housing provision and in the standard of amenities enjoyed by families. There was a marked rise in owner-occupation. In 1940 24 per cent of respondents (or their families) owned their own homes; this had risen to 66 per cent in 1970. The average for owner-occupation for the three towns in the 1971 Census was 62 per cent.[9] Some comparable national figures for owner-occupation were 26 per cent in 1945 and 47 per cent in 1966.[10] There were also significant changes in the rented housing sector, council accommodation tending to replace that provided by private landlords. In 1940, 59 per cent of respondents lived in privately rented accommodation; this fell to 10 per cent in 1970. In 1971 on average 13 per cent of the population of the three towns was in private rented accommodation. In 1940 17 per cent of respondents were council house tenants, this figure rising to 24 per cent in 1970. The average figure for the three towns in the 1971 Census was 25 per cent.[11]

It can be argued that in 1970, with regard to housing, the respondents as a whole group are representative of the three towns taken as one area. However, these aggregated figures disguise considerable variations, both in the housing available in the three towns and in that enjoyed by individual respondents. In 1940, for example, far more Lancaster respondents lived in council houses than did Barrow or Preston respondents. Although there are no Census data for 1941, it is clear from other records that these differences reflect to some extent the different housing provision of the three towns. Barrow built very few council houses in the inter-war period because of the problem of a declining population.[12] Preston built 2,639 council houses in the inter-war period but this was for a population estimated at 108,500 in 1940.[13] In the same period Lancaster built 1,748 houses for a population estimated at 52,000 in 1940.[14] The most startling differences were in owner-occupation. Far more Barrow respondents lived in their own homes in 1940 compared with those in Lancaster and Preston. It is clear that our Barrow group over-represented home owners and continued to do so throughout the period.

It should perhaps be emphasized that Barrow owner-occupiers were not necessarily living in palatial surroundings. Many of them lived in small terraced houses. They were beautifully maintained and decorated, but the rooms were very small and there were no back gardens. Frequently they opened straight off the street. Indeed, a different way of looking at housing provision might be to look at the size, age and amenities of properties. On one hand, there were the older pre-1914 houses, almost all terraced, although in Barrow there were hundreds of tenements built on the Glasgwegian model; these houses had no gardens and before the Second World

Figure 2.1   House interior, Preston, late 1930s
(Photo courtesy of the Harris Library, Preston)

War they rarely had bathrooms. On the other hand, there were the newer post-First World War houses, and here it is possible to group together both privately owned and council-owned houses, as they all tended to have bathrooms, gardens and more floor space than the older houses. In 1940 substantial majorities of the respondents in all three towns (indeed eight out of ten in Preston) lived in pre-First World War houses. By 1970, only in Barrow was there a small majority in such housing. Elsewhere the majority of respondents lived in newer properties. The transformation in the type of housing occupied by the Preston respondents (only a third of whom occupied pre-First World War housing by 1970) reflects the huge programme of demolition and rebuilding undertaken by the local authority. In 1971 32 per cent of all Prestonians lived in council houses.[15] Between 1955 and 1965 4,142 unfit houses were demolished and in the twenty years after the war no fewer than 6,614 council houses were built.[16]

Many of the people who bought houses in this thirty-year period were the first in their families to do so. Their parents had not been able to afford such an expenditure, and their children being able to purchase a house is yet another indication of rising standards of living. House purchase was becoming a norm for *some* young working-class people. Increasingly it was 'the

Figure 2.2   Nile Street, Preston (demolished in 1960)
(Photo courtesy of the Harris Library, Preston)

thing to do', an action not necessarily involving prolonged thought. Others became home owners for more positive reasons, welcoming the feeling of power, status and independence which home ownership gave them. In one major aspect of their lives they were taking charge, no longer subject to the possible whims of their landlords.

Mrs Wheaton was married in 1958 and she and her husband bought a small terraced house near Barrow town centre. She was asked why they had decided to buy a house:

> Oh no other consideration! I would never ever rent. My parents had a lot of trouble with the landlord who lived down in Birmingham. And Len's parents were having a lot of trouble with necessities which needed doing, never an easy path. If you got a burst pipe there was a load of hassle, a load of worry. I would never have rented a house even for one day. I had no intention of ever renting a house at any time in my life. In fact I've plagued my dad as to why on earth he didn't go out and buy a house. It's ridiculous this renting. He used to say, 'If you knew all the things we've had to go through.' I don't think he could have coped with the idea of borrowing money. He just didn't borrow money at all for anything, and I think that was the be all and end all.[17]

Certainly, the great majority of respondents in the earlier studies had a dread of being debtors and many perceived a mortgage as a colossal debt.

Mrs Hutton was married in 1950 and she and her husband, a painter and decorator, worked and saved very hard for six years to buy a newly built three-bedroomed semi-detached house in Lancaster. In contradicting herself about whether or not people bought their houses, she is perhaps reflecting the different and conflicting attitudes to home ownership which existed among her contemporaries. She is clear, however, about the status gained in being a home owner. She is interesting too in her assumption that it was women who were house buyers; this was a not uncommonly held view in the earlier part of the century:[18]

> Well, nobody bought their own house in those days. Everybody put their names down on the housing list and then got a corporation house. If you planned and got your own house, which quite a few women and girls did, that was another thing. 'It's putting a noose around your neck.' But it didn't matter. The done thing was to buy your own house, be independent, so it was nice. And you was looked up to if you was buying your own house. You know, 'She's buying her own house.' We had a house like a palace. And people used to come and visit us and say, 'Oh isn't their house posh.' And everything was spot on, it was so lovely.[19]

Although it is clear that home ownership was very much on the increase there remained a group of people who were very nervous of incurring the huge debt which a mortgage represented to them. Mrs York, referring to the late 1940s, said:

> I was frightened we wouldn't be able to. I said to him, 'Oh no, we can't take all that debt on, we can't do it.' All he wanted was a little house with a garden where he could put up a swing for his children and he was going to have a sandpit. No way would I buy a house.

Mrs York, her husband, who was a building worker, and their children continued to live in a council flat.[20]

Domestic Appliances

There were great changes inside houses and the transformations were greatest in the older properties, especially those which were owner-occupied. A large number acquired bathrooms and electricity, and underwent extensive refurbishment. Working-class families also acquired a whole range of domestic appliances in the years 1940–70. In 1940 the commonest piece of domestic technology was the gas stove. Houses with electricity may have had an electric iron and kettle. Few had a vacuum cleaner. By 1950 all respondents had an electricity supply, and domestic appliances came in a certain order. The electric iron, vacuum cleaner and television were usual by 1960. Nationally, in 1963, 82 per cent of households had a television and 72 per cent a vacuum cleaner.[21] The decade 1960–70 saw the widespread introduction of the fridge and the washing machine. Nationally 3.6 per cent of families had washing machines in 1942, 29 per cent in 1958, and 64 per cent in 1969.[22] All this domestic technology had the potential for transforming both housework and women's lives.

Mrs Hutton remembered her mother's washing day in the 1930s and 1940s:

> Monday was a dreadful day. Mother had basins and buckets all over the kitchen floor when we got home from school. On the way home we used to be saying, 'Oh it's left-over tea, mum will be washing when we get in.' And she had a bucket with dolly blue and a bucket with starch in and the sink full of water for rinsing. And there was the tile floor and water everywhere. She had a boiler lit with gas and a mangle you worked by hand. And most of our garden was just full of these lines of washing. She used to start off with the

lighter things and finish up with the muckiest things. To us it was such a
big job, you know. It was a horrible day.

Mrs Hutton's account of her mother's washing day was so long it has been
heavily edited. Her account of her own washing, by contrast was very
succinct. 'Funny thing is I love washing, it's my favourite job. I don't do it
now, the automatic machine does it.'[23]

Housework Routines

Although the arrival of domestic appliances had the potential for transforming both housework and women's lives, the transformation, in reality,
was somewhat patchy. Domestic appliances did not necessarily give women
more time, because now higher standards of cleanliness than ever before
were expected, as were more demanding levels of child-care.[24] Alva Myrdal
and Viola Klein, writing in 1956, commented that, 'Modern labour saving
devices seem to have raised standards of housekeeping rather than reducing
the time spent on housework.'[25] Mass Observation in 1951 reported that
suburban London housewives spent seventy-one hours a week on domestic
activities.[26] It is not possible to estimate how many hours respondents and
their mothers spent on housework but it is clear that it could be a substantial number. Many housewives still followed the traditional rigid routine of
doing the same task on the same day, washing on Mondays being the most
obvious example of this. But because an increasing number of household
tasks were being done more than once a week, timetabling in general
became more flexible.

Mrs Morrison was married in 1956. Her way of organizing her time as a
wife and mother was typical of very many housewives. She had two children
born in 1958 and 1961. By that time she had a fridge, vacuum cleaner and
washing machine. The family lived in a small, owner-occupied, terraced
house in central Barrow. Her routine was not so rigid as that of a woman of
an earlier generation, when each household task had an appointed time in
the week, but she and her children had a crowded schedule:

> I used to see to them of a morning. There again my mam used to do messages
> for me if I wanted anything for dinner. On some mornings I would get
> them ready and I would go down to the butchers or the fish shop. I
> would take them into town on a Friday morning. And then in the afternoon
> I would take them out to the park or up to Furness Abbey; most afternoons. Or
> to see my mum and dad or Bob's mum and dad. Yes, I liked to get them out

Figure 2.3   New domestic appliances in the 1950s did little to change attitudes to who
did the housework
(*Red Star Weekly*, 1955, by permission of the British Library)

every day. Monday was wash day. Of course with kiddies you have to wash
every day but Monday was the main day. I don't know about Tuesday.

Wednesday morning I used to go to the market. Thursday I always used to do my front. I did my window-sill and front door every morning and then on a Thursday I would give the windows and the front door and all the front a good wash. Sweep the front and then I used to wash right through, the tiles in the vestibule, the kitchen floor, then clean the windows and swill the yard out.

When asked about the vacuuming and dusting she replied,

I used to do it in a morning. I don't mean that it got done every day, some days you had to look to the kiddies if they didn't settle but I tried to do it in a morning. I mean, in the living room every day but not round the house, not with all the other jobs. In between times there were curtains to take down and wash. I used to like to do those. Put a different season's curtains up, you know. I didn't really spring clean but after the winter you always gave the paint a good wash and before Christmas it always had a good wash down and I put clean curtains up.

(She had two sets of curtains for each window.)[27] Mrs Morrison with her vacuum cleaner and her washing machine cleaned her floors and clothes more frequently than had her predecessors without such equipment.

Myrdal and Klein believed that many women expanded their domestic work to fill the time allotted:

Domestic work is expanded to an almost unlimited degree and there is sufficient evidence to justify the suspicion that housewives often unconsciously expand it in order to allay their feelings of frustration by providing evidence that they are fully occupied and indispensable.[28]

Some housewives absorbed the idea that their work was not automatically valued as it had been in the past and that therefore they had, somehow, to justify their existence, thus exacerbating the very problem Myrdal and Klein were trying to address.

In fairness to Mrs Morrison, it is clear that a lot of her time was spent with her children. However, she had worked in a full-time job for two years before the children were born and then the housework was all done at the weekends with a bit in the evenings, not every day or so thoroughly, as when she was at home.

In the earlier part of the century each room and its contents were cleaned once a week, not every day. It is possible that some women felt almost guilty about the easier life the new machines brought and that therefore jobs had to be done more often to compensate. Others retained a feeling that somehow work done by hand and/or the old technology, was 'better' than that done by a machine. In 1962 Mrs Kennedy got a washing machine, after the birth of her third child. Eventually she had six children and at certain periods two of them were in nappies at the same time:

> I always washed the nappies by hand even when I had a washing machine. I would wash them with green soap. I never used to put any washing powder in. I gave them three or four rinses and I boiled them once a week.[29]

Caroline Davidson, writing about women in the 1940s, was curious about why the majority of women did the washing at home rather than sending it to a laundry. The obvious reason must be that they could not afford a laundry, but Davidson offers another explanation: 'If cleanliness is next to Godliness, women wanted to create that moral worth with their own hands.'[30]

Despite the introduction of new technology old habits died hard, especially in poorer areas and among older women. Donkey-stoning steps was a time-honoured custom which apparently defied rationality. The doorstep (and sometimes the flagstones of the pavement) were scrubbed and, while still wet, were rubbed with a soft stone (the donkey stone). Depending on the type of stone used, the treated area was white or cream when dry. Unfortunately, this attractive colour-wash came off when anyone stood on it or when it rained. To the 'sensible' outsider this process may have seemed a waste of a housewife's time and effort. But donkey-stoning remained an act of deep significance to many women well into the 1960s. It also, as will be seen in chapter 11, served a social purpose.

Thus, for a variety of reasons, the arrival of domestic appliances did not necessarily lighten a woman's burden of housework. The technology may not have been fully applied; there were increasingly high standards of cleanliness; larger houses and more possessions entailed more work. No technology had been invented to do some jobs which were regarded as essential, such as window cleaning and dusting.

The Family and Housework: Children

It is possible that women may have had less help with the housework than formerly. Mrs Hutton, when speaking of her childhood, described how she was the 'washer-up' and her sister the 'cleaner-up'. She added: 'With a bit of luck I used to get my brothers to dry up. I probably used to nearly strangle them with the tea-towel to get them to do it.'[31] It was not at all unusual, in pre-war families, for girls to be expected to do the housework while their brothers were excused; although in families where there were only boys they would be generally expected to help. In some families, in the post-war period, children continued to help; but frequently one heard of mothers *not* expecting their children to help with the housework. There was no evidence at all of the situation which Young and Wilmott reported from Bethnal Green; with reference to housework, they wrote: 'Children do more.'[32]

Some women felt that the children's homework was more important; others believed that it was their responsibility to do the housework because they were at home. Others, regretting that they had had to do so much housework when they were young, wanted to spare their children and allow them to have a 'better' time. Mrs Peel, who had four children in the 1940s and 1950s, spoke for many when she replied to a question about children doing housework:

> No, never, no. This was because when I was a youngster, I used to have to do quite a bit of work in the house especially when my mother took in boarders. And I always thought, 'Well, if they go out to work and if they go to school and do their homework, they have done enough.' I just used to get on with everything myself. No, I had no help with the housework off the girls or off the boys.[33]

Some women were more ambivalent. Mrs Critchley's three children were born in the 1950s. They never did any cleaning:

> Oh no! I've always been one of those who didn't think that they could do it like I did it, which isn't a good way to be. I'd rather do it myself because they don't do it right. I think sometimes it's not always a wise thing. I think in some ways it is better to make them do it.[34]

Mrs Critchley's uncertainty about aspects of her children's upbringing was very commonly heard in parents' evidence. Mrs Warwick was almost unique in believing that her mother had been too 'soft' with her and her sisters; but this belief did not make much difference to the upbringing of her own children in the 1960s:

> We have always said that my mother was too soft with us. She just did it herself. As we got older when we left school, we used to do our own ironing, and shopping on a Saturday and that was it.

Of her own children she said,

> I always used to make tham wash up, but that started when James was in the Cubs. And they would keep their own rooms tidy.
> Did they do more than you did or less?
> Perhaps a bit more but not a lot because I didn't work so I didn't really expect them to do any housework.[35]

Ellen Ross, writing of an earlier period, suggested that love in working-class homes had to be seen as taking the form of service and that the *reciprocal* obligation of mother and children in respect to labour should not be seen to be without emotional content.[36] In both the earlier studies and in the current one there is much evidence to support this view. But the question needs to be asked about what happened to family relationships when the work and services were not offered on a reciprocal basis, but only by the mother. Did this result in a mother resenting her children? Or did children come to undervalue their mothers? There is not enough evidence to answer these difficult questions about relationships, but it is clear that some children growing up in the 1940s and 1950s did not value and esteem domestic work. Their mothers' insistence that school work and 'having a good time' should be put before the carrying out of household duties tended to give them different sets of values to those of their parents. It could be argued that some children were developing into a form of family pet. Some girls and boys grew up with ambivalent views, not at all sure if domestic work was of value. They tended not to learn traditional household skills. It can be argued, of course, that boys had never learned them, but this was not entirely true. Many of them were at least sufficiently involved with some household task as children to appreciate their mothers' work. Studies of the earlier part of the century indicate that copying mother was the most important way girls had had of learning domestic science. On the more positive side it can be argued that a few girls, but still only a few, were not being conditioned into being 'little wives and mothers' as their predecessors had been.[37] For the long-term effects of this lack of domestic training in some homes, it would be necessary to study household management in the years after 1970 when the boys and girls growing up in the 1950s and 1960s began their own housekeeping.

The Family and Housework: Husbands

The role which husbands played in housework was a complex one. Historically the great majority of working-class men had done no housework, except in dire emergencies. This did not mean that 'good' husbands spent their time being idle or in visiting the pub; they worked around the house or, if there was one, in the allotment or garden. The work done by men and women, however, was based on gender. There was men's work and women's work, and these divisions survived in some families until 1970. Many women did not expect their husbands to do 'women's work' and felt no resentment at the state of affairs, accepting the gender division of labour as a basic tenet of married life.[38]

Mr Rowlandson grew up in the 1940s and 1950s, and was asked what jobs his father, a shop-worker, did about the house:

> Everything really, decorating, repairing things, like most men do. He built the greenhouse and the garden shed. He did all the gardening of course.
> Did he do housework at all?
> Oh no. There was a strict division. My mother did the cooking and the housework and the washing and the ironing – the wifely duties, should we say, and that was that. He never did that, he was never asked.
> Did she expect him to?
> Oh no. She never said, 'You never do a bloody thing' or anything like that.[39]

Some women did not just accept this division of labour as a norm, they preferred this state of affairs, regarding themselves as superior to men in housework. Men were not always unwilling to do housework; they were not allowed to do it. Mr Graveson was asked if his father, who was a labourer, ever did any housework:

> No. There was a strange situation there. My mother just didn't believe in men doing housework. She just didn't believe in it. I mean, if he picked up a duster he was in trouble. It was that sort of relationship. He had his cellar and his gardens (he had a part-time job as a gardener). But no, he wasn't allowed to do anything in the house. Many a time he would offer but never ever would he be acceptable. My mother always thought it was her job and that was that.[40]

Many women who got married in the 1950s and 1960s shared this 'traditional' view that for women to do the housework was somehow 'natural'. 'Cleaning, no, but I didn't expect him to, because I was at home with the children.'[41]

Mrs Webster was rather more ambivalent; her husband was a gardener and later a meter collector:

> He's not very domesticated is my husband. He doesn't want to be. Some men are willing, some aren't, but I don't mind. I wouldn't say I don't like husbands helping if they are willing, but he just doesn't want to know really. It's less trouble to do it myself. Well, I've never been at work and needed a hand.[42]

Ann Oakley, in *The Sociology of Housework*, has surprisingly little to say about women *not* wanting men to do housework but does mention that some of her female respondents believed that men who did a lot of house-work were 'unmanly', and that women were better at housework than men. She links these attitudes to the influence of the stereotype of the subservient female dedicated to the satisfaction of her husband's needs.[43] It cannot be argued that all the women who held these views in our study were subser-vient. In our studies of women in the earlier part of the century, it was clearly not the case that women who supported a strict gender division of labour in the home were powerless: many were extremely powerful.[44]

There were, of course, changes. Indeed, the picture of men never doing housework was not universal. In pre-war Lancashire, the husbands of textile workers often (but not always) carried out a wide range of household tasks which included scrubbing floors, bathing children, cooking, washing and bed-making. They rarely did work such as window-cleaning or donkey-stoning which exposed them to the sight and therefore the possible mockery of passers-by. Both husbands and wives dreaded the epithet 'cissy' being given to men.[45]

As will be seen in chapter 7, more and more wives had paid work outside the home in the post-war period, and this brought into sharp relief the question of whether husbands should help with the housework. In a few homes husbands did not help at all and this led to conflicts. It was more usual in these homes where the wife worked for husbands to help to some degree with the housework. It is significant that the word used by both men and women to describe men's part in housework is 'help'. No one described men as being 'responsible'.[46]

Although no one had described the husbands of Lancashire textile workers as being 'responsible' for housework in our previous studies, never-theless they had undertaken a wider range of domestic tasks over a more prolonged period than any husband in the present study. It is therefore ironical that the number of families in our study that might just be described as 'symmetrical' was declining rather than increasing in the 1950s and 1960s. This decline was clearly linked to the demise of the cotton industry and the falling numbers of full-time women cotton-workers. The phrase 'symmetrical family' was used by some sociologists in the 1960s and 1970s, and was linked to the quite commonly expressed view that house-work was being more equally shared. Leonard Benson wrote in 1960:

> The old pattern of male-dominated, female-serviced family life is . . . being replaced by a new and more symmetrical pattern. . . . our domestic ideology is quietly modified and a bloodless revolution occurs unnoticed in millions of home.[47]

Young and Wilmott also described a 'symmetrical' family in which there was equality between husbands and wives and where men participated much more than previously in housework. The men may have participated more, but given the evidence in their own survey it is difficult to see why Young and Wilmott wrote of a 'symmetrical' family in which work and housework were equally shared. In families where both husbands and wives had full-time jobs the husbands spent 9.9 hours per week in household tasks but their wives spent 23.1 hours.[48] The argument in favour of the 'symmetrical' family was attacked by Ann Oakley. In a devastating critique of men's role in housework, based on interviews with London housewives, she concluded that only 10 per cent of husbands had a 'high' participation rate in housework. This compared with 5 per cent with a medium participation rate and 85 per cent with a low participation rate.[49] Jane Lewis concluded that, 'The extent to which unpaid work in the family has remained women's work is seemingly one of the most unchanging aspects of post-war life.'[50] It is difficult, in view of the empirical evidence in this study, not to agree with the views of Oakley and Lewis.

Husbands may well have helped with the housework when they were first married and they and their wives were both in full-time work. The position changed dramatically when the children arrived. As will be seen, fathers were much more involved with their children than was the case in the previous generation, but they neither played an equal role in doing housework nor did they share equally in the responsibility for it. Housework remained the woman's sphere, an area for which she had the responsibility and in which she was judged to have the greater competence.

Mr Rowlandson's comments on his parents' attitudes to housework have already been noted. He himself was married in 1966 at the age of 22, having just completed an engineering apprenticeship, and his wife continued in work as a machinist until the birth of their daughter in 1968:

> Well, we both worked. I used to do more than I do now because I used to come home from work before Christine and get the tea ready. Yes, I used to dust, but I don't do it now as Christine is at home all day and I'm out. Christine is like my mother, she says it jokingly but I think she believes it. 'My job is to look after you, to cook your meals and to do your washing.' I vacuum of course and I wash the windows at weekends. Well, Christine is an excellent cook and if I did it it would be a hell of a downward step. She has banned me from washing because I broke the last washing machine.[51]

Most couples still adopted the 'traditional' view that it was equitable for the wife to take charge of the housework when she was at home and her husband was out at work. But although most accepted this division of labour, an increasing number of wives resented the lack of help from their husbands. Mrs Hutton's husband had also helped before the children were born but offered very little after their arrival:

> My husband was under the impression while we were both working . . . if we were both bringing money in, we both shared what was to be done at home. But he did make a rule that once I had stopped working the ball was in my court as regards cleaning, cooking. He may have changed a nappy for me and he may have washed up sometimes but after that he never did anything.[52]

The reasons for husbands not doing much housework and wives resentment at the paucity of the help offered are perhaps not difficult to understand. What appears to be more difficult to explain are the motives of women who positively refused to allow their husbands to do more than a limited range of household tasks. It was and is all too easy for observers to be patronizingly critical of women's domesticity. Some writers in the 1950s tended to irritation when surveying women's domestic role: 'The domestic setting as the accepted framework of women's lives still underlies the pattern of women's roles to an irrationally large extent.'[53] It is more useful to attempt to find explanations for women's attitudes. Women in general bore the weight of generations of conditioning which led them to believe that their place was in the home, cleaning their houses and caring for their families. Most little girls were still conditioned by their mothers' examples into believing that their lives should be spent doing housework (although as has been seen, conditioning through being expected to *do* housework was weakened in the 1950s and 1960s). Caroline Davidson concluded that:

> From the perception of the 1980s it is remarkable how content women were to spend their lives doing housework. . . . Women's attitude to housework did not undergo any fundamental change between 1650 and 1950. The vast majority accepted housework as their main occupation through three centuries.[54]

One would doubt if everything changed overnight *after* 1950. Ann Oakley found in her women respondents a 'firm belief in the "natural" domesticity of women and a corresponding belief that domesticity in men is "unnatural" '.[55] One of the youngest respondents, and certainly the most successful from the point of view of a career, was not asked about her adult life as she was still in the educational system in 1970; yet totally unprompted, she felt it necessary to insist that she had never rejected a domestic role.

Some wives, who were not in full-time work, regarded it as a 'fair' and mutually advantageous arrangement to have husbands working outside and women working inside the home. Other women, like their predecessors, continued to believe that they were more skilled at housework than their husbands. (No one suggested that men might have become more competent with more practice.) It is interesting that the very few husbands who are recorded as doing any cooking were not doing so because of any deliberate attempt to blur gender roles, but because they were experienced cooks having been trained as such during their time in one of the armed services. Presumably they were judged to be fit to do the cooking.

Lastly, and this point is rarely made in womens' history, some women appear to have felt that it was important to have areas of work over which they had complete control, for which they were responsible, and in which, compared to the rest of the family, they were expert. Their dignity, self-respect and self-confidence demanded it.

Family Activities in the Home

The separation of roles within many families meant that individual members could spend a lot of time physically apart; mother in the kitchen, the children playing outside, and father in his own particular space carrying out gender-related activities: carpentry, working with metal, doing repairs and gardening. The site for these activities depended on the family's circumstances, but might be the cellar, washhouse, garden shed or the garden or allotment. In these places men made things like toys for the children or items for the house. They also mended a variety of articles ranging from bikes to shoes. Mr Graveson's father, who was forbidden to do any housework, was perhaps typical of many:

> He used to love going down the cellar and he used to make things, tools for the garden, stick dolls. He was very clever really and we didn't realize it at the time.[56]

Some fathers clearly found this kind of creative activity satisfying. Mr Norton, who had a variety of jobs, had four children to provide for in the late 1950s and early 1960s, and spoke of Christmas when they were small:

> We hadn't got a lot of money so I had to make a lot of toys for the kids, typical examples would be the doll's bed and cradle for the girls; and for Danny a soldiers' fort which was literally two margarine boxes one upside down and the battlements cut out. Actually it was quite good when it was finished. I painted it grey and black and I went to a local toy shop, there was

one in the window and I used that as a pattern, followed it more or less precisely. While the paint was still wet I put some sawdust on to give it a rough exterior as they had done but I put on a few more refinements. Mine had a drawbridge and tower. Their mass-produced one hadn't got them. I found I got very interested in that sort of thing.[57]

The growing interest of fathers in playing with their children is further examined in chapter 8. It is interesting that Ann Oakley found similar evidence in her study in London. She concluded that a good father was one who played with his children. 'The physical side of child-rearing is a mother's responsibility. Fathers are there to play with the children.'[58]

It had never been the case, of course, that family members spent all their time in gender-related activities, physically separated from other members of the family. Most obviously, they had come together for meals. In the post-war period there were various factors which tended to cause the family to spend more time together in the same place, regardless of age or gender. The arrival of television in the 1950s resulted in families spending much more time together. Children spent an increasingly large part of their out-of-school time in either their home or garden. In earlier times they had only used the house for eating and sleeping; there had been too many children and too little space to enable, and too few toys to encourage, them to play indoors. In large, poor families this remained the case in the post-war period. For others different factors assumed some importance; smaller families meant more playing space in the home. For reasons of security or snobbery, or because they thought it was part of being a 'good' parent, more mothers chose to keep their children at home during leisure hours. Greater prosperity meant that there were more attractions in the form of toys and games which persuaded children to play at home. The increasing amount of homework which some children had meant that they were obliged to play out less and stay in more. Given the general absence of central heating in most homes, they would do this in the only heated place, the living room. In some families tension was caused by competition for use of the table, and conflicts arose over acceptable noise levels.

Meal Times

Meal times had always been an important focus for family life. The family had met round the table, although in large poor families the younger children may well have had to stand for their meal. In the post-war period it was very unusual not to have chairs for everyone. There were no dramatic changes in the style and content of the meals themselves. In this important area of social life the element of continuity is much more marked than that of change. Throughout the century a sign of prosperity had been the consumption of large quantities of meat. Improvements in family income had almost invariably resulted in an increase in the amount of meat eaten. This trend can sometimes be described as conspicuous consumption. Mrs Owen was married just before the Second World War; her husband was a tradesman, whereas her own father had been unskilled. 'I used to have the butcher's boy come every morning with the meat, you know. We had meat every day, yes.'[59] War-time rationing interrupted the trend to ever-greater consumption of meat, but as soon as supplies permitted, the trend was resumed after the war. A meat-and-two-veg main meal, usually eaten at midday, accompanied by a lighter, later meal which contained meat in some form (such as sausages, bacon, cold meats or a meat pie) became the realizable goal for very many families, instead of being the ambition to which they aspired in earlier and less prosperous days. Rather less was heard in this study of the traditional soups, broths, hot-pots and stews made with a small amount of the cheapest meat, a lot of vegetables and much patience and economy. But, if there was a shift in emphasis away from vegetables and towards meat, there was absolutely no evidence of any fundamental changes in taste. The only 'new' food which was widely accepted was the packeted breakfast cereal. Any other 'new' foods tended to be regarded with suspicion, not to say hostility. Those who have adopted 'new' foods have done so since 1970, but many respondents are still hostile to these changes.

Mrs Owen had not welcomed changes in the past, and continued in her rejection of new foods. She said:

> My daughter cooks all sorts of horrible stuff. I don't like Chinese or curries or pizzas. No. Yoghurts and that kind of thing. I like the good old things. My mum is the same. She doesn't like anything like that. No.[60]

Only listening to her tape can convey the venom with which she pronounced 'Yoghurt'!

Mr Warwick, like so many others, saw no change in his food preferences from childhood right through adulthood. The question was asked about his childhood:

> Do you remember any different foods being bought? Any slightly foreign foods?

No, I won't have it now, never mind ought else. Black pudding, liver, steak, beef. No, I'm not a lover of foreign foods, never have been. I've tried it when I've been abroad but it's nasty. I tried a bloody fish and I spat it out, anchovies! I just like basic simple foods, me. It was just corn beef hash, scouse, meat and potato pies, roasts on Sunday and that were it. Just the same as it is now.[61]

Food tastes may have remained unchanged but there were changes in the norms which governed the conduct of family meals. In earlier times most families had adopted the precept of children being seen and not heard. With the generally more permissive attitudes to children in the post-war period, many were encouraged to discuss the day's events at meal times.

Indeed, there are more accounts of family discussions than in the earlier study. Children did not have any real power but their voices were being heard, which was a very new phenomomen in many families. Mr Norton said:

We didn't get problems from the kids. Oh hell, we had arguments, of course, when we didn't see eye to eye, but I always encouraged argument and debate. And if there was a decision to be made within the family, we really brought the kids in, you know. We democratically arrived at the solution I had decided upon anyway. But we all felt better.[62]

As some children became more involved with home and family, they were less involved in the culture of the neighbourhood. In these families individual tastes developed at the expense of neighbourhood solidarity.

Conclusion

The theme of this chapter has been the changes in the physical environment, in the house and home, where so much family life, and especially the lives of women, was played out. Inevitably this survey has also introduced the question of family relationships, which will be looked at much more closely eleswhere in the book. But this chapter has already indicated that obvious conclusions are to be avoided. Modern houses and labour-saving appliances did not necessarily lighten the burden of housework. Many more women may have entered the labour market but gender divisions within the home remained strong. Closer propinquity between family members may have produced closer relationships but this was not inevitable. Watching television did not necessarily produce greater communication, and the competing claims of television and homework in a small living space could produce a degree of enmity. The period 1940–70 saw an unprecedented improvement in the comfort, convenience and attractiveness of the average home. It is not always possible to speak with confidence about parallel improvements in the quality of family relationships.

3

Growing Up – Relationships
with Parents – Getting a Job

For the teenager, the adolescent, the young adult, the years of growing up were dominated by three topics: their relationships with their parents; their jobs or careers; and their relationships with the opposite sex, which are considered in chapter 4. Friends continued to be very important to teenagers, and friendship is a continuing theme in much of the testimony.

Financial Interdependence

From at least the middle of the nineteenth century there had been a well-documented public debate about the 'independence' of the young. There was a wide-spread fear, especially among middle-class observers, that 'independent' young people would leave home and become delinquent.[1] Before the Second World War it is clear that young people from the working class continued to occupy their traditional place in both their families and in society. They were young workers and therefore wage-earners, experienced in the ways of the adult world of work, often long before their counterparts from the middle and upper classes. But they were not independent; they lived at home subject to their parents' rules and regulations, and most of their income went straight to their mothers so they had little financial independence. They can perhaps best be described as occupying a position of semi-independence. Older respondents growing up before the war remember this pattern well.

Mr Lodge left school in 1933 when he was fourteen. He worked in a butcher's shop and continued in this occupation until he was called up in 1939. He lived at home and gave all his wages to his mother:

> It was the done thing. Everybody, doesn't matter who they were, when they started work, they put all their wages on the table, and there was nothing

taken out. And some made an agreement. 'You can have twopence in the shilling back.' I was in a lucky position. I used to give it her and I'd say, 'I don't want anything back,' and she'd say, 'Are you alright?' And I'd say, 'Yes if I need anything I'll tell you.' Because you see as a butcher's lad you did a lot of delivering up and down and people gave you an odd threepence. And I found I could manage.[2]

Mr Lodge had little independence and clearly did not expect, nor indeed want, things to be different. Only at dances did he feel matters could have been better arranged:

At dances mother came. Well, she would dance with me or she would sit and watch. Have a good talk with everyone else. I didn't used to care very much for her coming because I would be speaking to a girl and I'd come off the dance floor and then she'd tell me what I'd said. Because she was a weaver and she could lip read every word I said to anybody in the hall.[3]

This lack of teenage independence can still be seen in some families after the war, especially in the poorer ones where the earnings of the young adults continued to make a vital contribution to the family budget. Mrs Brown and Mrs Kennedy were sisters in a large, poor Preston family, both became mill workers on leaving school; their father was a docker and their mother had no employment. Conditions were perhaps more difficult for the younger sister. Mrs Brown was allowed to board, that is to pay a set rent for board and lodgings and keep the rest of her earnings. Mrs Kennedy, however, was the last child to be at home, all the rest being married. She had to hand over all her money to her mother until she finally left home at the time of her marriage in 1957. Mrs Brown said:

You had a job to get married. She wasn't in favour of anybody getting married. She didn't want you to leave home because you were bringing home money you see. You weren't sent off with, 'All the best and happiness.' Oh no, no way.[4]

Mrs Brown's situation was comparable to that of many pre-war teenagers; what was new was her resentment, a recurring attitude in so many respondents' comments about their parents.

Teenage Affluence

By the 1960s, with increased parental prosperity and a consequently reduced need for children's wages, 'boarding' was the most usual way for young workers to contribute to the family income, leaving them with more disposable income. By 1960 there were indeed signs of teenage affluence, nationally and locally, a phenomenon previously unknown in working-class life. In 1959 Mark Abrams in his book, *Teenage Consumer Spending*, wrote, 'This is a distinctive teenage spending for distinctive teenage ends in a distinctive teenage world.'[5]

Mrs Lonsdale, a factory worker, after prolonged arguments with her mother, who was unmarried and who also worked in a factory, was allowed to board in about 1964 when she was seventeen. When asked what she spent her money on she replied:

> Records, stockings, cigarettes. I would go out and buy clothes when I could afford them, but I used to buy them more often than if she was buying them you know. Nights out![6]

Teenagers were becoming an important part of the consumer society, aware of an ever-increasing range of goods and services on which to spend their money. As always, it is difficult to assess to what extent their purchasing was affected by the media and advertising. What is clear is the way in which they were influenced both by what they saw in the shops and, most importantly, the spending habits of their peer group.

Challenges to Authority

As well as controlling a much larger part of their earnings, there were other signs of growing independence among the young. There was more independent thought, a rejection of some of the mores of a previous generation and with it a questioning of parental authority. Some of this independence resulted from the experience of evacuation in the earlier years of the war and so began long before the advent of adolescence. Mrs Wheaton was seven years old when she was evacuated in 1940. She was away from home for ten months:

> I can realize now that I never turned to my parents for help or anything at all after I came back; and looking at my life, what I can remember of it before I went away, I wasn't like that when I came back. If I had problems at school, I sorted them out myself. In fact, I attacked a boy who had previously bullied me. I grabbed him by the scruff of the neck and got him against the wall and he was crying and that was the end of them. They never bullied me after that.

Mrs Wheaton felt able, as a teenager, to confront her father with complaints about the way he was treating her mother.[7]

But greater teenage independence cannot be simply attributed to one factor, such as evacuation or greater spending power. The widespread challenging of authority in many parts of society was also important, and is a recurring theme in this book. Mr Kennedy actually fought with his father. No other respondent reports such an event but it is interesting that Mr Kennedy did not appear to think that his action was unique either among his peer group or in his own family:

> The only fight I had with my dad I got a bit cheeky with him. And I think every lad does this, every one of my lads has done it anyway, squared up to their father at some time and think like 'I'll put him in his place.' But I remember when I was about sixteen or seventeen, and I'd given him a load of lip and I had just started on the trawlers and I thought I was the bees knees. And he said, 'I've had enough of you. In that back yard.' And he started fighting and he was knocking hell out of me was my dad and he was only little. They were coming in from every direction. And I was glad when my mum stopped it you know.[8]

There were many arguments between parents and their children about what the young should do in their leisure time, who their friends should be, and how they should treat other people. Mr Rowlandson, as an apprentice engineer, was typical of the 'new' teenager and was much more confrontational with his father than, for example, Mr Lodge had been twenty years before:

> I had a lot of bother with my dad who always thought he was right and of course I'm the same with mine!'
> What did you argue about?
> Going out, spending money, girls. Yes, girls. He used to lecture me on girls. I used to treat them horrible. I don't know why. I'm not saying I had loads of girl-friends, I didn't, but I had no respect. I used to come home regularly with different women. I would come in late, two o'clock you know. I was never drunk; you can't do anything when you're drunk!
> Did he wait up for you?
> He did earlier on but when I had my own key I just used to come in and go to bed.[9]

Mr Rowlandson was different from his working-class, teenage predecessors in several ways: he had his own key; he stayed out far later than was traditional; he saw lots of women even when he was going out with the girl he eventually married; and he had a car when he was eighteen. He was a clear representative of the teenager as consumer. He did not contribute to the family budget; indeed, as an apprentice on low wages he was subsidized by his parents. He is typical of those of whom Tilly and Scott wrote, 'Children cost the family more and contributed less.'[10] He continued to ignore his father's warnings about his behaviour. Indeed, although there were the rows, it is clear that his father, like many other parents, was much more lenient than earlier generations had been. It is also fair to say that Mr Rowlandson had more freedom as a teenager than any other respondent (with the exception of Mrs Horwich – see below).

Mrs Rowlandson had problems with her family about her friendships; her father was a riveter and her mother acted as a child-minder; both were devout Catholics:

> One of my best friends at school, her father had interfered with her, and she kind of told us. We couldn't do anything about it, but eventually he did get put in prison. Now my mum found out and said I hadn't to speak to that girl again. They were funny you know, they were Catholics and Christian but they had a very funny attitude. I mean I was friendly with that girl for years and I wasn't going to give up my friendship just like that. I didn't tell my mum that. She said 'That girl, that's a very dirty family and you'll have nothing at all to do with them.' And the same thing when I met a boy and his parents were divorced, 'You mustn't have anything to do with them, they are a very dirty family.' And it was a kind of saying even though it wasn't their fault. The whole family got the stigma, not just the one person. And a girl was pregnant, it was in the last year so I had just turned fourteen. And I was frightened to death of her finding out; and she did. And it was a case of walking across the road if you see them coming towards you.[11]

Mrs Rowlandson continued to ignore her mother's dictats and later believed them to be one of the reasons for her rejection of Catholicism.

As they began to think for themselves other teenagers rejected the religious beliefs and practices of their parents, although this was far from a universal trend. Those who did reject their parents' beliefs tended to do so on the grounds that they were hypocritical or lacking in compassion. In about 1959 Mrs Horwich went to confirmation classes in her local Anglican church:

> Yes, I went to all the classes. I remember I threw these Catechism books that we had written in for about six months, over the banking down into the river when we had finished. I often had to hold myself back from shouting arguments at the pulpit. It didn't seem fair that you had to be talked to, to be so receptive without saying anything back.[12]

Continuing Dependence?

Despite these various manifestations of independent thought and action, it remains difficult to describe the majority of young people as being truly independent. None of those quoted above left home, except to be married, before 1970 (although Mrs Horwich did so after that date). The custom of young people living at home was not confined to this area. In 1959, 90 per cent of English children still lived at home two years after leaving school.[13] It is not easy to describe youth as independent when the great majority continued to live in their parents' homes and to observe, by and large, their parents' rules. Young people in the study, with the exception of Mr Rowlandson, also continued to contribute financially to the household. Although young people's financial contributions were less important to the family budget than those of their predecessors and, as has been seen, they were less likely to do housework, parents continued to expect more of their adolescents than those described by Klein: 'Parents expect and encourage their children even in adolescence, to do little to support the house in labour or in money.'[14] As has been seen in chapter 2, it may well have been that this observation *was* increasingly true about parental attitudes to younger children, and to those who continued in full-time education. Young wage-earning workers were not treated so indulgently.[15]

There were, of course, two groups who did leave home at eighteen: the young men who went to do National Service and those going on to higher education. Eighteen male respondents either served in the forces during the war or were called up for military service after it. Fourteen returned to their parents' homes when their tours of duty were over, three went home to their wives, and only one went to another town. Four more went into the Merchant Navy and they all returned home when their service was over. The next largest group of respondents to leave home were those going on to higher education; of these, seven were born after 1945 and their subsequent careers do not form part of this study. However, six older respondents went away to some kind of higher education, and of these only two returned home. It is tempting to see this small group as harbingers of the future. They were clearly untypical of their peer group, which continued to live at home.

Respondents, however, were aware that things were different for their own children. Mrs Burrell grew up in a family where there were constant arguments between her parents (her father was a welder, her mother a housewife); sometimes she joined in on her mother's side, sometimes she left. But her absences were temporary and she only went up the street to her grandmother's:

> I think children these days are more independent. They like to go and do their own thing. I left home but I only went to my grandma's. I wouldn't have thought of packing up and leaving home like they do now.[16]

Careers and Jobs: Parental Choices

Parents continued to play an important role in the choice of their children's job or career. As will be seen in chapter 9, parents could be roughly divided into two groups: those who expected their children to leave school and to find work as soon as possible, and a growing minority who were ambitious for their children and encouraged them to stay at school longer, and possibly go on to further or higher education. It was virtually unheard of at any time during this period for an adolescent to act in defiance of his or her parents' wishes, prejudices or ambitions. Retrospective resentments about those decisions were not, however, unusual.

The respondents and their parents all shared one assumption in their choice of work: all jobs and careers were gender-related. There are references to males in Lancaster becoming nurses, but men had been attendants and nurses in the two hospitals for mental illness and mental impairment since the nineteenth century. By the middle of the twentieth century this had become a 'traditional' male occupation. Girls chose jobs from a predictable range of occupations; although one traditional job, domestic service, was much less popular than it had been at the beginning of the century. Respondents, reflecting the choices of the rest of the young female population (see tables 7.2, 7.3 and 7.4) became shop assistants, factory workers, clerks, typists, nurses and teachers. As will be seen, when they re-entered the labour market after having children their choice of occupation was even more restricted, and part-time domestic work became quite usual.

Mrs Atkin left a secondary modern school in the early 1960s and reflected on the jobs her classmates took:

> I don't think the school actually put forward any idea. I would say the town girls mostly went to the factories to be secretaries. The country girls went home to their fathers' farms to work on the land. Some went to the egg-packing factory. They never sort of looked beyond that and getting married. Then you got the middle of the road like myself who went into nursing or who wanted to be teachers. Maybe one or two went into the shops.[17]

There were a few examples of girls being denied a grammar school education because parents felt that such an education would be 'wasted' on a girl, but this was very unusual. Much more common were clear perceptions about which jobs would be appropriate for a daughter, given the family's traditions, status and aspirations. Mrs Peel was asked about her attitude to working in the paper mill. Her mother was a part-time shop assistant and her father was a borer:

> My mother would never have allowed me to go working in a place like that, no. They were considered rough. It was the same as the shipyard, certain parts of the shipyard were considered rough.[18]

In families and areas where factory work had been done by women for several generations, attitudes could be quite different. Daughters of mill workers increasingly did not follow their mothers into the mills, but this was not so much because of changing attitudes to mill work but because the numbers of mills still operating in the post-war period were declining reapidly. Mrs Brown entered a spinning mill in Preston in 1943 when she was fourteen. When asked if that was what she wanted, she replied succinctly, 'It was available.'[19] Her sister followed her into the same mill in 1950. She had more to say about how she came to be there. She had received no careers advice at school:

> I knew where I were going. Our Diane, she worked in the mill and my name just went down automatically. I had to go in the mill. Later on in life I used to think to myself, I'm sure I could have got something different. It's just that's where the money was.

When asked who thought of this she replied, 'My mum. Of course we all went in the mill when we left school, even the lads. But they didn't stick it like me.'[20]

Evidence of drifting into a job without much thought and little exercise of conscious choice, along with the importance of parental influence, is also well illustrated in the lives of girls who were academically able. Mrs Barlow's father had been a plater in the shipyard, but he was killed, leaving her mother a widow for most of her daughter's childhood. She had a struggle to manage on her pension and on the proceeds of taking in a lodger. She had been a teacher before her marriage and was determined that her daughter should have a good education. After leaving the grammar school in 1946, Mrs Barlow had obtained a place at a teacher training college with an excellent reputation:

She was very pleased, she thought it was the top college. I mean, she didn't know but people had told her. She was very, very good really because we had no money.

Do you remember making the decision to become a teacher?

No, no. I just drifted into it. She [her mother] was quite keen because in Barrow there weren't really any jobs for girls. If you were going to do anything, you were a nurse, a teacher, or went into the civil service. Well, I didn't want to be a nurse and I didn't know any other jobs. I mean I'm sure now I wouldn't have gone into teaching.[21]

Job Satisfaction and Dissatisfaction

It is difficult to generalize about whether girls enjoyed their work or not. Perhaps rather predictably, some girls enjoyed some jobs and detested others. There were no jobs which were either liked or disliked by all those who tried them. The factors which caused most discontent were low wages, and poor relationships with supervisors or employers. There were two major sources of enjoyment arising from work: the social contacts with other women, and pride – either in the skills being acquired and/or in the advancement being achieved. The following accounts of working lives illustrate both these points and those made above.

Mrs Lodge left school in 1936 aged fourteen. Her mother was a mill worker and was determined that her daughter should follow her:

I went when I left school for twelve months and I hated it. I really hated it. She said everybody had to go in the mill. I don't mean it snobbishly, but some of the girls used to tell jokes and I suppose I was a bit straightlaced, I didn't particularly like it. It was noisy and I didn't like the work. Didn't appeal to me at all.

Mrs Lodge left the mill and went into domestic service:

Now, I really loved it when I went into service. I love to clean up, I like working on my own. I wasn't over-fond of a lot of people and some of the people were a bit rough. These people I went to work for were good people. I loved them, I really loved them; but I didn't live in.

Mrs Lodge was conscripted into munitions work during the war. Initially she was in a small foundry making shells. She was happy there, partly because it as a small firm, partly because she knew a lot of the girls there, and mostly because of the big increase in her wages:

Just before I left [service] I got fifteen shillings. Now my first week's wage was five pounds something. I ran all the way home. I couldn't get in fast enough to show her this wage slip.[22]

Mrs Lodge and her mother then embarked on a spending spree, mostly buying things for the house. She disliked her next job in a much larger munitions factory, and after her marriage in 1945, settled for casual part-time domestic work.

Mrs Jenkins was the only other respondent to be a full-time domestic servant. She left school in 1945 and went as a living-in parlour maid in a house in the Lake District: 'Cleaning, washing up, laying the table, waiting on at table. It was a big house and a lot of cleaning.' The cleaning was made more burdensome by the mistress's decision not to have a vacuum cleaner. Mrs Jenkins was allowed half a day a fortnight to visit her mother, and two half-days off in a week. She liked her employer but only stayed a year:

I didn't like house cleaning. I went there originally because I wanted to go in the Forestry Commission or Land Army which was still in operation then, and I thought this was the nearest thing to it till I was eighteen. But after twelve months I found that probably because I had quite an active brain I didn't like house cleaning all the time.

She worked for a time in a small corner shop in Barrow:

Then I went and got a better job in Dewhurst's the butchers. I was a clerk and that was my smallest book, my first book-keeping. I quite enjoyed it except that they were all men and boys and I felt a bit isolated.

When she was sixteen she went to live with her much older sister in London. (Her parents also moved but because of accommodation difficulties lived with other relatives in London. Mrs Jenkins was not leaving home.) She was again a book-keeper:

I loved it. I was earning £3 a week. I had £1 to myself so I was going to all these musicals, opera, ballet for two or three shillings; so it opened up a whole new life for me.

Sadly, it was not to last long. Mrs Jenkins developed tuberculosis and spent two years in a sanatorium, after which she married and returned to Barrow. When, many years later, she went back to work, she again became a book-keeper.[23]

Mrs Emery went to work in 1952:

My first job was at Berry's slipper works; and I hated it. It just depends who your boss were. We had an Ethel and she gave us scissors to cut this leather and your fingers were sore and that. And I said to my mother, 'I want to come out. I want to go in the mill like you did.' I went as a doffer and I loved it. You had a good time with the other women, we've had many a laugh. We used to go for a smoke in the toilets. And the tackler used to say, 'You've been in there long enough.' And if you didn't come out he would throw a wheel at the door. We used to walk about in our bare feet. And we really enjoyed it. And there was the time that we all went on strike and Curly Helm had a landau and you could have a ride in it. It were sixpence. So we hired him out to take us to the dole! And we dressed one of the girls up as the Snow Queen, oh laugh![24]

Mrs Rowlandson left school in 1959. She wanted to be a children's nurse but her teachers appear to have had a low (and false) idea of her capabilities:

What I wanted to do was a children's nurse and they just said, 'Well you're not clever enough, so I wouldn't bother with that if I were you.' They more or less wanted you to go into the factories. I enjoyed sewing, so I went to work at Hawkins in the sewing department. It was aprons and eventually you were making tailored shirts. But it was slave labour, you know. It was £2 a week and you started at 7.30 and you finished at 6 o'clock. It was like that until you finished your time which was two years later and then you went on piece work.

She left after six months when a friend told her about the Mullard factory in Lytham which made television valves. A special bus was put on to take workers from Preston. Mrs Rowlandson stayed for six years until her marriage:

When you went there they put you on a training course. They showed you films of what they did in the big Mullard factories, what your valves were used for. You had someone permanently sitting with you, talking to you and explaining everything. And that person looked after you until you were out of your time six months later. So it was a brand new factory and it was very well organized. There was a union if you wanted it but no one pushed you into it. The hours were quarter to eight and it was a half past four finish. So you got more money for less time.

Mrs Rowlandson was pleased to be earning £5–£6 per week. She also enjoyed the company of the other girls.[25]

Mrs Lonsdale, unlike the four women mentioned above, went to the grammar school. She disliked it intensely and left in 1961 to avoid sitting her O Level examinations:

It was the K shoe factory. It was a horrible job, I was staining shoes. I soon got fed up with that. And the job didn't pay much so I kicked that into touch. I went down to Nelsons [an artificial fibre manufacturer] where my mother worked. I was putting the bobbins on the warping machines. I enjoyed it and worked there for quite a while. Eventually worked up to being a warper on a machine. I quite enjoyed it. Well, when I first started we used to have a laugh with all the girls. And when I got on a machine it was a sense of achievement. This is my machine and I am working it. When anything went wrong with the machine and you used to have to get the fitters in; I knew that machine like the back of my hand. 'It's so-and-so you know. Can I do it?' 'No don't you do it, you will get me the bloody sack.' And I used to stand there watching him and I used to think it would be great to get my hands full of oil.

Eventually she had a dispute with a supervisor:

> There was one of them that was a bit offish and me and my friend left. I think it was a dispute about wages. And we sort of said, 'Well stick your job. We're going.' But I mean at that time you could do that. You could leave a job on a Thursday and get another job on a Monday. Not like now.[26]

Young women who went into offices appear to have had a quieter time than those who were in factories. They gained satisfaction from the skills they had and some were proud of having work which was generally regarded as being 'superior' to either shop or factory work. Mrs Adderley said, 'It was mainly shop and factory work, a few got into offices but I think from a secondary school you didn't get a lot of chance into anything like that.'[27] Mrs Adderley, whose father was a farm labourer, was very pleased to have an office job which she obtained through her uncle's influence. Mrs Sykes, whose father was also a labourer, went to a grammar school but did not do very well there. She left at fifteen without taking any exams and went to work in Woolworths. 'Everybody gets a job in Woolworths don't they?' After three months there she started taking private lessons in shorthand and typing. She had jobs in two building societies and listed her various achievements: typing, shorthand, using the duplicator and addressograph, and book-keeping. She was especially pleased with this particular skill and commented simply, 'I liked that.'[28]

When young women disliked a job, for whatever reason, they were much more likely to leave it than have a dispute with the management or owners, either in person or via a union. There might have been arguments, but that was all. In the study there was only one example of a woman seriously challenging the management of her firm. Mrs Needham left school in 1933 and was sent by her mother to a variety of local mills, all of which she left

after a very short time. Eventually she was found a job in an artificial silk
factory where she stayed:

> If we had run short of silk and we had nothing to do, we used to clean up;
> you know, clean the factory. Well, we had done all that and we were just
> stood about talking. And the chargehand come up and told me and swore at
> me, told me to get some work done. And I said, 'Well, we have nothing to
> do.' And she said, 'Well, you find something.' And there was a to-do and the
> boss come and told me to collect my cards and go home.

The 'to-do' was clearly quite dramatic as she went on to say, 'We had to
stack bobbins on these wooden things and I threw that at her and it hit her
on the hip and she pretended to faint.'

When Mrs Needham went to collect her dole it was refused on the
grounds that she had finished the job. She challenged this decision and the
matter was heard by a tribunal. What still rankled with Mrs Needham after
so many years was being sworn at, and she repeated this grievance several
times in her account. The tribunal granted her dole and she felt that her
complaint about the swearing had been justified. She added, however, an
interesting postscript to her account: she claimed that the boss and the
married chargehand were having an affair:

> We knew it. Me and these three workers, we worked overtime and we saw it.
> And we used to giggle about it. 'What are they doing behind them stacks?'
> Anyway, when it came to this tribunal I told them about it. I knew I was
> going to lose so I said, 'Well, he would send me home, he would sack me, he
> was having an affair with her.' And they said, 'You can't say things like that.'
> And I said, 'But I've got witnesses.' And I brought these witnesses. So with
> that she got finished, he got finished and I was offered a job back there. I went
> into knitting but I couldn't take to it so I finished there. I did my bunk.[29]

Changing both the place and the type of work were common features of
women's employment in this period. Only one respondent, Mrs Brown, had
a continuous record of employment staying for twenty-five years at the
same mill as a full-time worker, both before and after marriage. She was
made redundant in 1968.

Conclusion

Many of the features of young women's work can be illustrated by the
assumptions they made about their lives. Girls' ambitions did not centre on

work, but on marriage and children. Work may have been enjoyable, but it was not seen as a lifetime commitment. Fifteen-year-old girls envisaged a job with or without training, then marriage with a continuation of paid work until the birth of the first child. The great majority could see no further than that. Young men had different expectations: they left school assuming they would work until they were sixty-five years old. Although they expected to marry, they never envisaged marriage and parenthood interfering in their working lives. The least ambitious, least well qualified, did not foresee what jobs they would do, but they did expect a future of full employment. More ambitious men thought in terms of a trade, work in an office or, for a minority, a profession. Whatever the occupation, it was expected that they would follow it for a lifetime. Girls had no life plan which included full-time paid work. In 1968 Eva Figes was dismayed to find, in essays written by London grammar school girls, an absence of long-term planning and assumptions about the ultimate female role being a domestic one: 'A basic assumption in all these essays, and one made by the whole of our society, is that the care of a man and of children is a woman's duty and that any other interests she may have must be curtailed by the demands that these duties make on her.'[30]

4

The Opposite Sex: Courtship and Weddings

Relationships with the opposite sex were, predictably, very important to young adults. Friendships and romances, however, were all too often blighted through ignorance, embarrassment and mutual misunderstandings. A consistent thread running through the evidence of many respondents was the feeling that relationships with one's own gender were much easier and more relaxed than with people of the opposite sex. Pre-marital sex and illegitimacy were still frowned upon and, indeed, were regarded as disgraceful by many families. Weddings continued to grow in lavishness and social importance.

The Facts of Life

A small number of women in the earlier study who had had their children both before and after the First World War were so ignorant about sexual matters that they approached the birth of their first child with quite erroneous ideas about the nature of the event. No female respondent in the present study described such a degree of ignorance, but both men and women, probably the majority, remembered very inadequate instruction in such matters from their parents. This accords with Klein's view: 'Even today, few working-class parents seem to tell their children anything about sex.'[1] The fact that respondents were not as ignorant as previous generations appears to have been the result of greater openness about sexual matters both in schools (although schools had widely differing policies about what they told pupils) and in society at large. Young people had always learned something from their friends; now they learned rather more.

Mrs Hutton, when asked if she had been taught 'the facts of life' at her Catholic school in the 1940s, replied:

No, that would have been a taboo subject. The facts of life, I was never ever told them. I just knew them through what other girls told me. When you get your periods, I think my mother told our Sheila [the eldest sister] and then told her to tell me about it when it was my turn; but my mother never actually spoke to me about it.

She remembered a brother being born in 1942, when she was eleven:

We were quite naive really. I don't think we knew where babies came from. I mean, we were running up and downstairs with these jugs of water. We used to think they were scalding my mother to death.[2]

The inability to speak to children about sexual matters persisted in some families throughout the period. Mrs Boyle had five children. When asked if she ever spoke to them about these matters, she said: 'No, I didn't, no, because I knew they were learning it all at school.'[3] Her daughter, Mrs Gerrard, who was born in 1958, and who was interviewed separately, confirmed her mother's reticence and went on to say:

My friend told me. I started my periods one day and my mother had to tell me. I was screaming. I thought I was bleeding to death. 'You've only started your period, go and get a sanitary towel.' And that was it.

Mrs Gerrard went on to talk about her attitude to her own children. She had already spoken to her nine-year-old daughter because she was 'developing', but she was ambivalent about the whole matter:

All the years, I always said I would never tell them about it. I think it is the way I've been brought up. I was thinking they shouldn't tell them in schools either. You know it didn't do me any harm about periods. The more they know when they are younger, I think a lot of them go out and try it.[4]

Both Mrs Gerrard and her mother were pre-maritally pregnant, so it could be argued that their ignorance did not preserve their innocence.

The advice which was given by some parents was both confusing and rather late in the day. Two of the youngest respondents were Mr Monkhouse and Mrs Horwich; both were teenagers in the early 1960s. Mr Monkhouse was given no clear information:

Not directly, no, good gracious no. Not by my parents. Father was basically too shy and mother was too prim. It was said, 'Don't you get a girl into trouble', but I didn't know what getting a girl into trouble was. I thought perhaps you threw a stone through a window or something.[5]

Mrs Horwich learned something at school:

I think the school did it via the rabbit. My mother tried but she couldn't express herself. I can see her now at the old house, ironing, continually ironing at this cloth and telling me to always keep myself nice. And the explanation went on and on and on but didn't mean anything. But you'd to 'keep yourself nice'. So it was a puzzle really. I must have been about eleven or twelve.[6]

Mrs Sykes was twenty-five when she got married in 1952. On her wedding day, at breakfast time, she was sitting with her aunt who said, 'You ought to get a book and read it!' Mrs Sykes replied, 'Who says that?' And the answer was: 'Your mother.' Mrs Sykes ended the exchange with: 'You tell my mother she's a bit late now.' Then she added: 'Nobody ever said a word.'[7]

Some parents did of course talk to their children openly and with sensitivity, but the overwhelming impression given by respondents was of mutual embarrassment and non-communication.

Schools increasingly introduced some form of sex education into the curriculum, with, it appears, the grammar schools leading the way (although they may not have been as 'progressive' as outsiders thought). Mrs Critchley attended Lancaster Girls' Grammar School from 1937 to 1942:

> My husband [who did not go to grammar school] always said that girls who were at the Grammar School were very fast because they learned all about it at school. Well, I think that they did in the sixth form in biology, but we never did.[8]

However, pupils who attended a variety of grammar schools only a few years after Mrs Critchley clearly remember sex education lessons; and these were increasingly not just for the older pupils. Mr Christy attended Preston Grammar School from 1939 to 1946. While learning nothing about sex from his parents, he had gleaned some information from both his peer group and his brothers:

> I was in the sixth form when this thing happened; and it was an army major. He was called in to give the first sex lesson that had ever been given in Preston Grammar School. The only thing I can remember was the uproar from his first statement. He started off by saying, 'Sex is a very sticky subject.'[9]

Mrs Ruthven started at Barrow Grammar School in 1948 and recalled that new pupils to the school were spoken to in small groups by the headmistress, if their parents so wished. But feelings of embarrassment remained. Mr Thornbarrow went to the grammer school in the early 1960s:

> We did get facts of life lessons. They were given by the biology teacher, who was a young woman, which we probably found even more embarrassing than

she did. It was only one lesson and it was in the second form. Those who
studied biology at a later stage could catch up if you had missed out earlier.[10]

Boy meets Girl

Of course, eventually young people, whether well- or badly informed about
the 'facts of life', met and formed relationships. The most frequently
mentioned place for meeting a potential boy- or girl-friend was the dance
hall. Some met through church or church youth clubs, others through
work. Very few mention meeting in pubs; indeed, it still was not acceptable
for young women to go on their own into pubs, although it was acceptable
to accompany a man into one. Once a couple had started to 'go out' with
each other, in the 1940s and 1950s they were most likely to go to the
cinema, where they could be assured of an element of privacy. It was in the
1960s, with the decline in cinema-going, that alternative meeting places
were found, notably the pub and, for some, the disco. This significant
change in the pattern of teenage leisure activities is illustrated by the

Figure 4.1   A dance held as part of the Preston Guild celebrations, 1952
(Photo courtesy of the Harris Library, Preston)

comment of a respondent who was twenty at the end of the 1960s but who stopped going to the cinema rather earlier than that:

> I literally did not go for years. And as far as I am aware the people of my peer group at school didn't go much either. There was a period in the sixties when going to the cinema wasn't what young people did. It had no image at all. I remember going to the cinema and there would be about half a dozen or ten people in and it just seemed to be almost embarrassing somehow.

When asked about alternative meeting places he replied: 'When we went out it was either to a private house or to a pub.' Certain pubs became fashionable with the young for a while and then they would move on. He remembered dancing only at private parties.[11] The growing tendency for young people to meet in a private house is perhaps another sign of the decline in community-based activities. Earlier generations of adolescents were much more likely to have met in the dance hall, the church hall or the cinema. By 1970 the only public meeting place which was regularly mentioned as a meeting place for the young was the pub.

Attitudes to Pre-marital Sex

There was a perhaps surprising continuity in the rules governing the relationships between young men and women. Attitudes to promiscuity, illegitimacy, pre-marital sex and pregnancy were not noticeably different in the 1940s and 1950s than in the 1920s and 1930s. In the 1960s it is possible to chart some changes but not so many as is assumed by those given to using the overworked phrase 'the swinging sixties'. One man who was a teenager in the late 1960s said: 'It was beginning to oscillate in Barrow.'

The national picture also suggests that young people were not being promiscuous. Gorer's study, published in 1955, reports that nationally half the men and two-thirds of the women believed that neither partner should have sexual experience before marriage. In his later work, published in 1971, Gorer reported that a quarter of men and two-thirds of women claimed to be virgins when they married, and a further 20 per cent of men and 25 per cent of women claimed to have had sex only with their future spouse before marriage.[12]

Many respondents remember vividly their shyness and embarrassment with the opposite sex, often lacking the social skills to form a friendly relationship, still less a sexual one. This was as true for many respondents reaching adolescence in the 1960s as it was for earlier generations. Mr Mulholland said:

> It was implicit that what would make your night out was meeting a girl. Most of us, if I'm honest, hadn't the social skills. I was an absolute and utter total failure. I was far too shy to actually go and approach a girl directly. I was OK if you were fighting. I felt very much at home in a macho ambience, but that sort of thing, no. I was extremely gauche.[13]

Embarrassment continued to dog this young man even when he found the courage to take his girl-friend home unannounced:

> It had been a wash day and all the male underwear was on the fender being aired. Mother was not terribly pleased that men's underwear was on public show. We had only been there a couple of minutes when Linda had to go to the toilet. So I showed her where it was and when I got back it had been whipped. It had gone. So I thought no more about it. When Linda came back she sat on the settee and said, 'Oh it's a bit bumpy' and she lifted up the cushions and there was all the laundry hidden from view![14]

More confident young men were bolder with young women but must have often given the impression (perhaps correctly) of only being interested in their bodies. Mutual misunderstandings were common: boys felt girls were teases and girls believed boys went 'too far'. A kind of sexual warfare is observable, boys wanting what girls would not give.

Mr Trickett was a teenager in 1940 and has several accounts of adolescent sexual frustration:

> Some got a reputation more of a teaser. You could take a girl home from the pictures and she would hold your hand in the pictures and you could put your hand on the top of her blouse. And when you got her home you stood on the corner kissing and your leg was working in between her legs. Then you were getting all het up and you were sweating bloody cobs and then all of a sudden she would say, 'Oh I'll have to go now, there's me mam'.

When he was older and in the Navy he often went to dances, but his greater social poise and polish was no more successful than had been his adolescent urgency. At the end of a dance, he asked to take a girl home:

> Because of the blackout she linked arms with you. And you would tell her about yourself and ask her about herself. And then when you got to her door, 'Thank you very much. Good night.' You see, that was it! I've walked from Barrow to Dalton and back [about six miles] and never had a kiss. It's true, honest.[15]

Over twenty years later, in the 1960s, girls were still as careful in their relationships, and still as reluctant to go 'too far'.

Mrs Lonsdale frequently went dancing in Morecambe when she was a teenager:

> I always remember a grey skirt, a right tight skirt. I couldn't get it up to go to the toilet. But I thought that was great because if you got a lad and he was a bit randy he had no chance of getting up, you know. I could hardly walk in it, it was that tight. I thought I was the bees' knees in it, but I felt quite safe in it.[16]

A young man's description of this skirt may have been different.

Girls' reluctance to have a full sexual relationship with boys is easily explained. There continued to be a high value placed on a bride's virginity. A girl who was known to have slept around was in danger of not finding a 'good' husband. Even agreeing to have intercourse with one's fiancé was frowned upon, as it was felt that this would 'spoil' the honeymoon. Mr Trickett, whose youthful sexual ambitions have already been described, displayed a breathtaking double standard which was not at all unusual. After complaining about 'teasers' he added, 'Our motto was if she was not a virgin you did not marry her. She was second-hand goods, you see.'[17]

Mr Hinchcliffe, remembering the mid-1960s, said, 'All my male friends were still going out with nice girls and, believe it or not, it was still a big thing to marry a virgin.' His own interests were different, which may partly explain why he never married. 'I used to find all the girls I liked were the sort men would call slags.'[18]

Mrs Leighton was eighteen when she married in 1959:

> I was brought up that way; I just wouldn't. Sex before marriage just wasn't allowed, really no. I didn't want to. I must admit it was very hard, especially near to our marriage. But I still think my future husband wanted me to be a virgin, it was most important in those days. It was quite difficult at times but he didn't want to spoil things.[19]

Thus internalized norms played an important part in controlling sexual behaviour.

Being known to have lost one's virginity damaged one's reputation to some degree in an age when having a good reputation was still important. Sleeping around was judged to be much worse than having intercourse with only one person. Mrs Swallow spoke of how girls got a bad reputation in the late 1960s. 'I suppose being easy with boys. You know, to become pregnant or to have an affair with somebody; well, I think that would be the pits. I think that would be the end of your reputation, yes.'[20]

When Mrs Lonsdale was asked how she maintained a good reputation she replied, 'Well, I maintained it by not going with guys. I would let them kiss but not go any further.'[21] Boys were much more likely to acquire a bad reputation by fighting or by getting into trouble with the police. The implication in all the replies about reputation is that gossip and fear of gossip still played an important part in controlling sexual behaviour up to 1970.[22]

Parents also continued to play a major role in controlling their children's sexual activities. As has been seen, the great majority of respondents lived at home until their marriage. This meant that all relationships were carried on under the gimlet gaze of parents, and that opportunities for sexual intercourse were far fewer than those enjoyed by a later generation with their own flats and bed-sitters. Age-old warnings against the evils of pre-marital pregnancies were regularly issued to both boys and girls. Mr Monkhouse said:

> I remember my sister being warned never to bring something like that to our doorstep and my dad saying to me, 'Don't you ever bring a girl to the doorstep in that condition.' Being threatened and intimidated.[23]

Parents continued to be strict about when young people came in at nights. Before the war the general rule had been 9 o'clock. This had been extended to 11 o'clock by the 1960s. Those who broke parental rules could expect retribution. Mrs Lonsdale loved going to dances when she was sixteen and seventeen, in the mid-sixties:

> And she always used to say, 'Be in this house at 11 o'clock.' 'Oh it's just getting going then'. 'Be in this house; if you're not, the door is locked.' I've had to wake her up and then I've had a good hiding.[24]

Corporal punishment for girls of that age, in the 1960s, was relatively unusual, but reprimands were not.

Some parents went to what can only be called bizarre lengths to try to control their children's sexual activities. Mrs Needham said this about her mother's behaviour in the late 1930s:

> She didn't trust anybody. She didn't even trust my brothers. Well, I mean, if they had been out, she would examine their clothes when they had been with a girl. She got hold of George and said where had he been because of his trousers, inside of his trousers. You know George.[25]

This was the most intrusive example of parental interference in an adult child's sex life and perhaps significantly took place in the pre-war period when parents in general were stricter with their children, whatever their ages. The passage of time, however, did not mean that all mothers stopped being investigative. Mrs Emery spoke of her experiences with her mother in the mid 1950s:

> She used to have a calendar up on the wall. And she used to know when your period started and if you didn't start she used to say, 'You should have started.'[26]

Pre-marital Pregnancy

There were, however, changes in sexual behaviour and attitudes. Despite the mores, fear of gossip, fear of parents' reactions, fear of pre-marital pregnancy and the continuing importance of being or having a virgin bride, some unmarried couples did have sexual intercourse which sometimes resulted in pregnancy. This was hardly a new phenomenon but more female respondents were pre-maritally pregnant than in the earlier study, when only one woman said she was. It may well have been that pre-marital pregnancy was under-reported in the previous study, but the apparent increase in its incidence in the period 1940–70 does suggest some changes in sexual attitudes and a real change in sexual behaviour.

Klein suggested that one in eight babies were conceived out of wedlock in the decade 1950–60, with 60 per cent being made legitimate by the subsequent marriage of the parents.[27] There was a smaller percentage of declared pre-maritally pregnant brides in this study, but, as no one was asked directly about pregnancy before marriage, the real total could have been greater. What seems to be significant is the increase when compared to the earlier study. Six women respondents and the wife of a male respondent were pregnant when they got married, four in the mid-1950s and three in the 1960s or later. In all cases the respondents made it clear that they had had every intention of getting married and that they saw anticipating marriage as being very different to being promiscuous. Mrs Jenkins was married in 1954:

> I mean, I was a virgin when we got engaged. And I think a lot of my friends were. I think it was just a case of how long you waited.[28]

Mrs Boyle was also married in 1954:

> I were three months pregnant when I got married.
> Did that worry you?
> No, because we were going to get married in July really and Barry's

mother asked us if we would hold it back until December, which we did. And if I had got married in July I wouldn't have been pregnant! And no, I weren't bothered because we both knew that we were going to get married. I daren't tell my dad I were pregnant, by the way.[29]

Mrs Boyle's last throw-away remark indicates that the family situation was not as relaxed as her account would suggest.

Two of the pre-maritally pregnant women had particularly strict parents and have already been quoted. They were Mrs Emery and Mrs Lonsdale. Mrs Emery was married in 1955:

He was the first boy what ever touched me. Once I went to a dance and somebody wanted to take me home, long before I met Tony, and somebody shouted out, 'Don't bother to take her home because wherever you take her you'll get nought.'

When she realized she was pregnant she could not tell her parents. Her mother cross-examined her about the absence of circles on the wall calendar and she made up an excuse about having an accident at work which gave her a shock which in turn stopped her periods. Eventually, as she gained weight, she screwed up her courage to tell her mother:

I said, 'I'm going to have a baby,' and she said, 'Mary, Jesus and Joseph. You'd better get yourself upstairs. I'll have to tell your dad.' And he come home and she must have said something to him. And I thought, 'Oh here goes.' And I came downstairs and he just looked at me and said, 'Now you can get back to bed and I'll deal with you later.' And then in the morning when I came downstairs he just said, 'What has to be will be. If you don't want to get married, don't.' And it just carried on from there and I did get married.[30]

Mrs Lonsdale was married in 1967. She could not understand her mother's shock:

I think she was just shocked. I think it hurt her. She wouldn't speak to me for a few days. I can't understand it. I mean the way she lived. She lived with a man. She had me out of wedlock. She lived with another man, she had another child who she put up for adoption. And yet for me, just to get caught even though I was getting married. She just couldn't accept it.[31]

Despite the widespread and continuing condemnation of pre-marital pregnancy, parents, with very few exceptions, were supportive of their sons and daughters when the dreaded condition actually occurred. There was only one example in the study,[32] of parents rejecting or even of being particularly critical of their pre-maritally pregnant adult children.

Mr and Mrs Whiteside found themselves expecting a baby when they were unmarried teenagers in 1960. They were very innocent and believed that they were successfully disguising Mrs Whiteside's condition. Rather inexplicably, neither set of parents mentioned it until they did. Then there was a rapid rushing around and a wedding took place. 'So we was married, and had a family and got him christened all in eleven days!'[33]

There may have been an increase in pre-marital pregnancies among respondents as compared to the respondents in the earlier study, but was this a symptom of increasing promiscuity in the wider community? There is certainly official evidence to support this argument, especially in the 1960s. The Barrow Medical Officer of Health (unlike his colleagues in Preston and Lancaster) published figures for venereal diseases in the second half of the 1960s and wrote this comment:

> The rise in the number of cases of venereal disease is undoubtedly due to the increase in promiscuity. It should be remembered that the Pill, although it prevents pregnancy, does not prevent venereal disease, and the other methods of birth control are more effective in this respect.[34]

The total number of cases of venereal disease in Barrow rose from 59 in 1965 to 174 in 1970, while in the same period the figures for gonorrhoea rose from 5 to 65.

Illegitimacy

The 1960s also saw a dramatic rise in illegitimacy rates in all three towns. In 1960 the rates were as follows: Barrow 1.4 per cent, Lancaster 5.6 per cent, Preston 8.0 per cent (the figure for Barrow was peculiarly low: the average for 1959–61 was 2.9 per cent). The rates for the three towns in 1970 were 9.2 per cent, 10.3 per cent and 13.2 per cent, respectively.[35] These figures suggest that there was a more marked rise in illegitimacy in this area than in the United Kingdom as a whole. The national average was 5.8 per cent in 1961 and 8.4 per cent in 1970.[36]

Whether these official figures are indicative of greater sexual freedom or increased promiscuity is a debatable point. However, almost all the respondents would deny that, in the 1960s, they were either promiscuous or sexually liberated. Indeed, the dramatic rise in the figures for illegitimacy and venereal disease still represented changes in the life-styles of only a small minority of the population. As has been seen, the pre-maritally pregnant were characterized more by their naivety and innocence than by worldliness and sophistication; and most did, of course, subsequently marry.

Among the respondents and their families the incidence of illegitimacy remained very low. Two respondents were illegitimate, but only one had an acknowledged illegitimate child in the period 1940–70. The mother of one respondent in the 1920s had a long-standing relationship with a man, but her mother forbade her to marry him because she was a Catholic and he was not. She preferred illegitimate grandchildren to the shame of her daughter contracting a 'mixed' marriage. Perhaps the most surprising aspect of the story was that the daughter acquiesced in her mother's decision (although not happily). Mrs Lonsdale was also illegitimate; she was born in 1947. Her mother was in the process of being divorced when she met Mrs Lonsdale's father. 'She just said that he was someone she met a few times and that he didn't come from here.'[37] Later, still unmarried, the mother again became pregnant and had the child adopted. Only one respondent had an illegitimate child and she was the victim of frustrated marriage expectations: Mrs Needham became pregnant in 1940; unfortunately her partner was not of a similar social background to herself. He was also under twenty-one and therefore not able to marry without his parents' consent:

> Well, I met him at a dance. I was going with him and he knew that I was
> having this child and we went down to face his mother and father. And his
> mother's words were that she didn't want her son to marry a labourer's
> daughter. They were high up in society. They moved away to Plymouth and
> he went with them.

Her family made some efforts to find him but with no success, so Mrs Needham was left to face poverty and the anger of her mother: 'My mother put me in the workhouse because she thought it was wrong what I had done. When you were put in there, while the time come to have your baby, you had to work. But I couldn't work because I was ill.' Her mother continued to be unpleasant after she returned home with the baby, and eventually 'arranged' a marriage between her daughter and the son of one of her friends.[38]

Change or Continuity in Sexual Mores?

A very small group of respondents spoke of changing sexual mores in the 1960s. Three respondents, all born in the 1940s, spoke about sexual relationships with people other than those one expected to marry. One woman spoke of her contemporaries in the sixth form learning to drive as soon as they were seventeen. She felt that this gave them much more sexual freedom than had their non-driving predecessors:

> There is so much countryside round about, you have only to park anywhere and you have lots of opportunities for all sorts. So driving was the big break-through in terms of opportunity for sexual experience.[39]

Mr Rowlandson would perhaps have liked more sexual freedom. He defied his father by taking out a lot of girls, but as he continued to live at home he was unable to be as free as he would have liked. He went to a lot of parties. 'You know, it wasn't the type of party for a sex orgy, it was a dance, a drink and a laugh. And then you might walk home with a girl.' Then he added: 'There was no Pill in them days. It was a great myth, the sexual freedom.'[40] The Pill *was* available, as was indicated by the Barrow Medical Officer of Health, but it is doubtful if many doctors in the late 1960s were prescribing it for unmarried girls. The Family Planning Association did not give out contraceptive advice to the unmarried until the 1970s.

Only one respondent appears to have had some degree of sexual freedom. Mrs Horwich, when asked what she remembered about the 1960s, said, 'Well, certainly enjoying clothes and hair styles and freedom, sexual freedom, that was the sixties wasn't it?' Later in her interview she returned to this topic:

> It was a confusing period really. It was very exciting but it was also very confusing. There was a huge values conflict with what I'd grown up with right through teenage. And then suddenly at the age of about twenty all the values changed and all sorts of other things were encouraged and smiled upon. I see myself as fairly conformist but who would like to be different. I'm neither one thing or the other.[41]

This respondent felt the conflict between traditional values and newer freedoms so acutely that by 1970 she could be said to have been in a state of 'anomie'. She collapsed, and greeted the new decade, during which the sexual mores of more respondents and many more citizens would change, in a psychiatric hospital.

It has been suggested that nationally, in the 1960s, young people were much less permissive than has sometimes been thought. 'During the 1960s attitude surveys showed young people to be much more conservative in their ideas about sex and marriage than press reports about "Promiscuity and the Pill" indicated.'[42] No equivalent local surveys about attitudes to sex and marriage have been found. However, a newspaper report in 1966 suggests a far from 'swinging' life style for Preston teenagers. A survey was carried out of 593 boys and 587 girls in the 15–20 age group. Of the twenty-year-olds 80 per cent of the boys but only 50 per cent of the girls went to the pub at least once a week. The percentage going to the pub declined sharply as one went down the age group. A surprising 45 per cent said they attended a religious service once a week, but the most popular leisure time activity was watching television.[43]

On balance, there is far more evidence to suggest that local young adults in this period were behaving in a socially conservative way, rather than experiencing a brave new world of freedom from the conventions which had ruled the lives of their parents.

Weddings

Marriages began with an increasing amount of ceremony and expenditure than in earlier times. Weddings, especially with regard to the clothes worn and the style of the reception, became grander and more elaborate affairs (although the custom of having an expensive and prolonged honeymoon to exotic places appears to have become more common after 1970). 'Never before had so many married and with such elaborate ceremony.'[44] It was claimed that nationally, by the 1950s, 58 per cent of skilled workers and 45 per cent of unskilled workers were married in the 'grand manner'.[45] It is difficult to define what was meant by the 'grand manner', but almost all the respondents had a larger and more expensive wedding than had their parents. None, in this period, were married in a registry office. In the first decades of the century weddings had been constrained by financial considerations. Increasingly in the post-war world the overriding criterion was fashion.

It has been suggested that all the 'traditional' ingredients of the big white wedding were introduced in the nineteenth century and that none precede this date. The Victorian wealthier classes created the 'traditional' wedding to emphasize their ideal of conjugal love and the nuclear family.[46] It was not usual, however, for the bride to wear white, 'the universal symbol of feminine purity and virtuous womanhood',[47] until the 1930s. Working-class brides rarely appeared in white at this time, not because they wished to appear lacking in virtue but because of the expense involved. They

Figure 4.2   A wedding reception, 1960. Buffets were not as popular as 'sit down' meals
(Photo courtesy of Popperfoto)

continued to be married, as had the wealthy of the eighteenth century, in
their best clothes. However, increasing prosperity in the post-war period
made it possible for more and more brides to be married in white with 'all
the trimmings'. For them, too, the white dress had become the symbol of
purity and virtue and yet another middle-class Victorian fashion had spread
down the social scale.

Weddings were never, of course, totally stereotyped; there were always
individual differences resulting from family expectations, financial and
religious considerations and individual choice. It is not therefore possible to
say that Mrs Morrison's wedding in the mid-1950s is absolutely typical of
the time, but it makes an interesting contrast with that of her mother, Mrs
Sharp, which took place in 1920. Mrs Sharp's wedding was considerably
livelier than many of her contemporaries, who often had a simple ceremony
attended only by the closest family, followed at home by a very simple meal,

probably consisting of sandwiches and cake. Mrs Sharp described her wedding outfit and the proceedings:

> A costume; my sister and I made it; it was bluey-grey. It had a long skirt and the coat was rounded and we made it between us. Everyone said what a nice costume it was. There were about fifty there. We had it at the house, you didn't go out. I got about fifty wedding presents. The living room was full, the back kitchen was full and the front was full. We had a meat tea and they were carrying to them. Some sat at the table and then others took a turn. The men went out and brought a barrel of beer and put it up in the yard. Oh gosh! I think they came from all over. You never saw such a crowd, and it went on till six o'clock in the morning. I was going to live at his mother's and we were going home at six o'clock in the morning. At supper time m'aunt made a rabbit pie. I'm the only one who had a big wedding like that.[48]

Her daughter, Mrs Morrison, was asked what kind of wedding she had:

> A white wedding; three bridesmaids, my cousins. I had a long dress with a veil. And the bridesmaids had cherry red, for the winter wedding, you see. And then we had our reception at the Co-op because that was the place at the time. It seems awful now. And we went and stayed at my brother's house. Of course, we didn't have a lot of money, but we had bought a house of our own, so we just went away for a long weekend and then came back to our home to settle in.[49]

Ten years later, in the late 1960s, Mrs Rowlandson's wedding was different again. Her family were not well off, her father was a riveter and her mother a part-time childminder, but they had a small inheritance which was used to finance her wedding:

> It was a straight white satin dress with a train; and they were bouffant veils in those days with a pearl band. My husband wore a grey suit and grey winkle-picker shoes. My wedding was typical of the time because I was working with the same age group as myself. One by one people were getting married, so we used to go to each other's weddings and it was typical of the time. It was eighty guests. It wasn't very big, it was just an ordinary church. A white wedding with an organ; no choirboys, because that wasn't in then. The reception at a country pub. So we hired a bus! We came back here because we had just got this bungalow; and then we hired a car and went to the Lake District.[50]

Weddings were seen as predominantly female affairs; arranged by women and very much in accordance with the bride's and her family's wishes.

Bridegrooms appear to have agreed to whatever was decided, and there seems to have been little, if any, dissent. Mr Graveson was married in 1960 at a time when he held an unskilled job. His family was clearly working-class and yet he wore, somewhat unusually, a morning suit for the occasion:

> Because Rita's mother and father wanted them. I certainly wouldn't have done. I'll be quite honest, no way. I thought myself it was probably a bit 'poncey'. Women always win on their wedding day. And I suppose it's right in some ways. Yes, I remember both my brothers weren't really impressed.[51]

Conclusion

It would seem that the elements of continuity were more striking than those of change when considering relationships between the sexes up to and including the occasion of weddings. There was continuing ignorance about sexual matters and embarrassment in close social relationships. Pre-marital sex and especially pre-marital pregnancy were widely condemned, although they clearly occurred. Weddings were more expensive and had become formal family and social occasions; a development which to some extent reflected both increasing prosperity and raised social expectations. Before 1970 it appears to have been unthinkable for couples in our study to set up home together without 'the benefit of matrimony'.

5

Family Planning and Role Relationships in Marriage

There was a generally optimistic note struck by those writing about marriage in the 1960s. Ronald Fletcher, having considered much of the then contemporary evidence wrote,

> All in all then, in spite of the problems brought about through change, the picture of marriage in modern Britain which emerges from statistics and from these qualitative studies alike is, surely, a picture of considerable health, considerable stability, and an enlarged degree of opportunity and happiness.[1]

Was such enthusiasm justified? There had clearly been changes in the state of marriage since the earlier part of the century but were they all changes for the better? More particularly, how did they affect the role and status of women? This chapter considers the way in which couples planned their families, and changing role relationships in marriage.

Contraception and Family Planning

A fundamental element of the relationship between husbands and wives was their attitude to and practice of contraception. The overall decline in the birth rate shows an increasing tendency to limit family size, but aggregated data tend to hide the uncertainties, the difficulties in long-term planning and the anxieties which affected families and had a direct and critical bearing on the lives of many women. The fact that they had less than perfect control over their own fertility had important implications for their lives, both as wives and mothers and as workers outside the home.

Respondents, surprisingly like their parents from earlier in the century, showed some reticence in discussing sexual matters; this extended to questions of contraception and family planning. It would appear that most, indeed almost all, couples planned their families, but they were reluctant to discuss the methods they adopted.

Only one respondent claimed not to have limited her family in any way. Mrs Kennedy had six children between the late 1950s and 1970: 'I never planned any of them. They just came, yes. I never thought, it just happened. I mean you can plan them nowadays can't you?'[2] Mrs Kennedy's child-bearing was only ended when she had a hysterectomy. This quotation might give the impression that Mrs Kennedy was a passive victim of her own fertility, but, as will be seen elsewhere, she was a very fulfilled and happy woman who had thoroughly enjoyed her large family. She was not the only respondent who appears to have believed, erroneously, that contraceptives were difficult to obtain in the post-war period.

Among the parents of respondents the practice of not using contra-ceptives, even in the post-war period when they were widely available, was probably quite common. Mr Monkhouse was born in 1948, one of eight surviving children, there being two more who died. The youngest was born in 1960. He and his siblings, as they got older, were both mystified and amused by their parents producing such a large family. 'It became a steady joke when we were older, that every time my dad hung his trousers on the bedpost my mum got pregnant.'[3] He speculated about his parents' lack of family planning, and in so doing revealed something of the changing attitudes to contraception apparent in his and other families:

> The obvious way to get out of the poverty trap was not to have so many children, but contraception in those days wasn't the common thing. I suppose it was there. God knows, dad had been in the forces and I'm quite well aware that the forces issued servicemen abroad with prophylactics, as they were politely called. But they weren't commonly available. I think that working-class people would not only find it difficult financially to have afforded them, but a lot of them may quite well have been ashamed to have been seen buying them. . . . Mother occasionally, when she was deeply frus-trated – and there were quite a few times when dealing with a financial crisis, she would rail and would go about saying 'Bloody kids' – and for mother to swear was quite unusual – 'Why was I cursed with so many bloody kids?' And yet as we grew older and less dependent, to both mum and dad their real pride and joy was their family, and they took very great pride that most of us have done quite well really.[4]

Ignorance, poverty and embarrassment all contributed to the absence of contraception in some families. Condoms were on sale in a variety of shops (including barbers) in post-war Britain, but there was still a feeling that their use was not entirely respectable or acceptable. Indeed, the government did not sanction official support for the provision of contraceptives until 1967.[5]

Did religious beliefs also influence couples' decisions about family planning? Preston in particular had a large Roman Catholic population (which was well represented among our respondents). Mrs Rowlandson was brought up in a very strict Catholic family. Her aunt had eight children:

> If you had more than seven the bishop baptized every child. 'Well,' I said, 'you've got to go through a heck of a lot just to get the bishop to baptise them. . . . it's just not worth it.'[6]

It is very likely that other Catholic couples shared Mrs Rowlandson's point of view. Certainly, her parents had only two children and she herself had only one. In the earlier study virtually no difference was found in the size of families born to Catholics and to non-Catholics, but the same is not true of the present study. The respondents were divided into two: those born before 1935 and those born after. They were further sub-divided into Catholic and non-Catholic. The Catholic parents of the earlier cohort had an average of 4.8 children while their non-Catholic contemporaries had 3.8. The children of these Catholic parents had 2.0 offspring while those of the non-Catholic parents had 2.4. In the second cohort (those born after 1935) the Catholic respondents' parents had 5.0 children and the non-Catholics 3.2, while the Catholic respondents themselves had only 1.5 children but their non-Catholic counterparts had 1.6. Clearly our sample is not statistically valid, but it has some interesting pointers. The most obvious conclusion must be that an increasing number of people from all Churches – and from none – were limiting their families to a greater or lesser degree. Therefore, it can be argued that many factors which had inhibited the use of contraceptives, and these must include religious beliefs, became less and less significant in working-class life as the century progressed.

Attitudes towards, and methods of, contraception

Contraception was not infallible, and women, however much they wanted to limit their families, were not at all confident that they would succeed in so doing. Mrs Wallington was married in 1946 and had three children:

> You didn't plan in those days like you do now. You didn't say, 'I'm getting married and having three children,' or 'I'm getting married and I don't want any kiddies.' You just took what came along.[7]

Mistakes could happen and unfortunate children were sometimes told that they were an accident. Mr Morrison, who was born in 1932, said:

> My parents were old when they had me. My mother was thirty-eight and my dad forty-three. An accident.
>
> Did they tell you that?
>
> Oh well, they were married fifteen years. I could have worked it out for myself. They never hid the fact. No, they didn't think that the world was a suitable place to bring children into.[8]

Couples used a variety of contraceptive methods. Mrs Leighton was married in 1959: 'I went a few days before I was married to have the cap fitted. That was the normal thing to do. That was the contraceptive to use, or the sheath.'[9]

Mrs Hutton and her husband, married in 1950, practised *coitus interruptus*, a traditional method of contraception in working-class families. She even used, as her predecessors had done, a transport euphemism to describe it. 'Even before we had children we never used anything. No. It was like getting off at the roundabout instead of going to Morecambe.'[10] This system 'worked' for her for eight years.

Occasionally couples failed to limit their fertility and had to seek more drastic action. Mrs Jenkins was married in 1954 and was pre-maritally pregnant:

> The first one wasn't wanted because we weren't married; the second one was. We didn't particularly go for it, it was only two years later. The third one . . . you just couldn't plan. We didn't do anything. No. My husband wouldn't do anything and he said it was up to me. I used to go to the doctor . . . things were sort of . . . you were very embarrassed with the doctor. You've got to have your husband's permission when you're sterilized and he immediately jumped at it. And my mother-in-law said, 'You know, what a good idea, otherwise you will be having one every year.' I'm very glad I did, because all those three children went on to university. So I mean, if we'd had a big family we couldn't have done that. It was a struggle as it was.[11]

Right up to the end of the period under consideration, even with the introduction of the Pill and the coil, women were still finding themselves unexpectedly pregnant. Mrs Turnbull had three children between 1953 and 1962. In 1970 she found herself pregnant again, at the age of thirty-eight, and she was very upset:

> I was learning to drive, and I was an auxiliary nurse going in for training, but of course it didn't come off after that. It just knocked me off. It puts you

back, you see, because you've got to be at home. It was a shock. And I wasn't
very happy about it, to tell you the truth. I was on the Pill and I came off the
Pill and then I had the coil done, and that was the result of the coil. About
eighteen months I had the coil in, and I had it checked regularly, and I just
couldn't understand it because it was always in place. I just couldn't understand it.

Mrs Turnbull was eventually sent to a specialist. She was late in seeking
medical advice because of the presence of the coil and because she was still
menstruating. The specialist told her that he would have done an abortion
had she come sooner, and she said that she would have accepted this offer:

Well, I would, because honestly I didn't want another one. I just didn't want
that baby. But when she was born and I saw her I just bawled my brains out.
How awful I'd been. The poor little thing didn't ask to be born, you know!
I mean to say, we had planned. We had never been able to plan a lot of
things, you know, we had just plodded along through life, and we were
going to have a different life in a way, but of course it didn't come off.[12]

Mrs Hunter, who had relied on *coitus interruptus* until the birth of her third
child in 1965 then went on the Pill (which she described as a new development). 'I went enormous. I went fat, big round fat face, and headaches. I was
in a terrible state, and the doctor took me off.' As a result of not using any
form of contraceptive she became pregnant when she started living with a
new partner. He disliked children and certainly did not want the baby.

'He said, "I don't want it." And I was so wrapped up in him at the time
that I did what he wanted. I regret it, you know.' Her own doctor agreed to
a termination and sent her to the hospital. She was very upset by the
interview she had there:

He made me feel like a loose woman. I was in tears. He said, 'OK. If we get
rid of this, how do I know you are not going to be in next year for the same
thing?' I was so upset that I nearly threw myself under a bus when I came
out. I cried all the way home on the bus.

Eventually the termination was carried out. 'At the time I was glad I was
having it done. But I think that anyone who has had a pregnancy termin-
ated always looks back and thinks, "Would it have been a boy or the girl I
always wanted?" '[13] Mrs Hunter is one of only two respondents who chose
abortion as a solution to her dilemma. The other respondent was still so
distressed about her abortion in the late 1960s that she would only talk
about it, and then with great reserve, with the tape recorder turned off. She
claimed that her mental health would have been totally jeopardized if the

pregnancy had continued. It was, of course, only at the end of the period, after the 1967 Abortion Act, that abortion became legal. No respondent admitted to an illegal abortion, whether self-administered or done by a back-street abortionist.[14]

Despite the evidence of unwanted and unplanned pregnancies, it is clear from the birth rates and from individual life stories that the great majority of couples were successful in limiting their families. The reasons given, or implied, for family limitation were closely related to economic aspirations. Respondents believed that they would be better off financially, either at that time or in the future, if they had a limited number of children. What the statistical evidence does not show is the uncertainty many couples showed about planning for the future. They might plan their families, but the unexpected pregnancy could not be ruled out. Retrospectively they would say, 'We were lucky, we wanted two and that is what we had.' But they could not be completely confident during their childbearing years. This uncertainty particularly affected women's plans for the future, making them more likely to take up casual, unskilled work and less likely to seek a job requiring any length of training. There was a much greater likelihood of their giving up work if they had an unplanned pregnancy rather than seeking an abortion.

Infertility and Low Fertility

Generally falling birth rates tend to obscure the problems of infertility or low fertility. At first sight what would appear to be an unusual number of respondents failed to have as many children as they would have liked. These findings are not so surprising when compared to those given in the *Report of an Enquiry into Family Limitation* which was published in 1949. This claimed that one in eight of all couples in the survey who were married before 1944 were infertile, that is, they had no children – for whatever reason.[15] In this present study only three couples failed to have any children before 1970, although among those married after that date another nine respondents had no children. It is not possible to say whether this was voluntary or involuntary infertility, as respondents were not asked about details of their lives after 1970. Four of these respondents formed two married couples, so therefore, in our study, there were ten couples with no children, which was slightly more than 10 per cent of the total number of respondents, given that two were unmarried. The respondents who were married before 1970 had more to say about low fertility than unfertility. Six women had only one child and would have liked more, two had two children but had been unsuccessful in their attempts to have a third. A few women reported being frightened of being infertile because they had been slow to conceive, although they subsequently achieved their desired family size.

Mrs Owen had a bad time giving birth to her first child in 1940, having been badly torn: 'At first I said to my husband, "We'll have no more." But later on we would have loved another one, but nothing happened.'[16]

Mrs Whiteside had her child twenty years after Mrs Owen. She was pre-maritally pregnant and only seventeen. She was married a short time before the baby's birth:

> You were upset, everybody in the family was upset. And at first, after I had Kevin, I was a bit frightened of getting pregnant again being so young, and thinking you're going to have a houseful of babies. And then I never had any more after that. But it's not that I wouldn't have liked to have more. They just didn't turn up. Nature . . . it tricks you doesn't it? I've always loved babies, but you know I just never had any.[17]

Not all women attempted to find explanations for their problems or indeed remedies. Resignation and fatalism, the characteristics of so many women's lives over the centuries, were not uncommon. Others took positive steps to change and improve their situation. One woman, fearing that she would never have any children, adopted two before having one of her own. Mrs Peel had the most complicated childbearing history: she had one child by her first husband before the marriage ended in divorce. Failing to conceive with her second husband, they consulted a specialist who decided that the husband was sterile, therefore they adopted a child. Ten years later Mrs Peel was again referred to a specialist for a hysterectomy only to discover that the reason for the 'growth' was that she was seven months pregnant; she later gave birth to a healthy child.[18] Mrs Hunter also sought and received help. She had been married seven years without conceiving and went into hospital in the early 1960s for an operation: 'I had been married all those years but apparently my vagina wasn't open properly. I had a flange of skin that they cut away. I was only in hospital four days.'[19] A year later a child was born, but no more followed.

Role Relationships in Marriage: the Earlier Part of the Century

In the previous study, covering the period 1890–1940, three models of role relationships in marriage were discernible. In the first and most usual model the husband was the wage-earner and the wife the household manager, with prime responsibility for the upbringing of the children. The home was the wife's sphere, and within it she tended to be the dominant person. In the outside world (with the exception of the immediate neighbourhood), husbands were dominant, whether in the world of paid work or in trade unions or in politics. Men's and women's roles were almost entirely separate, but there was an equal division of power: that of men resulting from their role as wage earners, that of women from their role as financial, household and family managers. They may well have earned money, but that was seen as an extension of their role as financial managers; their usually small and casual wages 'topping up' the family income. It has been suggested that women did not have power but simply responsibility. Certainly, it would be difficult to envisage a situation in which women had power in the home without responsibility. Whatever our feminist analysis may be about the siting of power within marriages in the earlier part of the century, it is clear from the empirical evidence that the majority of both men and women firmly believed that women were the 'bosses' in the home and family. They not only had the day-to-day running of the home and family in their charge, but they were the ones who made the important decisions about such matters as where the family should live, whether a house should be bought or rented, and what jobs the children should have. There is an overwhelming mass of oral evidence on this topic.[20] It is supported both by the evidence of contemporary observers and historians looking at other areas.[21]

Klein came to a similar conclusion about power relationships in 'traditional' marriages:

> We conclude therefore that male dominance and female dominance are not necessarily mutually exclusive and to be contrasted with one another. Where there is role segregation and a strict division between the spheres of the two groups, each may be sovereign in his own sphere.[22]

A second model was observable in the much smaller group of families where the woman was a textile worker. Here husbands and wives had equal roles and equal power. Both worked full time, both earned wages (sometimes the wife earning more than the husband) and both shared the housework and childcare. Not all husbands of women textile workers were domesticated, but a surprising number were. Although they tended to have roughly equal power, the women still controlled the budget.

In the third model of marriage, observable in only a very small group of families, there was a total separation of roles, as in the first model, but there was no equal division of power, the husbands being dominant, controlling the major part of the income and frequently bullying their wives and children.

Some of these findings are in accordance with those of Elizabeth Bott.[23] She related the degree of seperateness of conjugal roles with the degree of interconnectedness in the couples' social network. She argued that the more integrated the latter, the more separate the former. This model, however, was not really applicable in all cases. In Preston, for example, where both partners were textile workers the roles of husband and wife were not at all separate: they were very similar and interchangeable. But their social networks were also very integrated, neighbours and kin living in close proximity and being very interconnected. In the third model, where husbands and wives had separate roles and very unequal power, couples were conspicuous for the lack of an integrated social network. Indeed, they had few contacts, especially with kin. In this geographical area only the first model, with equal but separate roles for husband and wife, was in accordance with Bott's model.

Changes in Role Relationships: the Decline of the Powerful Woman

Patterns of role relationships in marriage become much more complex as the century moves on. It is possible, for example, to describe yet another model, one in which the partners had separate roles but unequal power, but not one in which the wife was bullied or ill-treated by the husband. On the contrary, in these marriages the wife was cherished and protected by her husband; but in return for these 'benefits' she relinquished much of the power of decision-making. This type of marriage was modelled on the one widely adopted by the middle classes from the time of the Industrial Revolution onwards.[24] Domestic ideology, so beloved by the Victorian bourgeoisie, with woman seen as 'the Angel in the Home' was increasingly viewed as an ideal state of marriage by working-class men and women. It remained unrealizable while wages were low and women's managerial and earning skills were so essential for the survival of the working-class family.

A dependent, slightly helpless, female simply could not be afforded in most working-class families. But in the more prosperous families this ideal was being increasingly realized before the Second World War, and the trend became more pronounced in the post-war period with its continually rising standard of living.

In the earlier studies many of the older respondents, born before the First World War, remembered very powerful women. Some respondents were very powerful themselves. In the present study powerful women appear much more infrequently, mostly as grandmothers, rarely as mothers and almost never as respondents. Mrs Lodge's grandmother, in the inter-war period, forbade her daughter to marry, and as a result she had two illegitimate children:

> My grandmother was an Irish Catholic and you only married Catholics, and if you didn't marry Catholics you didn't get married at all. Yes, her life was spoiled through religion. It wouldn't happen today.[25]

Mrs Hutton's paternal grandmother also dominated the family. Her daughter had died when only sixteen, again in the inter-war period, and at that point she had vowed never to comb her hair again. This subsequently grew in a mass of bright red curls. She also gave up her religion:

> Actually she was a very good Catholic, but when her daughter died she refused to go to church any more. She thought that God had done that to her and so consequently my father and mother were married in the Church of England. But then this priest came to see grandmother [who lived with her son and his family]. I don't know what he said to her, but he must have persuaded her to go back into the church, because all of a sudden: 'If I'm going back in the church, my son has to go back in,' and of course his wife too. So they were remarried in the Catholic church.[26]

The children remembered their parents' wedding and their own sudden removal from the state school to a Catholic one.

Several other dominant co-resident grandmothers are recorded and there were some dominant mothers too. Mrs Needham's mother has already been mentioned (investigating her son's trousers). Her husband in the pre-war period did almost all the housework as well as earning a living:

> He did everything, my mother did nothing. My mother had all those children [nine] and hadn't a varicose vein in her leg. And nails like a lady. She'd sit in a rocking chair, she'd sit all day long. He did all the work. He

used to get up at about a quarter to four, blacklead the fire place and polish
right through the house, prepare everything for the meal in the evening. And
then he used to come home and we all got fed and he made it. I think that
my mother was the boss of him. Well, he had to do it, yes. She treated him
as though he was still in the army. She even called him by his surname. Yes,
it used to be like a sort of bullying. This is why I was more for my dad than
for my mum. I was the one who felt it was wrong. There was only me that
spoke out.

(It is interesting that both Mrs Needham and other relatives who were
interviewed remarked that all the sons in the family had taken after their
father, and had relied on their wives to tell them what to do.)[27]
Apart from a few examples, why was there an apparent decline in the
number of dominant, powerful women? More importantly, why did there
appear to be a lessening of women's power in most marriages? It could be
that it was no longer 'fashionable' for women to be strong, capable and
managing. With the exception of the war years, one of the potent images of
women portrayed in films and magazines throughout the 1920s to the end
of the 1960s was one of a pretty, feminine, dependent person. In families
where there was a daily struggle for survival such images had little power
or influence; a wife and mother who was strong, capable and managing was
both needed and admired. However, with increasing affluence, men and
women alike adopted this model of the ideal wife who was 'feminine'.
Jacqueline Sarsby, in a survey carried out in the early 1970s, found young
working-class girls wanting a man to be dominant as well as kind. They
spoke of marrying for security and about husbands taking the decisions in
a happy marriage.[28]
It is always difficult to know to what extent respondents were influenced
by external fashions and standards, rather than by their own experiences.
Several male respondents with dominant mothers resolved not to marry
similar women, and women with similar mothers were determined not to
be like them. Mrs Needham was herself married in 1941; later in her
interview, she was asked:

Do you think women were stronger than they are made out to be?
I do. They were the dominant factor then. His mother was, my mother
was.
So your mothers were really the bosses in their households?
Yes, and that's why I'm not. I'm not the dominant factor with you [to her
husband].
[Mr Needham:] I know.[29]

Mr Warwick, who was married in 1959, said of his parents. 'He wasn't one of these chauvinists, you know. He couldn't be, could he? My mother was the gaffer. Father handed over his wages to mother, received his pocket money and helped in the house.' Mr Warwick was determined not to be like his father:

> I think there should be somebody who runs the place. I think if you start all this sharing you get in a hell of a muddle. I know blokes who used to hand all their wages to their wives and finish up with nought. They just have spending money and I don't agree. I don't think that is right. The man should run the money. I thought my father was henpecked.[30]

Mrs Warwick was also interviewed. She had grown up in a family where her mother had run everything. The reason for this was that her husband was in the Merchant Navy and was rarely home until he retired in his sixties. There was no suggestion that either she or Mr Warwick's mother were anything but excellent managers, but Mrs Warwick agreed with her husband that it was better for the husband to be in charge of the finances and to be the dominant partner. She was not downtrodden, and at one point in the interview when her husband said: 'She's the boss now, she's getting her own back', she intervened sharply: 'Nobody could be the boss of you.' She took a job when her children were teenagers, first as a shop assistant, later as a domestic, but felt compelled to add: 'I enjoyed being at home though, you know. I've no great desire to go to work, because I always did a lot of sewing and knitting, so you know I could always find plenty to do.' As Mrs Warwick was in paid work this defensiveness was not perhaps simply on her own account, but was a more general defence of those women who chose a purely domestic role. It could also well have been that she continued to feel that paid employment was somehow improper.[31]

Mrs Morrison, married in the 1950s, expressed support for notions of femininity. She did eventually return to full-time work in the early 1970s but said, 'It's nice to be taken out and looked after and have the door opened for you and people caring for you. I just like the homely things, yes.'[32]

Mr Graveson expressed his admiration for femininity thus (he was discussing clothes in the 1950s):

> Girls dressed like girls. I still prefer to see her [his wife] in a dress rather than anything else. My daughter wears a lot of jeans, but to me they don't look like women.
>
> Women's trousers did arrive in that thirty-year period.

They did and to me they are not a good thing. I like my women to be women and I think they are much nicer for it.[33]

Mrs Morrison's mother was interviewed in the early 1970s. She had coped with grinding poverty in the inter-war period when her husband was out of work for many years and she had three boys to bring up. Her own mother brought up ten children on a labourer's wage with great resourcefulness. Both women were endowed with a well-developed sense of humour. It would not seem likely that either of them would have shared Mrs Morrison's perception of what being a woman meant. Somewhat ironically, it is clear from their interviews that the women who perceived themselves as being very feminine were also excellent managers.

Table 5.1 Average age at marriage

| Year | Barrow | | Preston | |
	Male	Female	Male	Female
1911	28.3	25.8	26.9	26.7
1931	27.2	25.6	26.7	25.5
1951	25.6	22.0	25.8	21.7
1961	24.6	21.2	25.3	21.0
1971	23.6	20.9	24.4	21.2

Source: These figures were calculated from census data on the formula developed in J. Hajnal, 'Age at Marriage and Proportions Marrying', *Population Studies*, vol. 7 (1953).

A rather less important reason which could explain why some women seemed to be less powerful than their mothers and grandmothers was that more women than previously were choosing to marry men who were older than themselves. Alternatively, men were choosing younger wives. This, of course, could be another sign that the romantic idyll was being pursued. The older man could be seen as one who would care for, and cherish, a younger, less worldly wife. The age at which people married fell in both Barrow and Preston, as it did nationally,[34] but it fell relatively more for women in Preston (see table 5.1). This age difference made the man the senior partner in many regards, not least of which was his superior experience of the world of work. He was likely to earn more than his wife, which had by no means been the case earlier in the century, when an experienced woman weaver in her mid-twenties could well have been earning more than her husband, especially if he was unskilled. An older husband was more likely to take charge. (It is unlikely that the falling age at marriage is related to changes in women's job opportunities. With more women in paid work there were more opportunities for financial independence. It is difficult to see how this employment situation could be responsible for women marrying younger.)

There are some examples in the study of older husbands adopting an attitude towards their younger wives which some might describe as patronizing, but which they saw as protective. It is, of course, difficult to use evidence which may be open to more than one interpretation. Mr Stephenson saw himself as a caring, helpful husband. He appeared to take over the family shopping in the late 1950s. He used his car to tour the countryside buying vegetables in bulk, and when the first supermarkets appeared, he took his wife every week and directed her purchases. He was proud of his ability to spot a bargain, but unsure of women's ability to do the same:

> Well, if I saw a bargain, I used to buy it. But the women are conned you know. It's marketing, isn't it? You've got to have a mind like a calculator. So a lot of women they miss, they could be took for a ride.[35]

His wife was five years younger than him and only eighteen when they married. He claimed that they shared decisions about budgeting, but it is hard not to conclude that he was in charge. He was asked about the old custom of the husband handing over his wages to his wife:

> Well, I always thought that to be a bit cruel, because sometimes it doesn't work out, does it? And if you both know what is happening then you solve the problem together. I explained to my wife when we first got married, I said, 'There is one thing I disagree with and that is hire purchase and anybody coming to the door.' And I told her about the corner shop, 'Never let them put you on the slate.' I explained it all from the word go. That's what I told my children as well.[36]

The juxtaposition of his wife and children is interesting.

Changes in Women's Role: Financial Control and Household Management

The factors which affected power relationships in more marriages than either age differences or the cult of femininity were those related to budgeting and financial management. Historically much of the working-class woman's power had been derived from her control of the family finances. This role was weakened, in some families seriously, in the post-war period.

There were changing views on the ownership of money. In earlier times, in the great majority of families, all the money coming into a household was regarded as family money, which would be spent, by the mother, for the good of the whole family.[37] She would take from each according to his/her means and give to each according to his/her needs. A different way of regarding money is observable in some families after the Second World War. Increasingly, young couples, when first married, spoke of 'his' money and 'her' money. When the wife stopped working it was all too easy for 'his' wages to remain his and for them not to become 'theirs'.

Mrs Leighton was married in 1959 and worked for several years before having her children:

> It was alright when I was working and I always had my own money, but unfortunately when I wasn't working he sort of handled the money and held the reins. His parents always gave in. He was just completely spoiled.[38]

Men gave a variety of explanations as to why they tended to regard their wages as their own property out of which they gave their wives an allowance and retained a sizeable percentage for themselves. Mr Warwick's view, that it was only fair to do so, was echoed by others. Some argued that their fathers had had to hand over their wages in their entirety because they were so meagre that their wives needed all of them just to ensure the family's survival. This was no longer seen to be the case, and as men had earned the money they felt entitled to keep some of it for themselves. Occasionally a man admitted that he needed the money to 'keep up' with his friends. Mr Muldoon said:

> Most dockers, I think, opened the wage packet and you kept a penny or two, you know. We can be big spenders. We had to keep up with the Joneses.
> What would you spend it on?
> Oh just the booze, just booze, not so much on food, mostly on booze.

He reported going out with his mates at weekends and 'just the odd night or two'.[39]

It is impossible to generalize about the basis on which a man's income was divided up in these families. In some, the husband simply kept his 'pocket' money; in others, he was responsible for settling a variety of family bills; but where these arrangements were adopted the woman no longer had her old power of 'allotting' where the money went.

Many couples rejected the idea of either husband or wife controlling the budget, preferring to share responsibility. They began their married lives with the idea that sharing was the hallmark of a good marriage; neither partner would be dominant. In practice this arrangement tended to weaken the woman's position, because she was again losing her previous sole control over the budget. It is possible that some women welcomed the lessening of the responsibilities which earlier generations had carried, but only one, Mrs Morrison, expressed such views:

> Well, when we got married we decided that we wouldn't use my wages, they went straight in the bank. Because we said that one day we will have to live on one wage, so it is best to start from the beginning. So we discussed matters you know, and he decided to how much we would put away after gas and electricity and that. He dealt with accounts, you see, and he always did that side.

When asked about the very different experiences of both her mother and mother-in-law, who had organized their own accounts (involving the keeping of marvellously detailed account books), she simply replied 'Yes', but added in a tone of sympathy for her mother, 'Mam, she had her money and she had to pay the electricity, the rates, the gas, everything out of the money, you know.'[40] Mrs Morrison was clearly happy with her own arrangements, and felt sorry for her mother.

Some women, however, became sadly disillusioned because the ideal of sharing did not seem to work out. Mrs Atkin, who was married in 1967, went on working for some time. She recounted how her husband shared out their wages and allocated where they went, to gas, electricity, mortgage and so on. There was some left over, and, to her fury, her husband put it in a bank account which was in his name alone:

> Because he didn't trust me with money. He didn't trust women, full stop. No, he got very silly about money, which annoyed me a lot, because I'd always had to save. We've been married twenty years and now we have a joint bank account.
> How did you feel?
> Cross. I thought that marriage was trusting and sharing, and obviously it wasn't going to be altogether totally trusting. But it didn't matter, I'd got my little house.[41]

Lastly, women tended to lose control of the budget because of the way in which wages were paid. Although there was a tradition of men handing over the cash in their wage packets, it was not considered appropriate for the man's wage to be paid into his wife's bank account. Joint accounts or accounts only in the husband's name meant that women lost their sole control of the family finances. Mrs Webster, who was married in 1959, spent the first few years of her marriage in charge of the finances, as her mother and grandmother had been; the only difference being that she managed with an account book whereas they had relied on a series of tin boxes:

> Yes, I paid the bills, until he started with the brewery and that altered things, because until then we had had a weekly wage which I like, and I would still prefer a weekly wage. Then at the brewery he got a monthly cheque. It all went in the bank and my husband has sorted it ever since.[42]

Increasing prosperity not only adversely affected women's financial control, it also tended to marginalize women's traditional management skills. Working-class women had previously taken immense pride in being able to make 'something out of nothing' or very little. With great ingenuity old clothes were transformed into patchwork quilts and 'peg' rugs; orange-boxes into furniture; adult clothes into children's clothes; bones and a few vegetables into broth. Rationing and shortages during the Second World War produced a final and very important flowering of these talents, but they became less and less necessary as austerity faded and prosperity grew. Some of this increasing wealth was, of course, because more women worked for wages, as will be seen in chapter 7. Gradually, earning skills became as important or more important than managing skills, and the ability to purchase a new object became more important than recyling old ones. Historically, the ability to buy meat had been a sign of affluence and, with more disposable income, more meat was purchased, thus rendering redundant the old skills of making cheap, nutritious meals out of unpromising ingredients. For some, possessions and conspicuous consumption became a matter of greater pride than the practice of 'making do and mend'.

Josephine Klein wrote of the 'traditional' working-class family:

> Just as the woman's role is domestic and her self respect and status depend on her performance in keeping house, so the man's role is financial and his status in the household depends rather stringently on his ability as a bread-winner. His self-respect is clearly tied to his financial independence.[43]

If Klein is correct about male and female self-respect, and there is considerable oral evidence from the earlier studies to suggest that she is, then her statement raises interesting questions about the respective status of men and women in the post-war period. Clearly, men's self-respect, given virtually full employment and substantial increases in real wages, must have grown substantially. But women's self-respect could well have been eroded as their skills in household management were perceived as being of less importance than before. Many women tried to build their self-respect on a different basis by creating a beautiful, well-furnished and equipped home. Ultimately this made them even more dependent on their husbands; because to fulfil these dreams required far more money than they themselves could hope to earn.

Continuing 'Traditional' Roles

By no means all marriages, of course, were different from those observed earlier in the century. Although there were no very powerful women in the study, there were those, although probably a minority, who continued to run their families and homes in the 'traditional' way. They took pride in their skills in household management. Their roles were separate from those of their husbands but they had more or less equal power. Mrs Sykes said succinctly, 'He says his motto is, "I'll earn it if you'll spend it." And we have always done that.'[44]

Mrs Lewthwaite throughout her married life, which began in 1948, enjoyed budgeting:

> The responsibility, yes. But I like a bit of responsibility. Well you feel you have achieved something in life don't you? The pay packet was never opened. I can say that about him, he never opened the packet.[45]

Mrs Lodge, married in 1945, was an excellent manager of the old school. Her husband was an unskilled labourer, and they had a struggle to bring up their four children, to ensure that they had further education, and eventually to buy their own house. 'And when I got my wages I always used to write down what I was going to spend at each shop, and I used to sew for the children.' She had a box into which she put money for the gas, electricity, rent and so on and added:

> Otherwise we wouldn't have managed. And I made all my own jam and bottled fruit. We used to go into the countryside and collect blackberries and make blackberry and apple jam. So it hasn't been easy. I mean we are fairly comfortable in our old age but it hasn't been easy. But I enjoy a struggle![46]

(It is interesting that she refers, as did respondents in the earlier study, to 'my wages' which were in fact her husband's wages.) Couples like the Lodges continued to work on the assumption that income belonged to the family, not the individual wage-earner. The husband had the satisfaction of supporting the family by earning the money, the wife took pride in supporting the family by a judicious use of the money.

Mrs Britton was younger than Mrs Lodge, she was married in 1954, but she too controlled the budget. She was asked if her husband gave her his wage packet:

> Yes always. I gave him something back but he didn't want to be bothered. He wanted me to pay all the bills and be responsible. He didn't want the worry. He had never organized his own finances; his mother had looked after him. But his brothers were all the same when they got married. Yes, the nicest sort of men on the whole from the working class used to hand their money over.[47]

Conclusion

There were significant changes in the role relationships between husbands and wives in the post-war period. Many women were not as powerful as they had been, either because of their husbands' determination to gain more autonomy and authority than had their fathers, or because wives, also rejecting the role models of earlier generations, chose to be more feminine and less managing than had their mothers and grandmothers. Probably one of the key reasons for women losing some of their previous power was the relinquishing of their hitherto sole control of the family finances.

6

Marriage: For Better? For Worse?

In the post-war years there was optimism about the state of marriage. Commentators spoke of a new kind of partnership between husbands and wives which was widely described as being 'companionate'. This chapter attempts, first, to examine whether or not such marriages did in fact exist, and secondly, to look at some of the reasons for marriage breakdown. Marriages which collapsed cannot be said to have done so simply because they were not companionate. If this had been the case there would have been considerably more divorces. But this group of marriages exemplify, in a rather extreme way, some of the problems which were not widely discussed by the optimistic contemporary observers.

Companionate Marriages

Writing about eighteenth-century marriages, Lawrence Stone identified a relationship which he called 'companionate'.[1] This type of marriage was characterized by companionship, affection and equality. Stone suggested that companionate marriages first manifested themselves among the upper bourgeoisie and that they appeared much later among the poor. It is not clear how much later he had in mind. In the section on role relationships in marriage (in chapter 5), four models of marriage were identified; is it possible to regard companionate marriage as a fifth model observable in our regional studies?

Contemporary observers in the post-war period appear to have believed that the companionate marriage had arrived in working-class homes and was becoming more established with the passing of each year:

> The general view from a range of such community studies was first that companionate marriage was the modern form of marriage and inherently desirable; second that it was filtering down from middle-class families to the working class; and third that it was becoming more widespread as the years passed.[2]

Klein, throughout her book, suggested that companionate marriage was the result of growing prosperity and social change in the post-war world.[3] Young and Wilmott, writing in 1957, found 'a new kind of companionship between men and women reflecting the rise in status of the young wife and children which is the great transformation of our time'.[4] As will be seen in chapters 8 and 9, there can be little doubt that Young and Wilmott were correct about the changing status of children; it is much more doubtful if the status of wives enjoyed a similar improvement in the same period.

Finch and Summerfield summed up the post-war literature on companionate marriages thus:

> Although the phrase 'companionate marriage' had been employed as early as the 1920s, it is in the post-war world that it appears more widely being used to summarise a set of ideas about marriage which ranged from the notion that there should be greater companionship between partners whose roles were essentially different, through the idea of marriage as teamwork, to the concept of marriages based on sharing, implying a breakdown of clearly demarcated roles. 'Partnership' and 'equality' in marriage can clearly mean very different things and both can be traced in the literature of the period.[5]

It was, in fact, difficult to find many examples of companionate marriage in our study. This was partly because, as Finch and Summerfield point out, there was no clear understanding of what was meant by the term. The second difficulty is that, in achieving one of the criteria, couples may well have been jeopardizing another. The blurring of conjugal roles did not necessarily result in equality, but may well have meant women having to share the control of areas where they had previously had sovereignty. It has already been seen how attempts to 'share' financial management all too often resulted in a loss of equality between husbands and wives, because women lost some of the power which they had previously enjoyed. If the criteria of sharing, companionship and equality are strictly applied, it is questionable if any marriages in this survey can be described as companionate.

Affection

No direct questions were asked about affection because we believed our respondents would regard this as intrusive and would, in any case, be likely to produce a 'public' rather than a 'private' answer.[6] Many couples appear to have been comfortable with each other. There were very few unsolicited romantic memories. Mr Kennedy was a Preston docker who described his first meeting with his wife thus, 'Well I think it's being a bit sloppy and sentimental, but I never believed in love at first sight then. But she came to the door and I went "Oh" and that were it.' He always spoke glowingly about his wife and, after listing her many achievements as a housekeeper and mother of six, he added, 'I don't think she's a saint, you know, but she is absolutely unique.'[7] Mr Muldoon, another docker, said simply about his wife, 'She was very attractive. I fell in love very soon.'[8]

It remains difficult both to comment on the presence or absence of affection in individual marriages and to make meaningful generalizations when surveying a large group.

Companionship

Undoubtedly, two people can be companionable in a passive manner, by simply being together and enjoying one another's company. Very few respondents mention this kind of companionship and there would be difficulties in trying to report on such relationships. It is easier to examine more active pursuits and to see how many or how few were shared by both husbands and wives. It was seen in chapter 3 that, apart from during a childless period early in a marriage, there is little evidence of couples sharing housework. There was, however, some sharing of childcare when the infant was past its early months (see chapter 8). It is in its leisure-time pursuits that it may be possible to identify a companionable family. If companionship is an essential ingredient of a companionate marriage, what evidence may be found of this in husbands' and wives' shared activities?

Courtship and the early years of marriage

In the earlier part of the century courting couples had spent time together, but not often alone. Once married, the common assumption was that men and women worked and took their leisure in their own spheres, living out their separate roles.

In the post-Second World War period there was clearly the expectation, at least among some people, that companionship was an important element in a relationship between a man and a woman. When couples were courting, they were almost always companions as well as sweethearts and lovers. This companionship lasted in many marriages for some time, household tasks and leisure activities being shared and enjoyed together. The delayed birth of the first child could give time for this relationship to become well established.

Mrs Webster was married in 1959 and it was six years before she had a child:

> What did you do in your spare time after you were married and before your daughter was born?
>
> Well, we had a gay time. We had the motor-bike and we had various friends who didn't have children, and we used to go to a village pub on a Saturday very often. We packed in the motor bike and got a Hillman Husky instead and it was before the days of 'don't drink and drive'. We had loads of friends and we fitted them top to tail in the back of this Hillman Husky. And one of us could play the piano and we'd have a good sing-along and just enjoy the night. We'd end up in someone's house. One of my friends used to talk to spirits and we had a good time doing that, pushing the tumbler round the table. Yes, we had some good times. And then one after another they had families. And if you have to stay in with a family you kind of drift your own ways after that.[9]

Mrs Hutton, married in the early 1950s, waited for nine years before having a child:

> We would come home and make a meal together. There was a lot of togetherness then between him and me. We shared everything, the house-work, and we had a home like a palace. We were both working, plenty of money to go out. So we never stopped in. Then when we had William, that was when we had to stop in.[10]

The arrival of children

In many marriages the arrival of the first child resulted in a significant separation in the roles of husband and wife, and an end to shared activities outside the home.

Men were excluded, or excluded themselves, from the process of child-birth; in the study only one father attended the birth of his children. A much more common attitude was that of Mr Rowlandson, whose daughter was born in 1969: 'He dropped me off and said, "Have a good time," and went back home again. Among our group none of the husbands did [attend the birth] because it wasn't done. It was the woman's personal thing wasn't it?'[11] The birth did not go smoothly and at one stage Mrs Rowlandson was pronounced technically dead and had to be resuscitated, so in fact she did not 'have a nice time', however her husband may have defined this term.

The whole area of childbirth was regarded as a woman's sphere. Women who, following the birth, went to be churched, either went alone or with a female relative. Men whose own wives had been churched were sometimes unfamiliar not only with the practice but even with the expression. As will be seen in chapter 8, childrearing remained principally a female activity, although fathers were increasingly involved both in home-based activities and in outings.

The birth of a child need not necessarily have ended the companionship which had previously existed and, of course, in some cases it did not. Mrs Lucas, growing up in the 1950s, listed her parents' separate leisure-time activities, but also said:

> They had a regular night out together at the local theatre. They used to enjoy that; and my mother's mother would come and sit with us. She was quite pleased to do it and she felt that it was good for my parents to get out together.[12]

Gendered Leisure Activities

In rather more marriages the birth of a child meant the end of any regularly shared leisure activities. Not only was the wider circle of friends lost, as in Mrs Webster's case, but couples stopped going out together. This did not necessarily mean that they stayed in together, for often the husband went out in an all-male group; sometimes this resulted in resentments. This gendered nature of leisure activities persisted long after 1970.[13]

As more children arrived, women increasingly relied for companionship on other women, whether neighbours, relatives or friends. Both men and women adopted the separate, segregated roles described by Bott.[14] It was possible for couples to do this because they retained their close-knit social networks which provided alternative companionship to that of their spouses. It can be argued that these networks removed the stress which might have existed in some marriages if the couple had spent all their time together rather than with friends and relatives, but such separate roles did not produce companionship.

Men tended to revert to the traditional pattern of associating with their male peer group in sports and social clubs and in the pubs. Recent work on rural pub cultures, which could equally well apply to smaller towns like those in this study, emphasize the importance of the public house as an arena in which to display masculine bonding behaviour.[15]

Mr Warwick spoke fondly of his old pub, which was demolished about 1970, but one he frequented all through the 1960s, a period when his children were small, his wife was at home and he was away working a lot of overtime:

> I used to work. I used to come home, and then I used to go down the pub 9 o'clock every night, for two pints and a game of dominoes and darts. That was my relaxation. It was scruffy, it was clean. Floors sand, wooden tables – the old iron leg tables – and just a bar. In the best room they had some soft chairs.
>
> And was it basically for men?
>
> For men's refreshment, there was no women allowed, only in the snug. We used to have some songs depending on how much beer the lads had had; but it was mainly dominoes and just banter – *men's* banter, the usual mickey-taking.

After the pub closed down he went to another one, but it was not the same:

> Ladies went in and spoilt it all. They cause trouble, don't they? You can get twenty blokes in a boozer, all half-cut, but if a woman walks in there is always plenty of trouble, and I don't know why. It's probably nought to do with her is it? They don't cause the trouble, it's just because they are there.

Mrs Warwick added that she had only been twice to the pub with her husband, but that they frequently went to the cinema on a Saturday when the children were small.[16]

Mr Whiteside was married in 1960 and his son was born soon afterwards:

> I used to work shifts quite a lot and quite a bit of overtime. I got into the football [he was secretary of a club]. So after that it was just a matter of football and pretty little else. Actually, work, football, home, in that order. I've got to be honest about it. It took a lot of hours, a lot of hours, all day Saturday, Wednesday night training. It has taken a lot of my life, a lot of energy that could have been used better. Yes, it's been my life has football.

Both Mr and Mrs Whiteside agreed that she had been much happier once she had developed her own interests outside the home. He said to his wife, 'Prior to that, it was difficult for you, accepting me spending so much time at football, because you didn't understand what I was interested in.' Mrs Whiteside replied, 'Yes, because I always spent such a lot of time here on my own with Kevin [their son].'[17]

Strains and Resentments

Traditionally, this separation of male and female leisure activities had been accepted. While it remained a 'normal' state of affairs for some women, others, probably influenced by the ideal of the companionate marriage, came to resent it. The gap between the ideal and reality was particularly hard to bear when a respondent had parents who had shared their leisure time, but she and her husband did not.

Mrs Hunter's parents, in the 1930s and 1940s, had been great cinemagoers and in fact went several times each week: 'My Mum and Dad went everywhere together.' On another occasion when discussing her mother's non-attendance at church she said, 'I don't think she wanted to leave him. They went everywhere together. They were very close.'[18] Certainly, when Mrs Bibby, Mrs Hunter's mother, was interviewed several years ago, she was still very upset about her husband's death although he had been dead for twenty years. In a later interview Mrs Hunter was asked about her views on what, if any, changes there had been in the lives of women. 'Well, marriage is more of a partnership for a start. I mean, it never has been with Fred and me. I don't want to sound unkind.' Mrs Hunter was married several years before the birth of her son but even in that period she did not feel her marriage was a partnership:

> The girls I worked with, the husband would get up first one week and the wife would get up first the next week. Well, there was none of that with Fred, and I didn't finish work until 5.40. He was home about 4.15, and he just sat there waiting for me to make the tea. And he never once changed a nappy. Fred and I have never done things together really. His mother said it was my place to go with him. [His hobby, aeroplane spotting, took him to some out-of-the-way places.] And I used to think, 'Hell, why should I?' To go to these God-forsaken little fields and sit there all day. I preferred to be in my garden. This is where my mum came in. My mum was my companion. We used to go places together. I mean, I'm not saying we haven't had a happy marriage, it's just that it's been an unusual marriage.[19]

It was not as unusual as Mrs Hunter believed, but she raised an important point. Some couples had incompatible leisure interests. Mrs Wheaton, a teenager in the 1950s, complained that her father, who was a fitter, went out every evening to the pub, sometimes to play darts, usually to drink:

> And that got to annoy me, because I didn't think he should. I used to have a go at times about it. It wasn't fair! Then he got his own back, 'Well I bought

a bike for your mother and she wouldn't learn to ride it, and she wouldn't do
this and she won't do that, so if she won't do all these things I'm going to go
my own sweet way.' That's how it developed. She used to like going to the
theatre. And when I got older she started taking me to the pictures. I saw an
amazing amount of pictures with my mother. And I went to the theatre with
her. If I didn't go she went on her own. She didn't seem to object, and my
Dad didn't object, but I didn't think it was right.[20]

Ironically, Mrs Wheaton's husband, as will be seen, had exclusive leisure
activities, but Mrs Wheaton viewed them differently from those of her
father.

Problems of Baby-sitting

The difficulties of couples sharing leisure-time activities was exacerbated by
the problem of baby- and childminding. In a sense some couples created
their own dilemma. Their perception of being a 'good' parent meant that
father or mother was always with the child or children. Some women
reported with pride that they had never left their children until they were
old enough to look after themselves (usually in their early teens). Others
reported relatives who were unwilling to 'baby-sit'; others appear to have
been reluctant to be beholden to the extended family. Others again had
mothers who flatly refused to help out. Very few had paid baby-sitters or
even the unpaid services of friends and neighbours. Mrs Webster, who had
had such a sociable time after marriage, was asked about baby-sitters for her
children:

No, I had plenty of relatives around here but none of them ever baby-sat.
Mother always had her own interests and father sat at home, and then my
sister had her own family. So you just tend to get on with life, you know. On
the odd occasion they would come, but nothing regular [thus slightly
altering her claim that they *never* sat]. She added that her friends were all in
the same position.[21]

Mrs Wheaton, who had been so critical of her father going out on his
own, said:

We didn't go out apart from John and his band two nights a week, and a lot
of concerts at weekends. We never went out, and it didn't bother me. I
wouldn't ask my mother to baby-sit, because of the things she said about
my brother calling on her to baby-sit, 'Oh not there again.' It got me to the
point of thinking, well, she had only to go round the corner to them, and if

she objected to that, I wasn't going to put myself in the same position. So I never asked her, only when we were forced to do so. So consequently we didn't go out.[22]

Working Patterns

Working patterns also made companionship difficult in some marriages. As has already been seen, increasing prosperity in some families was the result of husbands working overtime. In other families women worked evening shifts. In these marriages spouses saw little of each other.

Mr Norton was married in 1952; his wife worked in her parents' fish and chip shop. 'We worked it so that she went to the shop in the evenings and obviously I stayed in and looked after the babies.' (There were four eventually.) When asked if he and his wife ever went out together he replied:

> Oh hell, no. Just the odd time to the pictures, just the odd time. Because we had a commitment, we produced them and so we would look after them. If you said three times a year that would be about it.[23]

Mr Ingham, married in 1957, also saw little of his wife. He often worked shifts; she had a full-time job and also attended night classes. Mr Simpkins, married in 1953, regarded his evening classes as being essential for his work and went regularly, leaving his wife at home. She had a full-time day job. It could be said that these last three marriages represent those where there were equal roles for the partners, but no companionship. Mr Norton, Mr Ingham and Mr Simpkins were all eventually divorced.

Leisure in the Home

Not all couples worked long hours, and not all husbands went to the pub or club on a regular basis, but both being at home did not necessarily result in conjugal companionship. As has been seen in chapter 2, there was a marked physical separation of spheres in some households. Men spent time in their own private domain, which could have been a cellar, an outhouse or their allotment or garden. Here they pursued a variety of hobbies, from toy-making to gardening. However, this physical separation appears to have been more usual among the parents of respondents. Undoubtedly, the arrival of television in almost all homes by 1960 brought about a significant

Figure 6.1   A family watching television, 1957
(Photo courtesy NMPFT/Science and Society Picture Library)

change in the pattern of family activities. Home-centred couples sat down together to watch programmes and possibly discussed them afterwards. No doubt the cynical would question whether or not this represented an improvement in conjugal companionship.

Equality?

A third element of companionate marriage was equality. The nature of the empirical evidence makes it easier to comment on the presence or absence of equality in marriages, rather than the absence or presence of affection. As will be seen in the next chapter, more married women than ever before were going out to work, widening their horizons and enjoying earning money on their own account. Outside the home they could be described as having more freedom and choice in their lives than formerly, but they did not enjoy equality with their husbands in the world of work. Moreover, whatever gains were made outside the home were paralleled by a loss of power and status within it, as has been suggested in the previous chapter.

Did Companionate Marriages Exist?

It is difficult to find many companionate marriages in this study up to 1970. Those which were childless appeared to have had the best chance of being companionate, but in some cases it is perhaps questionable if these marriages could be described as happy.

Mr and Mrs Trickett, who were married in 1955,[24] had total role segregation. He went out to work and she stayed at home; Mr Trickett believing that a woman's place was in the home. He did not help with the housework and in this area there was clearly no sharing. Their degree of role separation should, according to Bott's model, have been related to a closely knit network of social relationships, but this was not the case. The couple were resolute in their determination to keep themselves to themselves, and had few contacts with relations or neighbours. However, they spent all their leisure time together, sometimes touring the countryside on their motor-bike. They could clearly be described as having shared leisure and they were good companions. Mrs Trickett was, nevertheless, extremely isolated, lacking during the day the companionship of other women, whether in the street or in her home.

Some marriages were never companionate. Others started thus, with a professed belief in sharing and team-work, but changed, usually with the arrival of children, which affected patterns both of work and of leisure. Earlier companionship was all too often destroyed, as was the woman's chance of equality with her husband in the labour market. Finch and Summerfield concluded that, in the 1940s and 1950s, the ideal of companionate marriage had many benefits for the husband but did not work to the advantage of the wife, and that indeed the ideal placed many pressures upon her.[25] Whether one examines the contemporary literature or the empirical evidence, it is hard to escape the conclusion that the changes which were occurring in marriage relationships were not, in general, to the benefit of women.

Marriage Breakdown: Domestic Violence

Quite possibly and understandably, some marital difficulties were not discussed. Difficulties which ultimately led to divorce were described, but there was a reluctance to talk about continuing, contemporary problems. In two families there were accounts of domestic violence, but it was not the husband or wife who mentioned them; rather, it was the close relatives. Mrs Gerrard, the daughter of Mr and Mrs Boyle, witnessed much violence in the 1960s and beyond. She variously attributed her father's behaviour to drink and being 'moody'. It was not our task to investigate such explanations, but Mr Boyle's own description of his childhood is illuminating. It is a graphic account of extreme poverty, malnutrition, violence from his mother, cold indifference from his father and a bewildering series of moves between relatives and unofficial foster parents. Mrs Gerrard was asked what, in particular, her mother had to see the doctor about and replied tersely:

Near enough the same thing; black eyes and being strangled.
Did she ever take you children away to avoid seeing him?
No, because he never came home before the pubs shut. And we were in bed, so she would probably think that we didn't hear it anyhow, but we did.
Did she ever consider leaving him?
Yes, but she had nowhere to go. My nana couldn't put her up, she didn't have enough room.
Did you say anything to him or ever interfere at all?
Yes. Well one night he had come in and it weren't like it usually was, it was really quiet. And I remember standing at the top of the landing screaming, and I jumped back into bed and my sister said, 'Aw, what'd you do that for? He'll kill you now.' I were really frightened of my dad. And he come up and told me off. And my mum said, the morning after, that if I hadn't screamed . . . he was strangling her and it had all gone black.[26]

Although there was little direct evidence of domestic violence, there was, in the replies of some respondents, an antagonism – sometimes faint, sometimes pronounced – which would seem to indicate a subterranean war of the sexes which rumbled on in some marriages.

Marriage Breakdown: Separation and Divorce

Some couples experienced a breakdown in their relationships. Respondents found it easier to talk about such events in retrospect, even when they resulted in separation or divorce, than to discuss any contemporary problems they may have been experiencing. The topic of marriage breakdown was not included in *A Woman's Place* because both separation and divorce were very rare among the respondents in the earlier studies. It is also important to note that, despite a national increase in the number of divorces

after legal aid was granted in 1949, divorce was still unusual throughout
the period (see table 6.1). In 1962 it was claimed that 93 per cent of all
marriages did not end in divorce.[27] Locally, as table 6.2 shows, only a small
percentage of women were divorced even in 1971.

Table 6.1 Number divorcing per 1000
married people: England and Wales

Year	No.
1951	2.6
1961	2.1
1971	6.0

Source: Office of Population Censuses and
Surveys, *Marriage and Divorce Statistics,*
1837–1983, Historical Series F. M.2.16, table 4.1.

Table 6.2 Divorced women: numbers and percentages of women
aged 15+, 1931–71

Year	Barrow	Lancaster	Preston
1931	9 = 0.03%	12 = 0.06%	43 = 0.08%
1951	126 = 0.47%	153 = 1.2%	340 = 0.68%
1961	182 = 0.7%	197 = 0.97%	450 = 0.98%
1971	390 = 1.5%	375 = 1.5%	780 = 2.02%

Source: Census data.

Separations and divorces were rare among our respondents, and one
should be cautious about the statistics which show a rise in the divorce rate
in the early 1970s. The Divorce Act of 1969 completely revised the existing
legislation, establishing what has been called the 'no-fault' divorce, leading
to a simplification of the legal procedures.[28] Seven respondents were divorced in the early 1970s. None of them mentioned the changes in legislation, although the fact that this made divorce easier to obtain could well
have influenced their decision. The root causes of the marriage breakdowns
which resulted in divorce at this time could possibly be traced back to the
1960s.

In a negative way this again illustrates the continuity and change in the
pattern of relationships: breakdown in some marriages is a continuing
phenomenon, but whereas in pre-war times this was likely to lead to
separation, after the war divorce was increasing likely to be the outcome.

Mr Trickett's[29] father was a soldier in the First World War and met Mr Trickett's mother when stationed in Barrow. After the war they lived in London, where he was a costermonger; but she was home-sick and could not settle there. Her husband could not settle in Barrow because he was unemployed. He finally deserted the family in about 1930, leaving her to bring up four children in considerable poverty. Mr Fleming's[30] father deserted his family in the 1920s leaving his son initially to be put in an orphanage and later to be brought up unsympathetically by an uncle. Mrs Wallington's[31] parents separated in 1939 but she continued to see a lot of her father as he lived near by. Mrs Hocking's[32] father returned from the Second World War very unsettled and almost a stranger, finally leaving his family in 1952 and not being seen again for another thirteen years. Obviously, it was difficult for these respondents to give a clear explanation for the breakdown of these marriages, of which they were the children.

Adultery

Respondents, speaking of their own marriages, make it clear that as far as they were concerned, the prime cause of marriage breakdown was adultery. However, in all the accounts of marriage breakdown, we only heard the views of the person who regarded him or herself as the 'wronged' partner. It is reasonable to suppose that there might, in some cases, have been another side to the story.

Mrs Peel was married in 1941 at the age of twenty. Her daughter was born the following year:

> We didn't get out together much. He played the piano in a dance band, so the times he wasn't working over he was playing in the dance band. Now my daughter was born in the June, and in the August it was the shipyard holidays and he went away for a week with two of the chaps out of the band. And he came back half way through the week to tell me that they had been up in the Lakes in this boy's auntie's house. And she had come back and found them with three girls and she was going to tell me. So he came home and told me himself. I left him that night. I waited while he went out and I took my child and all my clothes and I went. I didn't live far from my mother's and I stayed there for two years.[33]

What subsequently happened to Mrs Peel was not particularly dramatic but suggests why some women stayed in unsatisfactory marriages. Her husband threatened to cut off her maintenance unless she went back to him. She did not seek legal help or advice and felt she had no alternative. Her mother had initially offered accommodation to her and her child, but as she was a busy boarding-house keeper she refused to take on the responsibility of looking after her granddaughter while her daughter went to work. There was perhaps a little more to it:

> It was a case of nobody had looked after hers and nobody had baby-sat for her so you look after your own. It was as simple as that. And she would much rather I had stayed with him. My place was with my husband.
>
> What did she say about his infidelity?
>
> Well, she didn't actually agree that it was the right thing to do, but I should have been more tolerant. You see my mother was a Catholic. My father wasn't. And my mother believed that once you are married you are married and that is the end of it. She said you should stay with a man through thick and thin. But I wasn't prepared to share.[34]

The adultery continued and Mrs Peel finally got a divorce in 1946; but her mother never recognized it, or her second husband whom she married in 1948. Mrs Peel herself, however, did not feel that being divorced made her in any way socially unacceptable:

> I think, myself, that it was just coming about that people realized that they could become divorced if things weren't going right. I think, if anything, divorce was a bit more in fashion than it had been six years before. The war made a difference because so many folk had to get divorced after the war when the chaps came back and found them with someone else. There was so much of it after the war.[35]

Mrs Peel was correct in her view that there was a change in national attitudes to divorce. In the post-war period there was a rise in the divorce rates. 'England . . . where marriages contracted between 1940 and 1945 were not only dissolved by divorce at a greater rate than earlier and later marriages, but were dissolved more rapidly.'[36]

Mrs Leighton was much younger than Mrs Peel. She was only eighteen when she married in 1959. Like several other couples they waited some years before having their children and in the meantime travelled and worked abroad:

> He was stopping out a lot when the children were young. He did go out a lot and I stayed at home mostly. And gradually it got worse and worse. And then I found out that he was seeing other women. He denied it and I believed him. And I think it was easier on my feelings to believe it was the truth. But finally he got somebody pregnant, another married woman. I felt so strongly

about it that I couldn't have lived with him any more, when I found out that
he had been sleeping around. I just finished then.[37]

Mrs Hutton has already described the companionable early years of her
marriage. She and her husband were childless for nine years and then they
had three sons between 1959 and 1965. They had not wanted children until
they had their house and its contents just the way they wanted them. The
period of Mrs Hutton's childbearing proved to be disastrous for her
marriage:

> He was a bit of a bugger for the women.
>   When did this start?
>   Well, that always seemed to start when I was pregnant. Maybe because I
> wouldn't go out with him. I was just stuck at home all the time for a couple
> of years. He didn't really like women who were pregnant; he felt a bit
> ashamed of them. I think I looked ugly to him you know.

For a long time she tolerated her husband's adultery:

> Yes, putting up with it. You knew it was going on actually. You were a bit
> frightened to be on your own. You have got kids and you don't go out to
> work and you think 'What am I going to do?' You need a man so you just
> hang on to him. I don't think either of us wanted to be divorced. He wanted
> me to carry on turning a blind eye to it. He would have loved that.

Mrs Hutton, however, was not just a helpless victim. Like Mrs Peel, she
decided to fight back; but she chose a way of so doing that was still unusual
in the 1960s:

> I thought, I'm not going to carry on the rest of my life with this. I could
> visualize in years to come being really nasty with each other, and just
> carrying on. I didn't have any love left for him; he killed it all. I don't think
> it's right to keep going for the sake of the children although I'm inclined to
> think that they suffer. I always remember telling his mother that the only
> way to cure him was to do the same to him. And she said 'What do you
> mean?' I says, 'Well if I hear about another woman I shall just go right out
> and get another fella.' And I remember her being absolutely and totally
> shocked at the suggestion. I said, 'Just watch me.' And I did what I
> threatened to do. He moved out and he moved in. I never ever married him
> but I lived with him for nine years.[38]

While pre-marital sex was described by respondents as happening
throughout the century (as is evidenced in the figures for illegitimacy),
adultery, when committed by women, is only mentioned in the period after

1940. It is likely that, as Mrs Peel suggested, sexual morality was changed to some degree by war-time circumstances. Several relationships formed between women and servicemen stationed in the area have been mentioned. These stories, however, are usually told about neighbours, and only one respondent spoke of such a relationship within her own family. This affair did not, however, lead to either divorce or separation. Her parents had a Canadian soldier billeted on them. The mother was a deeply unhappy woman, married to a man who was totally dominated by his mother who lived with them. After her parents' death, Mrs Britton learned the details of this aspect of her mother's life from the aunt to whom her mother had fled when the crisis in her life developed. Mrs Britton was old enough in the war to form an opinion of the Canadian:

> He was a very cultured and educated man. He was so well mannered and polite, very nice person. My father liked him; they got on very well together. My father probably suspected that my mother liked him but I think my father just wanted a quiet life. I think that, provided my mother didn't leave him, he was prepared to put up with anything, provided it wasn't anything the neighbours would talk about; that would bring disgrace on him and make him look a laughing stock.

Inevitably, at the end of the war a crisis developed, the soldier inviting the wife to join him in Canada:

> She didn't know what to do, and she'd flown to her family on the train in a fit of absolute hysterics. Uncle was a church-goer and a church warden and absolutely religious and so was aunty, and they both said, 'You cannot do such a sinful thing. You cannot possibly desert your husband and go to Canada, and what is going to happen to Lilian? Are you taking her or leaving her behind?' In the end my mother just broke down, came back, and she never saw the soldier again. And I think she lived with that for the rest of her life.[39]

Mr Simpkins was married in 1953. His bride was pre-maritally pregnant and, as he explained, not getting married was not an option. He was a self-educated man and also an ambitious one. Much of his time was spent, on his own admission, either working or attending courses. In the late 1950s his marriage began to break down:

> While I was away in the evening I suspected my wife was having an affair, and that went on for a period of three years. Until I finally found out that she was. I came from a very rough background and I believed in self-justice so I sought out the offending culprit and gave him a good hiding. And I learned a lesson. I came away after giving that man a good hiding feeling totally and

completely empty. Then my wife cleared off. The only money we had was in my wallet and she stole it and she left me with the two children. Anyway, she came back after a week, in which I did a lot of searching for her. I went to Liverpool, Manchester and Preston because I firmly believed at that time that I was in love with her. I wasn't, of course, I was in love with an idea, an image which was totally false, it was of my own creation. I assumed that she would feel the same way as I felt, which is wrong.[40]

At this point the couple renewed their marriage vows in church as a sign of a new beginning. The affairs continued, however, and Mr Simpkins finally threw his wife out after more than ten years of marriage. Then followed an unpleasant battle for the custody of the children, which Mr Simpkins lost. Although remarried, he remained very bitter about his first wife and his feeling of betrayal appears repeatedly in his interviews.

Mr Ingham was married in 1957 and divorced in 1971. His wife had been anxious to follow her career as a secretary and Mr Ingham supported this decision:

> You couldn't keep Alice at home because she was a little bit of a career woman, a very intelligent person although she had a few faults like we all have.
> So it was always part of your agreement that she went to work?
> Oh yes. She was quite good at work but not a very good mother.

He felt that she did not spend enough time with the child when she came home from work and was too harsh with her. But this difference of opinion about childrearing was not the reason for the breakdown of the marriage:

> From time to time Alice had affairs with I think three chaps and probably more. I mean I don't really know. She formed a friendship with this gentleman, if you can call him that, and she came to me one day and just said, 'I think I'm going to have to pack this marriage in and we'll get a divorce.' And I had reached the end of my tether by then so it all went on.[41]

The child remained with her father, refusing to live with her mother. Mrs Ingham's almost casual announcement about a divorce contrasts with the more intense feelings generated by marriage breakdown shown earlier in the period.

Drifting Apart

Adultery was not the only reason for marriage breakdown. Couples drifted apart and found they had little in common. The lack of trauma in these last two cases is reminiscent of the casualness of Mrs Ingham. Mr Norton, who, like his wife, worked long hours, was married in 1952 and divorced in 1970:

> Well, nothing spectacular. We just drifted apart. Again I was working quite a lot. I was working like there is no tomorrow and it wasn't greed, you know. I believed in it. I was away from home more and more. Our son was sixteen when the wife and I called it a day. I had sort of questioned our marriage a couple of times before that, again not in an argumentative way. And I got a bit tired of saying sorry, but I meant it. And when we finally decided that that was going to be that, I said to my wife, 'Look find a house that you really like and I'll pay for it, and the contents.' She took all that with my blessing. I think she had worked as hard as I had and she was entitled to all that. And even now if she was in any kind of trouble – and my present wife knows this, I would help, no doubt about it.[42]

Mrs Paulson was married in 1970 when she was twenty-three. She and her husband had attitudes to marriage similar to those of Mrs Ingham but very different to those who believed in the indissolubility of marriage. The newly married couple moved into a new dormer bungalow:

> It was smashing. We had quite a bit of furniture given. My mum bought us some fitted carpets and his mum bought us some furniture. So we got it more or less sorted to move into. Basically, we were too young really. He was immature for his age. He wanted to go out more. He wanted to still carry on as he was when a teenager and I wanted to settle down and get the house together and have a couple of kids. But he just wanted to carry on and spend money and go out. And he was going out all the time and I was staying in. So we finally called it a day. And there wasn't any nastiness about it and there were no children to consider. So we just said we would go our separate ways.[43]

The house was sold and the furniture divided up.

Conclusion

Both the empirical evidence and the official statistics indicate that in this geographical area separation and divorce were by no means common even by 1970. But it is also clear that the institution of marriage was suffering from various stresses and strains. Phillips suggests that there was a connection between increased rates of women in employment and increasing divorce rates,[44] but the evidence from the respondents makes it difficult to reach such a conclusion in this study. Some couples had unrealistically high expectations of marriage; possibly the result of the prevailing emphasis on the idea of marriage being companionate, and emotionally and sexually fulfilling. This was Gillis's conclusion: 'People expect more of the conjugal relationship; it is made to bear the full weight of needs for intimacy, companionship and love, needs which were previously met in other ways. Couples expect more of each other.'[45] Others were unable to reconcile their wish for self-fulfilment with the demands of marriage. There was a constant tension between the growing emphasis on individual rights, on one hand, and on the other, the demand for some degree of self-sacrifice which marriages make. Even among religious people there was less belief in the indissolubility of marriage than there had been earlier in the century.

Couples may have expected more of each other but, unlike those described by Gillis, the needs of many young couples for companionship and love were met, not only in marriage, but also within the wider family. Relations continued to provide friendship and help. It is perhaps arguable, however, that those who had to rely heavily on this external support can be described as having companionate marriages.

7

Married Women's Paid Employment

When *A Woman's Place* was being written, it seemed clear that material on married women's paid employment should be situated in a chapter entitled 'Women as Household Managers' (a chapter which significantly does not appear in this book). Respondents interviewed about life in the earlier years of the century always spoke of married women's paid work in the context of the family's standard of living. Women's earnings were seen as one way of balancing the family budget. Women working for money was an important strategy in the endless struggle against poverty. In this present volume there are several reasons why it seems appropriate to have a separate chapter on married women's paid work. First, far more women worked for wages than previously; secondly, their reasons for so doing were more varied and complex than before; and thirdly, their work had an important effect on, and in turn was affected by, their position as wives and their role as mothers. Hence this chapter is placed between those on marriage and on parenting.

The Second World War and Women's Work

The Second World War marked a watershed in the history of married women working outside the home. In her seminal work on women's work in the war, Penny Summerfield concluded that women who were expected to do men's work outside the home had very little support in the form of government policies to help them cope with the double burden of doing a paid job and running a home and family.[1] From our evidence it would seem possible to argue that the demands made of women during the war, together with the dual role they were expected to play, symbolizes a bridge between the pre- and post-war worlds of women. During the war they were expected to be, as they had been earlier in the century, household managers *par excellence*. They were required to feed and clothe their families on meagre rations and an inadequate supply of clothing coupons. The war can be

Figure 7.1   Women mechanics at work near Lancaster in 1940
(Photo courtesy of Lancaster City Museum)

regarded as the apogee of the period of married women as household managers. But the other role of women at this time was as important figures in the world of men's work. It might be argued that the war had only a limited effect on the history of women in the labour market, as almost all of those doing war work lost their jobs at the end of the war; indeed, they expected to do so.

In 1941 Mrs Lewthwaite went to work at Vickers in Barrow on a capstan lathe making nuts and bolts. She enjoyed being a munitions worker and was aware that she and her colleagues were doing work usually done by skilled men. She left at the end of the war:

> Would you liked to have stayed in Vickers?
> I don't know really. I think we'd had enough by then. We enjoyed all the different jobs, but I don't think it was really a place for girls, no.
> Why?
> Because all the lads and men came back from the Forces. We had to go really to let them have their jobs back, you see.
> Were you told that or did you just assume it?
> No, we were told. We went under those conditions really, that it was just

while the war was on. And when they came back of course they had to have their jobs back.

Did any of the girls resent that? Did they feel that that was a bit unfair?

No, I don't think so. Some may have done but I don't think there was much of that really.[2]

Government Policies Towards Married Women Workers

The government appeared to share this expectation that women should give up their war-time jobs. Its initial post-war position was to 'rebuild the family' with women staying at home to bring up their children. One of the clearest 'pro-natalist' official views is in the Royal Commission on Population Report (1949). The Commission was set up just after the war when there were fears that the declining birth-rate would result in the population falling below replacement level.[3]

This trend, of expecting/encouraging women to stay at home, was not, however, the whole or end of the story. Even at the end of the war, when the pro-natalist policy was being actively pursued, the ban which had excluded married women from employment was lifted in teaching (1944) and in the Civil Service (1946); the government thus tacitly admitted that there would be labour shortages in these areas. Only two years after the war, in 1947, it was clear that the economy in general was suffering from an acute shortage of labour.[4] Consequently, the Ministry of Labour appealed to women 'who are in a position to do so' to enter industry. To further facilitate women's work the government changed the law in 1950 (the Factories (Evening Employment) Order), which made possible the evening shift worked by many housewives, including some of our respondents and their mothers. Even the 1949 Royal Commission eventually welcomed the idea of women doing two jobs, at home and at work. The labour market's continuing demand for women's work through the 1950s and 1960s was undoubtedly one reason for their increased economic activity.[5] Table 7.1 illustrates this national trend.

The Increase in Women's Paid Work Outside the Home

In the post-war world it was more usual for women to have paid work outside the home than before the war. The idea that women could and

Table 7.1   Women in the labour force: Great Britain, 1951–71

	1951	1961	1971
Women in labour force (% of total labour force)	31	33	37
Women in labour force (% of women aged 20–64)	36	42	52
Married women in labour force (% of all married women aged 15–59)	26	35	49

Sources: C. Hakim, *Occupational Segregation* (1979); Census Reports for England and Wales, 1951–81; O. Robinson, 'The Changing Labour Market', table 9.1; H. Joshi, 'The Changing Form of Women's Economic Dependency', table 10.1. The table is taken from J. Lewis, *Women in Britain since 1945* (1992), p. 66.

should work outside the home for wages was accepted by an increasing number of women and, indeed, men. The effect of this development on women's status and power was, however, ambiguous. Fletcher, noting the rise in numbers of married women in paid work, and assuming that male wage-earners in the past had held dominant positions of authority, suggested that increased wage earning would give women more power.[6] Both of these assumptions are open to question.

Oral evidence and census returns show that not only did more married women work for wages in 1951 than earlier in the century, but also the percentage of married women in work continued to rise during the next twenty years, with the interesting exception of Preston in the 1960s (Table 7.2). The differences in the percentages of married women in paid work (many of whom must have been mothers) in the inter-war period, as

Table 7.2   Married women in paid work (%)

Year	Barrow	Lancaster	Preston
1901	5.8	10.2	30.5
1911	6.9	11.0	35.0
1951	14.8	38.6	45.6
1961	32.6	n/a	55.3
1971	40.0	n/a	50.2

n/a = not available.

Source: Census returns. The figures for 1901 and 1911 include married and widowed women; the later figures are for married women only. The figures for 1951, 1961 and 1971 are for full-time and part-time workers combined; we do not know which workers were included in earlier years. It seems likely that many women who worked at home, or casually in other people's homes, were not included.

compared with 1940–1970, is reflected in the evidence of the respondents. Among respondents and the wives of respondents, 52 per cent worked for wages, some full-time, some part-time, at some period in the years 1940–1970. Another 14 per cent began work in the first few years of the 1970s.[7] Because of the age structure of the group, far more were working towards the end rather than at the beginning of the period. Overall, 63 per cent of mothers of respondents worked for wages at some time during their married lives; however, a closer examination of the evidence reveals that mothers were much less likely to work before 1940 than after that date. Only 36 per cent of those who were the right age to do so, worked in the inter-war period. Most of the paid work done by mothers of respondents was after 1940.

Characteristics of Women's Paid Work

The characteristics of women's paid work in the post-war world are well known. First, it was not well paid;[8] women's wages were less than their husbands'. This was not surprising for the women who worked part time, but even full-time workers were still were paid substantially less. From the early 1950s to the mid-1960s the average hourly earnings of full-time women workers was 59 per cent of men's.[9] Equal pay for teachers, civil servants and local government officers was agreed in 1955 but there was no relevant legislation until the Equal Pay Act came into force in 1975, five years after it had been passed. There is no evidence in our study to contradict the official view. 'Women workers were and still are less qualified and less well paid than men. The avenue to success is more likely to be through a husband's career.'[10] In some families in our study these differentials between husbands' and wives' wages were in fact increasing rather than decreasing. The Lancashire cotton industry paid weavers on the amount and type of cloth they produced. In the earlier studies it was not at all unusual to find skilled women weavers earning more than their husbands, who might have been unskilled labourers or workers in a worse-paid branch of the cotton trade.

Secondly, the work done by married and unmarried women during this period continued to be gender-related. Little changed throughout the century; nationally, in 1901 88 per cent of women who worked for wages were in occupations dominated by women. In 1951 the figure was 86 per cent and in 1971 84 per cent.[11] 'Thus the expansion of women's paid work

Figure 7.2   Young women working in a commercial laundry in the late 1940s
(Photo courtesy of Lancaster City Museum)

in the post-war years did nothing to lessen sexual segregation.'[12] Tables 7.3, 7.4 and 7.5 show the pattern of female employment in the three towns surveyed. In our study women were teachers, nurses, clerical workers, cleaners, waitresses, shop assistants, bar-maids, and factory-hands. Only

Table 7.3   Main female employment, 1931 (% of those employed)

Occupation	Barrow	Lancaster	Preston
Personal service	43	28	13
Textile workers	X[a]	22	54
Commercial/financial	21	13	8
Professional	9	11	3
Clerks/typists	9	5	3
Makers of textile goods/dress	4	5	5
Unskilled	X	4	3
Makers of paper/cardboard	3	X	X

Note:[a]   X indicates less than 2%.
Source: 1931 Census data.

Table 7.4   Main female employment, 1951 (% of those employed)

Occupation	Barrow	Lancaster	Preston
Personal service	28	24	17
Textile workers	X[a]	14	28
Commercial/financial	22	13	11
Professional	10	13	5
Clerks/typists	17	14	12
Makers of textile goods/dress	4	4	3
Makers of food and drink	3	X	2
Unskilled	3	5	6
Warehousemen (*sic*)	X	X	3
Health workers	X	3	3
Transport	3	X	X

Note:[a]   X indicates less than 2%.
Source: 1951 Census data.

Table 7.5   Main female employment, 1971 (% of those employed)

Occupation	Barrow	Lancaster	Preston
Service/sport/recreation	24	n/a	20
Textile workers	X[a]	n/a	18
Sales workers	20	n/a	14
Clerical workers	18	n/a	17
Professional/technical	12	n/a	6
Clothing workers	6	n/a	X
Warehousemen (*sic*)	3	n/a	4
Transport/communication	3	n/a	X
Health workers	X	n/a	3

Notes
[a]   X indicates less than 2%.
n/a = not available.
Source: 1971 Census data.

one, the mother of a respondent, had a non-gender-related job, being a drummer in a theatre band throughout the 1940s and 1950s.

Thirdly, women's work was casual and part-time; only a minority of women worked full time.[13] Tables 7.6 and 7.7 show not only the increase in proportions of women working, but also the disproportionate increase in women's part-time work in the period 1949–69. Summerfield argued that policy-makers during the war decided that women could do part-time work without neglecting their domestic duties.[14] This argument was widely

Table 7.6   Proportions of women in Great Britain with dependent children, working full-time and part-time at different dates, by age of youngest child

Age of youngest child	Work status	Year (end December)		
		1949	*1959*	*1969*
0–4	Full-time	9	8	8
	Part-time	5	7	14
	All	14	15	22
5–10	Full-time	—	20	23
	Part-time	—	24	33
	All	—	44	56
11–15	Full-time	—	36	31
	Part-time	—	30	29
	All	—	66	60

Source: Equal Opportunities Commission, *Childcare and Equal Opportunities: Source Policy Perspectives*, (London: HMSO, 1986) p. 87.

Table 7.7   Historical trends in the numbers of part-time and full-time employment (Great Britain)

Year	Full-time (000's)	Total of which female	Part-time[a] (000's)	Total of which female	Ratio of F/T to P/T
1951	19,239	6,041	832	779	23:1
1961	19,794	5,698	1,999	1,851	10:1
1971	18,308	5,413	3,341	2,757	6:1

Note: [a]   Except for 1951, part-time work is defined as working fewer than 30 hours per week.
Source: Select Committee on the European Communities, *Voluntary Part-time Work*, HL 216, ix (London: HMSO, 1982); and Employment Committee, *Part-time Work*, vol. 2, HC 122–II (London: HMSO, 1990), p. 157.

adopted in the post-war period, for example by the Royal Commission on Population in 1949.[15] It is important to stress that married women preferred part-time work, given their preoccupation with the well-being of their children, a recurring theme throughout this book. Employers, given their need for female labour, were prepared to offer part-time work.[16]

Fourthly, the pattern of married women's work was bimodal. Women usually worked until just before the birth of their first child. They then had a period at home before returning to paid work.[17] This represented a notable change in work patterns for many Lancashire women. Those who had worked full time in the cotton industry had continued to work full time when their children were small and when the family was financially in most difficulties. They had stopped work when their family finances allowed it and did not usually return.[18]

Decline of Paid Work in the Home

In the post-war world there was a marked decline in the number of women who earned money at home as compared with the earlier period, but some of the traditional home-based ways of earning money still remained. A few women continued to take in lodgers; the account of one woman indicates how significant a contribution this could be to family budgets. The family moved into their house in the late 1940s, the husband earned £5 a week. Out of this £1 10 shillings went on the mortgage and 10 shillings on mortgage insurance, leaving £3 a week for housekeeping. Two rooms in the house were let to a couple for £1 10 shillings a week. By about 1950 the wife did not let rooms to couples but started taking in lodgers who paid about £2 a week for bed, breakfast and evening meal; by 1960 there were two lodgers who stayed for some years, each paying £3 a week. For about two years she had at least four lodgers in quite a small house. She gave up having lodgers in the 1960s when one of the long-staying lodgers finally went back to his own town.[19]

There were several reasons why she abandoned having lodgers, although they had been a profitable source of income. She began to work an evening shift in the local mill, and she also decided that she wanted her two daughters to have a room each. One daughter explained that she felt some embarrassment at school about the family taking in lodgers and she passed them off as relatives.

Very few women now did dressmaking at home for payment. No mother after the Second World War is recorded as taking in washing; this traditional occupation being rendered redundant by the launderette and the washing machine. In view of the increased number of married women in work, it might be supposed that there would be at least as many women childminding as before the war. Among the respondents there was, in fact, a decline in their numbers, and they are of course impossible to trace in the census returns. The reasons for this decline will be looked at later in this chapter. Women who earned money were more likely than ever before to do so outside their own home.

Reasons for Married Women Working

There were not only changes in the place of work of married women; the reasons why they worked also changed. In the earlier surveys women who worked did so because of dire economic necessity. 'We worked because we had too', was a phrase often repeated. Given the low wages of unskilled men, especially before the First World War, this seems to have been a valid explanation; women's wages were needed in these families to help clothe, feed and house them, the man's wage being inadequate for these purposes. As has been seen in chapter 1, rising standards of living after the Second World War should not obscure the fact that there were still families where the father's wage was too small to support the family.

Mr Lodge was demobbed from the army in 1946 and found a labouring job with the Preston Corporation Electricity Board. His wage was £4 16 shillings week, out of which his wife had to keep herself, her husband and a small child; their rent was 10 shillings a week. They were very badly off and his wife had to work. Mrs Lodge said:

> Well, two of the teachers at school, I loved going to tidy up for them. Just little jobs, but not when Barry was a baby [he was her first-born]. I had to go to work because we couldn't manage. And I went back to the lamp factory and worked there. But after Ron was born I have only done little jobs like brewing tea at the British Legion, or cleaning up for someone. If it only bought the material for them to have some pants it was a big help, you know.[20]

Mr Norton[21] worked as a printer in a wallpaper firm in the 1950s and earned only £5 a week. He and his wife had four children by the end of the decade, and although his wages increased, his wife had to work. She helped out in her parents' fish and chip shop each evening and her husband looked after the children. When Mrs Wallington[22] married in 1946 her husband was a hospital porter earning £3 16 shillings per week. She had to work as a shop assistant to supplement the wages and eventually she opened a shop in her front parlour. Mrs Christy[23] remembered her father, a laboratory assistant, earning about £5 a week in the late 1940s and early 1950s. Her mother was a casual domestic worker. In addition to these families where the father's wage was inadequate to support a family, there were some women who had to work because they were widowed, divorced or separated.[24]

By 1970 there were virtually no two-parent families in the study where the mother had to work because of dire poverty. This was not necessarily true of the population as a whole. The Department of Health and Social Security found in 1970 that the number of poor, two-parent families, with father working full time, would have nearly trebled if the father's earnings had not been supplemented by the mother's.[25] Basic survival, however, was increasingly not the reason for women in our study joining the workforce. Why then did married women work?

One reason was the increasing demands of the labour market; but the women's own perceptions of their reasons for working are more complex. They were certainly influenced by changes in public attitudes to married women working outside the house for wages. There was a developing climate of public opinion which not only supported married women working but also increasingly believed it was their duty to do so. This attitude was, in turn, not unconnected with the demands of the labour market.

It is not suggested that respondents had read or even heard of the work of writers such as Viola Klein and Alva Myrdal,[26] but some women acted as if they had. The ideas which they developed in their studies appear to have both influenced and reflected attitudes which became widely accepted. Myrdal and Klein argued that the economy needed women's labour and that it was therefore their duty to work. They had less to say about women's need for fulfilment or about their right to work!

> Our modern economy cannot afford, nor our democratic ideology tolerate the existence of a large section of the population living by the efforts of others. Whether we like it or not the leisured class has passed into history.[27]

Women were thus presented with an alternative to domestic ideology. In view of this conflict it might be expected that female respondents would exhibit signs of stress and worry about which model to follow. However, only a few discussed their choice of life-style in terms of it presenting them with a dilemma. There was, however, more uncertainty about their role in life than had been observed among older respondents.

Mrs Wheaton did not work outside the home. At various times, however, she investigated doing paid work at home. She was deterred from such work as addressing envelopes and making up garments by what she considered were exploitative rates of pay:

> I wasn't desperately keen, but I felt guilty that other people should be going out to work and I wasn't; and therefore I wasn't doing my bit. It was guilt. It wasn't a desire to go out to work at all. I was quite happy in the environment I was in. I had no spare time. I was completely happy with my lot so I felt guilty.[28]

An increasing number of both men and women exhibited a different attitude to married women working outside the home than had their parents' generation. Several women mentioned financial need as the reason for their wage-earning work. As has been seen, for a small minority of women it was essential to work if their families were not to find themselves in dire poverty, but this was not the case for the majority. Interestingly the authors of a study of married women working in south London came to the same conclusion: 'In the great majority of cases the wives studied were not driven out to work in order to keep the wolf from the door.'[29] In our study most of those who gave financial need as the reason for their work had different perceptions of need compared to women of a previous generation. Mrs Hunter,[30] for example, said, 'We needed the money', but her husband was a teacher and they had been owner-occupiers since their wedding. Her return to work coincided with a move from a small inner-city terraced house to a suburb in a very pleasant area, but with a larger mortgage than that on their previous house. This was perhaps why she felt she needed to return to work. Mrs Turnbull, who was a council house tenant, was not as prosperous as Mrs Hunter nor as poor as Mrs Lodge; she returned to work in the mid-1960s as a part-time home help:

> The reason I turned out to work was that my husband was only on £8 a week and there were five of us to keep. I turned out to work because we needed the money. After he had got his little car, well they had moved the warehouse and he had to get there. We bought a car and we had to pay for it on the HP.[31]

Increasing prosperity and the availability of an unprecedented variety of consumer goods led to greater aspirations. Money had to be found for such items as family holidays, a car, domestic appliances, and an ever-expanding range of clothing (see chapter 2). In many families women earned the money for these extras, men concentrating on being the bread-winner. Historically, women who had earned wages had made a vital contribution towards feeding, housing and clothing their families. It can be argued that the trend for women's wages to pay for 'extras' rather than basic essentials tended to marginalize women's work in a way that had not happened before. Women themselves, and their families, tended to share this perception of their work and wages being of marginal importance to their families. The phrase 'working for pin money' sometimes had a pejorative ring.

An increasing number of domestic appliances meant that women had more time on their hands (although this was not necessarily so, as has already been seen). Paid work could fill the time no longer occupied by housework. In other words, some women worked to have the money to pay for appliances which then gave them time which they filled with paid work![32] Alternatively, they may have worked so that they could buy appliances in order to lessen the burden of housework.[33]

Some married women worked for personal reasons, giving explanations for their working which would not have been offered by those from a previous generation. Zweig, in his study of Lancashire in 1952, wrote: 'The social student often forgets that many women go out to work rather under the emotional pressure of loneliness than under the economic pressure of low wages.'[34] A small group of women claimed that they were bored and unhappy at home.

Mrs Hunter, as has been seen, at one point gave financial need as the reason for her return to paid work. But she also offered another explanation which indicates that she, like so many others, had mixed motives for going out to work. When asked about her husband's attitude to her working she replied:

> Oh, he didn't mind, but his mother objected. She had plenty to say about it. I went out partly for my sake. I was just vegetating at home and I felt I needed an interest again, and we needed the money. You see, my mother-in-law had never worked for all the time she was married. Now my mum had worked all her married life. She had needed to. I was much better going out to work. You know what it's like at home, you are always cleaning for cleaning's sake, sometimes I was so bored, you know.[35]

A small group of women suffered nervous breakdowns and only recovered by finding a job. Mrs Christy suffered a serious post-natal depression in the mid-1960s and had a range of treatments. When she married she had not expected to go out to work, as her own mother had done:[36]

> When I got married I expected to have children and spend the rest of my days looking after them. But obviously I changed my views. It was mainly because of my depression, you know. I realized that my children weren't going to fill my life until I was 60. That was one reason, and the other was that I felt I needed to get out of the home. I would have felt guilty asking people to look after the children while I went out. But it seemed acceptable to ask someone to look after them while I did a job.[37]

Mrs Christy found a part-time, later a full-time, post as a laboratory assistant, a job which she was trained to do.

Much more usual than these women with clearly stated personal unhappinesses were those who returned to work to earn some extra money, and who then stayed on because they so much enjoyed the company of the other workers.

Other women worked for other personal reasons. Some wanted their 'own' money; one wanted to escape a difficult neighbour. The few nurses and teachers returned to pursue the careers which they enjoyed; but it would be difficult to describe any but one of them as career-minded.[38] Indeed, their return to professional work might well have been for other than career reasons. Mrs Lucas was a qualified teacher but gave up work to have a child. Sadly, when the baby was only eight months old, Mrs Lucas's husband died and very soon after that she returned to teaching:

> So I didn't really need the money; I'd been left comfortably off, I could have managed financially but I was just so depressed I wanted to get back and take my mind off things.[39]

For some women, working outside the home was now seen as an aspect of emancipation; whereas for earlier generations of women who had worked in the cotton mills, emancipation was seen to be an escape back into the home, away from an insupportable double burden of hard physical work.[40]

In parenthesis, it should be noted that none of the respondents echoed or even hinted at agreeing with the forceful views of Myrdal and Klein: 'Modern mothers who make no plans outside the family for their future will not only play havoc with their own lives but will make nervous wrecks of their over-protected children and their husbands.'[41]

Mrs Atkin's evidence raises several interesting points. She married in 1967. Her first child was born in 1969:

> When did you return to work?
> Very soon after Peter was born. I didn't intend doing. I wanted one of those continental pushchairs and we hadn't money for one. A friend of mine said, 'Why don't you work in the evenings with me? I'm a telephonist. They're taking on summer staff.' And when I asked my husband then he did have views. He didn't want me to go out to work. He wanted me at home. I'd done my bit and we could manage. The house was paid for. I pointed out that we couldn't afford this pushchair, that was a real extra and it was only for six weeks. He said I could and I was there for nine years! I think it wasn't inconvenient for him anyway. I think he enjoyed the time with the children and popping them into bed.[42]

In this short account there is the distillation of the experiences of many women in the post-war period. Mrs Atkin was a trained nursery nurse but she had no career plan in mind when she married. She said she had no intention of returning to work; the impulsive, casual taking of a job for which she was not trained, and in which she had, at least initially, little interest, was a common experience for many women. Asking her husband's permission and then in a way breaking the agreement by staying nine years instead of six weeks was also not unusual and the appreciation of the additional income for 'extras' was widespread. Mr Atkin's attitude was also typical of many husbands. His opposition to his wife's working was token and short-lived rather than real. His enjoyment of his children was shared by other fathers.[43]

Husbands' Attitude to Working Wives

It is impossible to discern a common view among male respondents about married women working for wages outside the home. There was, however, one commonly held assumption: male wages would exceed those of the female. It is possible that, for some, male pride demanded that men should be the major bread-winners.[44] Some men clearly felt they should be the only bread-winners. Whether or not male pride was an issue, it was simply taken for granted that men would earn more than women and that therefore their wages were more important.

Some men shared Mr Atkin's attitude. They initially opposed their wives working but came to accept it without much fuss. There was another group which felt, just as strongly as had their predecessors in earlier times, that a woman's place was in the home. Their reasons for adopting this point of view were varied. Some men believed that their children were at risk if their wives worked. Their concern was not so much about the children's physical health but about their moral well-being.

Mr Watkinson was a policeman. He thoroughly disapproved of what he considered to be the permissiveness of the 1960s, when he himself had been a teenager:

A lot of emphasis was put on going out to work, children left to fend for themselves, nobody in when they came home from school. And this is one of the major causes of what we see today. And a lot of sexual freedom was talked about. All the main religions were disregarded. And this has all led to this breakdown of discipline we see today.

His wife had returned to work not long before this interview but had given up. 'And she has given up work again mainly at my insistence because of the behaviour of my youngest child [aged 11], that I consider needs control.'[45]

Mr Kennedy, who was a Preston docker, also had worries about the welfare of children, but was perhaps more concerned about the effect on men's wages of women working. His belief that men should be paid a family wage was a long-standing one.[46] His attitude was particularly understandable in the context of Preston where the existence of large numbers of women in the textile industry had been one of the factors which kept down the wages of unskilled men:[47]

Women having to go out to work when they've very young families. . . . I don't think that's fair on the kids. And a lot of them have to do it to keep a roof over their heads. And that to me is wrong. The husband's wage should be sufficient to keep them in relative comfort.[48]

A few men appear to have regarded their wives as little more than unpaid domestic servants, whose only role was to attend to their husbands' comforts. Mr Trickett was married in 1955; he and his wife had no children but he would not allow her to go to work: 'No, she never. I didn't believe in it. I always wanted my meals on the table. I was the old-fashioned type. My dinner had to be on the table at 12 o'clock and my tea at 5.18.' Vickers closed at these times and it took him four minutes to get home on his motor-bike.[49]

Some husbands changed their views; Mr Christy was one:

I felt that her place was in the home, but she always tended to be unsure of herself and I modified my views in the 1960s. I accepted the fact that she really needed some other interest outside the home. She used to get depressed at home on her own.[50]

Some men never seem to have doubted that their wives would be happier working outside the home. Mr Whiteside, who was married in 1960, felt that his marriage only really went well when his wife developed outside interests, first in charity work and later in a paid job. Until that point he found that she relied too much on him for support. He addressed his comments to her:

And it wasn't until you said, 'Well sod that, I'm doing this,' that sort of geed you up a bit and you took more interest in what was going on around you, rather than what was going on in here.
So you didn't mind her going out to work?
No, not in the least.[51]

Other men simply welcomed their wives working because their wages provided extra income. Mrs Jenkins went back to full-time work in the 1960s. She had three school-age children:

> Did your husband mind you going to work?
> Oh no. He was all for it because it was more money in his pocket. He preferred me to work. He could buy a car and things like that.[52]

A few husbands strongly disapproved of their wives *not* working. Mr Farrell was married in 1968 and divorced in the early 1970s:

> I didn't realise it at the time that it was trying to keep up with the Joneses. She definitely coveted, she still covets anyway. And she wouldn't get off her backside as well. If she did, it was only for a month or six weeks. Whatever was earned it certainly never went in the communal pot.[53]

Mr Simpkins was older and was married in 1953, but he too believed his wife should have contributed more to the family budget. Like Mr Farrell he too was later divorced:

> She had two part-time jobs. I think if I had been very well off she would have liked to have been a lady of leisure. There was a period when she didn't work.
> But you didn't object to your wife going out to work?
> I have always welcomed women working. I have always had the greatest respect for women. And if anything happened to me then I certainly wouldn't want my wife dependent on, say, a factory. And I think that was one of my reasons for encouraging my wife [i.e., his second one] to go into nursing, even though there were two small children, but I could work my time round them with working for myself. So I was prepared to encourage my wife to train, get her out and go on for further qualifications. So that if anything happened to me she would be financially independent. My wife wouldn't think of being at home. She would be absolutely bored stiff.[54]

Work and the Family: Women's Expectations and Priorities

Despite the fact that women increasingly joined men in the workforce, married women did not view work in the same way as men did. As has been seen, women from teenage expected to be married, to be mothers, and to fit paid work around these family and household commitments. Women may have had a fairly definite idea of how many children they wanted but were well aware from personal observations that the arrival of children could not be precisely arranged or accidental pregnancies be guaranteed against.

These factors tended to result in married women working casually, taking jobs they were not trained to do, being uninterested in promotion or responsibility and almost invariably giving reasons for working which were unconnected with the intrinsic merits or attractions of the job in question.[55]

In contrast, men's concepts of, and plans for, the future centred on work. Although they expected to marry, and the majority were family-centred, they did not expect marriage and parenthood to interrupt their working lives. Women, unlike men, did not have a life plan for paid work outside the home because, in the great majority of cases, they assumed that they would become mothers and that their children's interests would come first. A few respondents, especially older ones, would probably not have gone out to work when they were married women, even if they had had no children. They left paid work the day they were married and did not expect to return.

Indeed, some of them could not have gone back because of the marriage bar which operated against married women. Although this was more of a problem for women who married in the 1930s, the marriage bar persisted in some places for many years after the war. Mrs Wheaton was a clerk in Barrow Town Hall: 'I liked my work, I was there eight years but they sacked you when you got married then. We fought it and fought it.' She and her colleagues also had a concurrent battle to get equal pay:

> We were going to have equal pay because a lad came in at the same time as you, same age, same job and he would get so much extra a week. We fought like mad, in fact the man that came round the office for the union dues used to dread coming, we wouldn't let him out! So they got equal pay, and that was our first victory and I do reckon that it was our little clique that really ground them down, and we fought like mad for married women to be kept on, and six months after I got married [in 1958] it came in that they would take married women on.[56]

Mrs Owen was representative of some of the older respondents. She had only one child, born in 1940. She never contemplated returning to work, having given up her job as a shop assistant the day she was married in 1939:

> No, they didn't in those days. Women stopped at home to look after their children. And my husband had a very hard job. He needed his food when he came in. No, I never went out to work. They were satisfied with the money they got.[57]

The great majority of women who were married after the war had a more relaxed view of paid work. Almost all of them continued working after marriage until the birth of their first child. After that, however, the needs of the children became of extreme importance; their interests were their first consideration. As Klein and Myrdal wrote: ' "Children first" is the motto writ large over all discussions of the merits and demerits of married women's employment.'[58] But, starting with similar concerns about children's needs, some came to very different conclusions about their own paid work. Some decided to stay at home for the benefit of their children, sharing the kind of views expressed by Mr Watkinson.[59]

Childcare

Mrs Webster was married in 1959 and worked until the birth of her first child in 1964. She afterwards blamed her husband for her staying at home, but she appears to have agreed with his views at the time. It is only with hindsight that she felt she may have made the wrong decision:

> My husband is very old-fashioned. He doesn't believe in working wives. He said I must stay at home and look after the children. But they haven't grown up any better than anyone else's children for me doing it, which is very annoying. I mean, you don't really miss going to work. You make your life around the children and the home. The only thing is when they grow up and make their own lives, you tend to want to go back then. You feel a bit lost then when they go to work and they go out for long days. Yes, because I always had someone at home midday which helped. It breaks the day, you see.[60]

Most women did not share Mrs Webster's rejection of all paid work once the children were born. This is clear both from the oral evidence and from official statistics. The figures for married women who were 'economically active' in each age group are available only for Barrow and Preston in 1971. In the age group 35–55 the majority of women in both towns worked for wages, and common sense suggests that most of these women must have been mothers. The figures also indicate that women were returning to work when they considered their children were 'old' enough (table 7.8).

Assumptions that women would return to work some time after the birth of their children were widely held, not only by the women themselves, as is clear from the statistics, but also by writers on women's work, such as Myrdal and Klein. Their book, *Women's Two Roles*, was based on the assumption that as women were marrying at a younger age (a quarter of brides were under twenty years of age in 1956), childbirth and childrearing were concentrated in an earlier and shorter time, hence there were many

Table 7.8   Married women economically active in each age group, 1971 (%)

Age	Barrow	Preston	England and Wales
16–20	42	47	43
21–24	43	43	46
25–29	34	47	35
30–34	41	55	51
35–39	51	63	53
40–44	57	68	59
45–49	60	70	60
50–54	50	67	55
55–59	39	60	45
60–64	20	29	25

Source: *Census 1971: County Report for Lancashire*, part 1, table 18.

years in which a woman could return to work and become economically active.

There were considerable differences in mothers' views about how old a child should be before they returned to work. Their decisions were largely dependent upon the kind of childcare which was available to them. Respondents were not apparently influenced, as were some middle-class mothers, by the writings of John Bowlby on maternal deprivation;[61] but their desire for their children to be well and lovingly cared for by a reliable person was very strong.[62]

There were some differences in childcare arrangments over time (see table 7.9). These are partly the result of changes in the labour market, but they also reflect women's changing ideas about the relationship of their dual roles as workers and mothers. Paid minders were usually employed when mothers with pre-school-age children worked full time; their relative loss

Table 7.9   Respondents' childcare arrangements, pre- and post-Second World War (%)

Type of care	Pre-war	Post-war
Paid minders	26.3	10.6
Unpaid minders	21.9	22.3
Husbands	5.0	12.7
Child at school	10.5	31.9
Child at mother's workplace	Nil	6.3
Mother paid work at home	31.6	10.6
Nursery	Nil	5.3

of popularity reflects the decrease in full-time employment of mothers which resulted both from the decline of the cotton industry in Preston and from women deciding not to work full time when they had pre-school-age children.[63]

The decline in women working at home for wages has already been discussed. To replace these two 'traditional' ways of wage-earning, women looked for jobs either where they could take the child with them (which almost always meant domestic work in a home or in a pub), or in the evening when the father could look after the child; alternatively they delayed going out to work until the youngest child was in school. The unpaid minders were almost always relatives who may or may not have been co-resident. Occasionally they may have been friends, but they were asked to childmind on a unpaid basis only if they cared for the child occasionally and not regularly. Nurseries were rarely used, and then only in the later post-war period. Respondents' mothers who did war-work did not use nurseries.

Some of the respondents' solutions to the problem of childcare have already been indicated, especially of those who found work in the evenings. Mrs Kennedy and Mrs Rowlandson senior,[64] who had both been weavers, found work at Peter Craig's, a mail-order firm in Preston, where there was a special evening shift for women with small children.

Mrs Carter,[65] who, like her mother, had been a textile worker, went as a cleaner in a pub where she was able to take the children with her until they went to school. Very occasionally there were women who found it possible to go on working in a job which was not domestic work and still take their child with them. Mrs Burrell was a part-time secretary in a school for children with health problems. When she became pregnant (in the 1960s) she told the headmaster, who asked her to bring the child with her once it was born:

Yes, I took her in the pram and it worked very well. If she was a bit grizzly they used to let me come home with her. My hours were very flexible. I could just work it the way I wanted, so I used to do most of my work when she was having her sleep. And then she got to the crawling stage and to the toddling stage, and the headmaster then he made a big play-pen in the middle of his office; so we put her in that. Then she got to the running-about stage. One day she ran out and rang the bell before it was time for the end of lessons. So I thought, right, this is the time she should be going to play-school. So I used to take her to play-school and then go back and do my hours while she was there.[66]

In the early 1960s Mr Ingham's wife had a child and almost immediately resumed full-time work as a secretary. The child went to the only state-run day nursery in the district. Mr Ingham supported his wife's decision and was happy with the arrangements for the child's care, perhaps significantly because he saw it as being provided on a family basis. Three close relatives worked in the nursery at that time, 'So she was going home sort of thing.'[67] This is the only recorded use of a state nursery among the respondents.

The ideal childminder, in the opinion of many respondents, was a relative. Until the Second World War, in Preston, very many grandmothers looked after their grandchildren while their daughters worked in the mills, just as their mothers had done for them. In our earlier study of this pre-war period we found that all grandmothers or aunts were paid for this full-time work. Not to have done so would have seemed to be exploiting a close relative and not sharing earnings at a time when income was seen as a family possession rather than as an individual one. The position appears to have been rather different in the post-war period, both as a result of changing attitudes and of changing economic conditions. Some women believed strongly that, having had a child, it was their sole responsibility to bring it up, the concept of shared family responsibility appearing to have been lost, as was so much else in the move towards individualism.

Mrs Wheaton, who was married in 1958, never worked outside the home once her children were born:

> I would have had to have somebody to sort them out at certain times. And there was no way I was going to ask my parents or John's to do it. No way under any circumstance, it had to be desperate. It had to be a hospital case or something like that before I would ask either of them. My fault again.[68]

It is not quite clear why Mrs Wheaton felt it was 'her fault'. Indeed, in looking for explanations for the absent grandmothers in childminding it is perhaps more revealing to examine the changing attitudes of the grandmothers rather than those of their daughters or daughters-in-law. Hoggart described the 'young' grandmother of the 1950s thus, 'She is the pivot of the home, she holds it together.' He describes her as keeping contact with a wide range of relatives.[69] Similarly, Young and Wilmott described the grandmother as the pivotal figure in the families of Bethnal Green.[70] As will be seen in chapter 10, this region was not without similar grandmothers who held a dominant position in their families. But a different 'model' of the grandmother was also emerging, one whose attitudes tended to cause some resentment in their daughters. A small minority clearly believed that they had not had help from *their* mothers and were not therefore prepared to help their daughters. Some were placing their individual rights before their family responsibilities. It would appear that it was not working mothers who were neglecting their family responsibilities, but the elderly retired. Mrs Wheaton was a mother with a strong feeling of responsibility towards her children, but perhaps the real reason why she was so determined to look after the children herself was because she was aware that her parents were highly critical of being asked to baby-sit by their son. Mrs Wheaton did not wish to be similarly criticized.[71]

Grandmothers could be quite direct in their rejection of a childminding role. Mrs Emery was pregnant when she got married in 1956 and felt she had to keep on working after the baby was born, as the family needed the money. At first she claimed her mother was too old to look after the child (she was 56) but then added, 'She said: "You had them, you made your bed, you can lie on it." '[72] Grandmothers did not seem to differentiate between sitting in the evening and during the day. Mrs Sykes's mother would do neither:

> My mother didn't believe in looking after your children. She said, 'You have them, you look after them.' She wouldn't mind him so I could go back and do a proper job. She said that she'd brought hers up, and she wasn't bringing anyone else's up. There you are.[73]

There was possibly a difference between the towns in this respect; Barrow grandmothers were much less used to the idea of women working outside the home. They were more resistant to the situation than Preston grandmothers, who had been accustomed to childminding for working daughters or daughters-in-law. For instance, in Preston Mrs Grimshaw's mother worked as a shop assistant from shortly after her daughter's birth in 1944. Mrs Grimshaw and her older sister were cared for by their grandmother who lived up the street. In 1956 grandmother went to live with the family and stayed twenty years until her death.[74]

There is no mention of payment to grandmothers, nor is there evidence that this was a problem to either parents or grandparents. It might have been interesting to interview the grandmothers and try and discover if the lack of remuneration was in any way responsible for their refusal to childmind, since payment for such services had been the norm in pre-war cotton towns. Occasionally it would seem, however, that a grandmother might be exploited. One respondent, who was, perhaps ironically, a union official, admitted that his mother-in-law cared for his and his wife's young child for eight hours a day with no remuneration. The grandmother did not live with the family.[75]

There were paid minders, especially in Preston, where they had long been a vital link in the labour chain. As has been seen, they were less used than formerly, as the cotton mills declined and women preferred alternative ways of combining their roles as workers and as mothers. Mrs Emery, whose mother had refused to help, had a paid minder while she continued her work in the mill:

> Well, you didn't stop work for six months like they do now. Just a couple of weeks before you went back to work. My first baby, a lady up Blackpool Road looked after him, a childminder. It was a nurse that came round and she knew this lady was looking for a little boy. But I had a long way to take him because we didn't have a car.[76]

While the census returns and oral evidence indicate that some mothers must have worked continually (as is shown by the figures for those employed in their twenties and thirties), the evidence also indicates that some mothers did not work for wages at all. Several of these mothers have been heard from in this chapter and there are more in chapter 8 speaking about bringing up children. Mothers who did not work explained that they felt it was their duty to be at home for the sake of their children. Unlike their wage-earning contemporaries, they were more anxious about the harm which would come to their children if they left them.

We have seen both working and non-working mothers regarding the needs of their children as being of paramount importance. Is there any evidence to suggest that children of working mothers did less well emotionally and physically than the children of mothers who stayed at home? Certainly, no wage-earning mother considered that her children had been harmed in any way by her working. There is little official local evidence which can be offered. In the earlier years of the century high infant mortality rates had wrongly been associated with high percentages of married women in work.[77] In the post-war world infant mortality rates fell as the number of married women in paid work rose (see table 1.7). The number of children entering higher education also increased,[78] but so too did the number of juvenile delinquents.[79] Precedents should make historians wary of offering monocausal explanations of such complex issues as the factors that affect children's development.

Conclusion

Probably all historical periods can be justifiably described as transitional, but there seem to be particularly strong reasons for viewing the period 1940–70 in these terms. An increasing number of men and women believed, not only that married women had the right to do wage-earning work, but also that they had a duty to do so. An ever-growing number of married women worked after marriage. But they were not equal to men in the labour market; they had gender-related jobs and unequal pay, while their concerns as mothers tended to make them choose casual unskilled work with few prospects of promotion. With few exceptions, they were mothers first and workers second. These had always been characteristics of women's paid work. But, despite their greater participation in the labour market, women appeared to be curiously more marginalized and less powerful than in pre-war days. Interestingly, the authors of the report on married women working in Bermondsey came to the same conclusion: 'It was alleged that the status of the Bermondsey mother had declined, speakers pointing out that, in contrast to today, "It used to be Mums as were the bosses round here." '[80] The authors went on to suggest that this trend could be reversed if more women went out to work, an optimistic solution to the problem which would now be difficult to support. Much would seem to depend on the kind of work done by women.

There were several reasons for this erosion of women's power, some of which have already been outlined in chapter 5. First, although more women worked for wages they were not perceived as providing such a vital element in the family budget as had their predecessors. The dramatic rise in real wages benefited men especially; some worked long hours of overtime; their wages were seen as providing the essentials in the family budget: food, clothing and housing. Women were seen as contributing to the less important 'extras' in family life. Their contribution to the family economy was also diminished in another way. In less prosperous times women's budgeting skills and abilities to 'make something out of nothing' had been highly prized and very important; a well-managed family budget could mean the difference between, on the one hand, being adequately fed and housed and, on the other, sinking below the poverty line. Now, this kind of work, because it was unpaid, was increasingly perceived by some as having little value. With increased male wages a women's ability to make do and mend and to budget well became less important than in earlier periods. At the same time, the opportunity to make money in the home, which had made it an economic power base for many women, was also much eroded. Coupled with these developments was the growing belief that a woman's place was no longer exclusively in the home. In the midst of all this confusion women found themselves in a truly transitional phase: losing some of the power they had once had in the home and family, they had yet to acquire equality and any real power in the world of paid work.

8

Changing Attitudes to Childcare

While some ideas about the upbringing of children persisted from the earlier part of the century, there were also changes in attitudes to the care and nurture of young children. Families became more child-centred, parents more aware of the emotional, psychological and intellectual needs of their children. Professional help and advice was increasingly sought and fathers became more involved in their children's upbringing, although this remained primarily the responsibility of mothers.

Influences on Ideas of Childcare

While it is not difficult to find parents with 'traditional' views in the period 1940–70, there were some changes in parental attitudes, expectations and behaviour which, not surprisingly, reflected the changes which were taking place outside the bounds of the immediate family. Some publicly expressed and canvassed opinions referred particularly to the family. After the war some experts advocated that the family should be 'rebuilt', and that social conditions should be such that 'problem' families could not be created. There was an awareness that many families had suffered separation: children from fathers who had been away in the forces, children from mothers if they had been engaged in war work, and children from both parents if they had been evacuated. Others had suffered physical dislocation and some were homeless. Expert views continually emphasized the importance both of good mothering and of the 'correct' upbringing of children.[1] Virtually all parents in this study expressed an acute awareness of the need for 'good parenting'. There was no agreement, however, as to how best this might be achieved, or what in fact was meant by the phrase 'being a good parent'.

Parents were also influenced by more general changes in attitudes and standards which have been referred to in chapter 1. These in turn affected attitudes to their children, although again it must be stressed that it is very difficult to trace the exact way in which generally held ethical and/or philosophical views impinged on individuals.

In accordance with views on individual rights and personal autonomy, almost all the men and women in the study wished to make a positive decision about the size of their family. This appeared to be the final stage of a development which had begun in the late nineteenth century.[2] But ideas about individual rights increasingly affected parents' attitudes to their children. In some families children's rights became more important than their responsibilities. The majority of families became more child-centred than ever before, with a corresponding decline in the exercise of parental authority and an increased concern about the emotional well-being of the child. Parents may well have been influenced by the changes in world events, as Christina Hardyment suggests: 'Reaction from austerity, military discipline and sudden death made parents peculiarly inclined to indulge the new generation.'[3]

Undoubtedly, some were influenced by the theories and attitudes of the child-care experts of the time. It was rare to find a respondent who had read Dr Spock. (One who had read him had a row with the staff of her infant welfare clinic because they wanted to vaccinate her child against smallpox, whereas Dr Spock had written that children such as hers with infantile excema should not be vaccinated.)[4] However, in view of the fact that Dr Spock's book, *Commonsense and Baby and Child Care* (which was first published in 1946 and which appeared in a new edition approximately every ten years), was only outsold by the Bible, it is reasonable to suppose that he had some influence, possibly through magazine articles; more probably via individual members of the middle classes who certainly read Spock. The book made available, in an easily understood way, the ideas of Freud and Piaget on the psychological and intellectual development of children. Most importantly, greater prosperity and smaller families meant that more parents than before could afford the time and money needed to preside over child-centred families.

Christina Hardyment wrote of such families:

> Being a constant reassuring presence, considering one's child every need, creating a stimulating environment exactly suited to its current developmental stage, all these take up a great deal of time. Only with two children and a modernised house can these demands of modern childcare be confidently met.

She considered that the prosperity of the 1950s and 1960s enabled parents to give time and money to their children in unprecedented amounts.[5] It is doubtful if many parents actually achieved the standards outlined by Hardyment, but for some they were an ideal to aim for; and at least these goals could be partly realized with greater resources of time and money than had been available to earlier generations.

The great majority of parents in the study were determined that their children should have a 'better' life than they themselves had experienced, although there was little agreement about what constituted a 'better' life. Only a few discussed their children in terms of their psychological development. The absence of this discussion perhaps reinforces the argument that they were unlikely to have read Spock, still less Piaget or Freud. But virtually all acted on the assumption that a child-centred family was a 'good thing'. It has already been seen that mothers decided whether or not to work for wages and what form that work should take, in the light of the effect those decisions would have on their children. Parents spent more time with their children than had parents of a previous generation. A growing number of parents were anxious that their children should have a good education. Others wanted them to enjoy the treats and possessions which they themselves had never had. Others hoped that their children would not be so burdened, as they had been, with work and responsibilities, whether inside or outside the home. In other words, they believed that they should be allowed to be children for as long as possible, an idea long accepted and acted upon by middle- and upper-class parents, but a relatively new concept for the working class.[6]

Fathers played a greater part in the upbringing of their children, although this was far from being a universal trend, and, as has already been mentioned, they were much more likely to play with their children than change their nappies. Marriages may not have been companionate but families became more so, enjoying more outings and holidays than had been affordable in earlier times. It is possible to see the post-Second World War period as being the golden age of the small nuclear family.

Anxieties about Childcare

However, as with all golden ages, there were many problems. While some parents continued to handle their children confidently, others showed a degree of uncertainty in their parenting which was virtually unknown to the parents in the earlier study. This group tended to worry about their children's physical, emotional and intellectual development and to rely less on themselves and their families and more on the advice of professionals. Although it is impossible to measure anxiety, it is difficult not to feel that mothers in particular, but some fathers also, were more anxious about their children in 1970 than at the end of the war. There was also an ambivalence about the role of women, which affected them both as waged workers and as wives and mothers. There are other themes which can be teased out of the oral evidence. Although the nuclear family was in many ways stronger than before, it was also in danger of being undermined by various forces. Sometimes the children, whose intellectual development had received much parental attention and encouragement, left home to follow some form of tertiary education and did not return, as has been seen in chapter 3. Thus the close-knit nuclear family did not always evolve into the close-knit extended family of previous generations. Sometimes education resulted in parents and children developing few interests in common. Consumerism undermined the close-knit fabric of some families as young people contributed less to the family's finances and spent a larger proportion of their wages on themselves.

The Care of Infants

In so many marriages, as has been seen in chapter 6, the arrival of the first child marked a parting of the ways for the parents. Couples, who could have been quite companionate, adopted separate roles and began to spend more and more time with their own gender group.

This may seem to be at variance with the idea of the more companionate family. Certainly, many fathers were more involved with their families than had been an earlier generation of men, but on the whole this involvement was with older children, not with small babies, and was mostly confined to leisure-time activities. The family, as a result, may have been companionate but the couple no longer was, seeing themselves as having separate and gender-related roles. Men and women still assumed that the main responsibility for childcare would be carried by women. Even such 'progressive' writers as Myrdal and Klein, who consistently urged women to return to work, did not question women's role as the chief providers of child care: 'It is women's business not only to bear children but also to take the lion's share in their care and education.'[7]

Several references have been made to the probable effect the writings of childcare experts had on the upbringing of working-class children. It is arguable that the influence of professional childcarers in the area could well have had a greater effect on the attitudes and practices of young mothers. This influence is certainly clearly discernible in the oral evidence, especially of the younger respondents.

The Influence of Professional Carers

In the earlier part of the period mothers and mothers-in-law and sisters and sisters-in-law and female neighbours, all part of the supportive gender group, remained the most important source of advice on childrearing for young mothers. But increasingly, whether this advice, once given, was acted upon or not depended on the judgement of the young mothers. They listened to their elders' advice, they did not argue if they disagreed with it, but *they* decided what was best for their babies, rejecting or accepting advice at will and with considerable confidence. As the period progressed young mothers not only took less and less heed of their elders' advice, although there was still no evidence of open conflict about it, they also tended to take less notice of their own judgement. They preferred to listen to those they regarded as the experts on childcare: doctors, health visitors and clinic staff.

Few were like the mothers of St Ebbe's in Oxford whom Mogey described in the following way: 'Children are brought up in the traditional way. The advice of the clinic is accepted only after a thorough testing to see if it agrees with local folklore.'[8]

Mrs Owen is representative of the generation of mothers who had their babies in the earlier part of the period. Her accounts of childrearing illustrate the difficulty in categorizing women as 'modern' or 'traditional'. She accepted the advice and help of female relatives but only really believed in the professional services of the doctor; she chose to reject those available from other health professionals. When her only daughter was born, in 1940, Mrs Owen lived very near to her mother and, indeed, to several other relatives. She said:

Well, if she was ill I used to ask mum, but I think I managed. I had my mum handy and my aunty down the street, so I managed. If she had a rash, I'd ask my mum, but I think it's natural. You get to know.

So although emphasizing the importance of mum, she also indicates that she had her own common sense to fall back on. When discussing home remedies she said that she had none: 'No, not really. If something happened to her I used to take her to the doctor's and get the *proper* thing.' When asked about her mother's extensive range of remedies, for which she was well known in the neighbourhood, she added:

> Well, I let mum goose-grease her if she had a bad chest. Out would come the jar of goose-grease, an earthenware jar with a piece of brown paper over it and a rubber band round it. And she would rub her back and front. In the end I took her to the doctor's and he gave me some antibiotics and it cleared up in no time.[9]

Mrs Owen's faith in the doctor having the *proper* thing was shared by many other young mothers in the post-war period. It had been far from a universally held faith in their mothers' generation. A growing confidence in doctors did not necessarily extend, in the early part of the period, to the pronouncements of staff at the infant welfare clinics. In the inter-war period an increasing number of mothers had visited these clinics and had valued

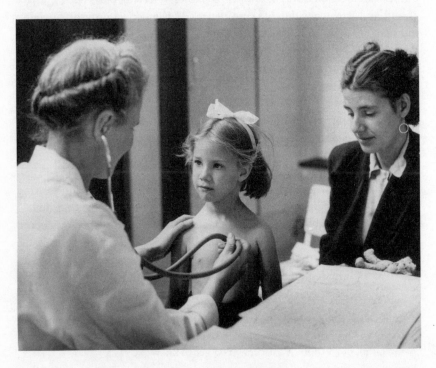

Figure 8.1   Mothers increasingly sought professional medical advice and treatment for their children (London, 1954)
(Photo courtesy of Popperfoto)

their advice, and this trend continued to grow; but some mothers continued to accept only the treatment and advice offered by doctors. After the advent of the National Health Service in 1948 it was, of course, much easier to adopt this strategy. Mrs Owen was asked if she visited the clinic:

> Yes, once or twice, not a lot. I thought it was a waste of time myself. They told me once that she was going to be bow-legged. I mean she's as straight as anything and I stopped going then. It used to upset me when they said anything was wrong.

Like many other mothers of her time Mrs Owen disregarded 'official' advice about infant feeding. When asked about regular time-tabled feeds she replied, 'Oh, in the hospital they used to tell me that, but my mother used to say, "Now when she cries, don't stick to time, if she is hungry she will eat." I used to give it to her when she was hungry.'[10] She added that her neighbours also fed their babies on demand.

Mrs Marley, like Mrs Owen, was an older respondent. She had her first child in 1939 and her second in 1943. Unlike Mrs Owen, she relied almost exclusively on her own judgement in matters of infant- and childcare, but she did take some advice from friends and relations. Her son was started on bottles of 'Truefood' in the hospital:

> He was bottle-fed and they hadn't found any food to suit him and he threw it back. I had a friend in Blackpool who had had two boys and she had them on 'Ostermilk'. And I had sense and I said to the matron, 'Well, I'll get a tin of "Ostermilk" on the way home.' And he guzzled it like mad. And he was fed every two hours, night and day. He was supposed to be on every three hours, the matron said! I know he went on to mixed feeding when he was about eight weeks old. My mother came and said, 'I'll give him something else.' So we tried him on 'Farex'!

After her daughter was born the health visitor came:

> She came in one day about 2 o'clock and asked when she was fed, and I said, '9 o'clock this morning.' She said, 'Oh you shouldn't leave her so long.' And I said, 'Look, the last one cried every half hour after he'd been fed and I'm not waking this one up, if she's hungry she'll waken.'[11]

Many mothers throughout the period continued to share the self-confidence of women like Mrs Owen and Mrs Marley. Occasionally a marvellously anarchic baby toddles through the memories; no doubt to the despair of the professionals but to the delight of their families. Mr Monkhouse's youngest brother was born in 1960. His mother, having already had seven children, was undoubtedly confident in her childrearing skills:

He would romp around in just a nappy. He loved tea, he had got a taste for it rather than for milk. He would have a bottle of tea; and he had this wonderful habit of drinking half his bottle and then sticking it down his nappy. He would toddle round with it and when he got thirsty he would take it out . . . by this time the tea was cold.[12]

There are clearly discernible changes in the attitudes of young mothers to professional advice and advisers throughout the period. Mothers' continuing and increasing reliance on the advice of doctors has already been referred to. There was a marked increase in references to infant and child welfare clincs among respondents whose children were born in the 1950s and 1960s. This trend can be seen most clearly in Barrow, and the respondents' experiences reflect those of the wider population. In 1956 the Medical Officer of Health reported that, because of the difficulties of mothers on new housing eatates attending the central clinic, a mobile one had been put into service. In 1956, 1,921 children made 12,445 attendances at it.[13] By 1965 the Medical Officer's report listed no fewer than 3,570 children making 23,632 attendances at the mobile clinic.[14] There are many references to this clinic in the oral evidence and they are frequently coupled with a mention of a health visitor whose advice was also increasingly relied upon. However, visits to the clinic were more frequent than calls from the the health visitor. Mrs Sykes is typical of many mothers:

Did you go to the clinic?
  Yes, well, it was a mobile bus. Well, they used to weigh them and measure them and all that. Then the health visitor used to come round and just check up to see if you were doing everything right. We used to take them until they were nearly school age. Mind you, a lot of it was a social afternoon out![15]

Mrs Jenkins was aware of a different attitude between herself and her mother-in-law who, because of fostering an orphaned child from within the extended family, had a child the same age as Mrs Jenkins':

Did you have a health visitor?
  Yes, I accepted her and took her advice. I took practically everybody's advice! But my mother-in-law wouldn't let her in the house. She said that she was an interfering busybody. But young people went to the clinic, my mother-in-law didn't.[16]

Younger mothers were likely to be much less confident about childrearing than their predecessors had been. Mrs Grimshaw had her first child in 1970:

She wasn't so old when I put her on solids. She never liked milk, it used to take me about two hours to get a bottle of milk down her.

Was that your decision or the clinic's?

Well, it must have been theirs, because with my first one I don't think I had the confidence. No, you sort of do everything they tell you, don't you?

Did they tell you when to feed her?

Every four hours, I used to wait every four hours.

And did you wake her up if she was asleep?

Yes.

Would you leave her to cry if the four hours wasn't up and she was hungry?

I suppose I must have done.[17]

Mrs Priestley was one of the youngest respondents, being born in 1950. She had her first child in 1977 and was clearly dependent upon the advice of professionals, and was also influenced by what she called 'advertising'. Her child was breast-fed:

It was sort of put across to you by all the advertising and the nurses that really it was the best thing to do. Nobody had to persuade me you know. It was just something I wanted to do.

The child was put on to solids at three months on the advice of her health visitor:

Yes, but it was my first baby. I didn't know what to do. I was totally ignorant myself really; and I did ask the health visitor what to do.

Did you ask your mum?

Oh yes. She helped me a lot. She was always there; I would always ask her.[18]

The mother–daughter relationship had undergone a subtle change. Mrs Priestley's mother, like many other mothers, did not tell her daughter what to do. Rather she offered reassurance and support: 'I used to ask, "Do you think she's alright? Have I done this right? How long should she sleep?" Just reassurance, you know.'

Very few of the younger mothers record any traditional remedies. If they had any doubts about their children's physical well-being, then the doctor or another professional health worker was consulted. In this thirty-year period there was a noticeable shift from reliance on one's own judgement, and the advice of relations and neighbours with some support from the experts, to a strong dependence upon the professionals with a corresponding diminution of self-reliance and self-confidence. From the beginning of the century the medical establishment had been urging mothers to seek and heed their expertise; high infant mortality rates being offered as proof of what happened when the professionals were ignored. It could be claimed that by 1970 they had won their campaign to be heard and heeded by the mothers. In the more important war against high rates of infant mortality, both professionals and, more especially, parents who had the day-to-day care of babies, must be recorded as winning a great victory (see table 1.7).

Mothering

In many ways the post-war period was a unique time for mothers and children. Working-class mothers earlier in the century had had so much work to do that there was little time for their children. Mothers saw their role as one of ensuring that their children were fed, clothed and housed, that they were obedient and well-behaved, and that when they were older they were fitted into a 'steady' job. They worked endlessly, washing, cleaning, shopping, cooking, sewing and knitting. Much of the work was made even more burdensome by the size of their families. Some women's responsibility was increased by their need to work outside the home in order to supplement their husbands' wages.

After the Second World War and, indeed, for a growing number of families before it, this burden of physical work was being reduced. Women had fewer children than their grandmothers had and, with increasing real wages for men, had less need to work outside the home for financial reasons. Housework became physically easier with the ever-increasing number of domestic appliances (see chapter 2). Women had more choice about how they spent their time. As has been seen, an increasing number chose to go out to work, but this was an almost inconceivable decision to others who made a different choice. These women either wanted, or felt it was their duty, to spend as much time as possible with their children. Only one mother mentioned the work of John Bowlby,[19] but it can be suggested that a somewhat over-simplified version of his ideas, and indeed those of other experts writing about the importance of good mothering,[20] was absorbed by many mothers. They believed that they themselves had to look after their children if they were not to grow up with some psychological damage. Some believed that this maternal care was vital until the child attended school. Others felt that they were needed to be always available until the child was much older. Mr Graveson expressed a view that was typical of many, both fathers and mothers:

The day our daughter was born [1963] she finished work. Well, you know before. And she didn't work again until our son was nine [1975]. We agreed, we thought it was the most sensible thing. They were our responsibility, it was our responsibility to bring them up. She ran a catalogue, but, no, she stayed at home and looked after them . . . It is a very important point.[21]

It cannot be emphasized too strongly that going out to work did not preclude loving one's children. Nor did being a devoted mother exclude one from going out to work. The great majority of women in the study did not see any inconsistency in being both a working mother and a caring one as well. They went out to work at a time when they judged that their children would not be harmed by their so doing.

There can be no doubt that many women found great happiness and contentment in bringing up their children. Mrs Kennedy, who had the six unplanned pregnancies, said, 'Mind you, I've enjoyed every one of them. I've thought many a time that I would love to turn the clock back and start all over again. I'd love to, yes. I really enjoyed them.'[22] (Mrs Kennedy eventually had a wage-earning job.)

Mrs Morrison had two sons in the late 1950s, and when speaking of women going back to work said:

I think there is a lot of women don't want to be at home. They want to get out to work as soon as they can. I can't understand them, being as I am. I can't understand people wanting to go out just after they have had a baby and going straight back to work. I think they miss such a lot, such a lot, with their baby; because you can't capture these moments again can you? But there again . . . everybody is different and do their own thing.[23]

(Mrs Morrison returned to work when her children were teenagers.)

Mrs Boyle was an abused wife who found considerable consolation in her five children, born in the 1950s and 1960s:

I got more enjoyment out of my kids than anybody else I know. Because I used to love being with them. I walked miles and miles with them. I used to help them play 'Hide and Seek' and 'I Spy' and learn them to knit and sew.[24]

Mrs Boyle simply enjoyed her children, she had few ambitions for them.

Women who found mothering totally fulfilling sometimes find it difficult to understand those for whom children are not their only interest. Women like Mrs Hocking reflect domestic ideology and look back with nostalgia to what was, for them, the golden age of the nuclear, child-centred family. Mrs Hocking had two children in the 1950s and, as a grandmother, she was quite critical of her daughter and son-in-law, comparing their parenting unfavourably with her own:

> She goes to tap dancing, he goes training, they are going out for a meal . . . so the kids have got to be geared up to get undressed ready for bed. Everything is geared to time. Whereas in my children's younger days, it was just relaxed; they could be in bed when they wanted; they could sit up and play when they wanted, and they could get mucked up. I just don't know. Life is a rat race, and it brushes off on the children. It's not right. Children are uptight, mothers are uptight. In my day the children came home from school, mother was there, never went out, father came home, never went out.[25]

Few women were as willing as Mrs Hocking to let their children please themselves to such an extent about their timetable, but many were as likely as she was to have lives centred on their children rather than on themselves.

On the other hand, there were many mothers who could not share either Mrs Hocking's relaxed attitude to childrearing or Mrs Boyle's enjoyment of her children. As has already been seen, some mothers were lacking in confidence; they felt insecure and needed the support of professionals in the handling of their children. Others, while not necessarily lacking in confidence, were aware of a rapidly growing literature on childcare, and believed that their job as mothers included the duty of seeing that their children developed properly, especially psychologically. A few mothers were anxious about their off-spring 'fitting in' with other children, an anxiety which tended to grow as both nuclear and extended families shrank.

Mrs Wheaton had two children in the early 1960s. She said that she consulted several books on childcare and, while claiming that she found them confusing and contradictory, clearly was influenced by some of the ideas on child psychology which she encountered. She worried for years about her eldest, a boy who appeared not to be sociable and who preferred not to play with other children:

> Our David was one that didn't play out. He didn't play with toys, he'd rather get the *Radio Times* and teach himself to read. He was the odd-ball. I tried for seven years to make him play normally, but I gave up after seven years and he was a happy child after that. I brought children in and he used to be sat in the corner doing his own thing and they used to play with his toys. I can remember when he was seven I suddenly decided, 'What are you doing? Why try to make him something he doesn't want to be?' The little lass was completely normal, she'd play out and I just came to realize that it wasn't my fault. I hadn't made him like that and I should let him be like he wanted to

be, without forcing my ideas of normality on him. I switched to letting him go his own sweet way.[26]

Some women not only worried about their child's psychology but their own as well. They found it difficult to reconcile what they perceived to be the child's needs with their own needs, which grew with their increasing self-awareness. Some found it difficult to balance what they saw as their own rights with those of their children. Women who failed to make this reconciliation expressed feelings of resentment and frustration, although it should be stressed that such women formed only a small group out of the total number interviewed. Mrs Hunter had one child and she clearly expressed feelings of ambivalence and resentment:

He was always very clinging. I had trouble when he went to school. Mind you, I couldn't get him off the breast. My mum, this sounds terribly disloyal, but my mum was one of those: 'If he wants to suck let him suck.' And it does create a great bond. I always felt we were very close. I loved feeding him, one of the nicest things about him being little, but I had trouble getting him off. And I think that made him a bit insecure when he went to school.

Mrs Hunter was very close to her mother but found it difficult to reconcile her mother's advice with her own needs:

Well, she never used to like him crying. 'You can't leave a little boy to cry, they rupture themselves.' And he never slept the first few months, it was awful with him. I was like a zombie. Maybe I was just over anxious, I probably was. I went to the doctor and he said, 'Let him cry a bit, don't keep going to him.' And this particular day, I decided to let him cry and my mum came up, and she took one look at him and she could tell he had been crying; he had for half an hour. And it didn't sound a bit like my mum, we were so close, but my mum was going to report me to the NSPCC for letting him cry.

Mrs Hunter clearly found it difficult to reconcile her own perceived needs with the obligations of being a daughter and the responsibilities of being a mother:

I didn't enjoy it. I felt I was vegetating really. I couldn't go to the loo without him. I wasn't used to this, you know. And if he was ill I used to worry. I love reading but I don't remember much time for myself when he was little. I resented very much the lack of privacy. And you know what my mum used to say to me? 'You are not eating enough; you must eat more because what is going to happen to that child if you are ill? It's that child that matters now.' And I used to have that rammed down my throat, as though I was a nonenity when I produced my son, and I used to resent that.[27]

Ironically, given their hard work and devotion, the unhappiness felt by some women about their role as mothers was possibly related to a perception that a mother's work was not so important as it had once been. Mothers no longer had to combat the dire poverty known to many of *their* mothers. Although these words were written about women in a different area of England, they could equally apply to women in this region: 'All those wives who brought their families through the Depression period give an impression of strength, patience and consistency of character which asserts itself, despite weariness and strain.'[28] Women in the post-Second World War period were spared the struggle against such terrible poverty, but they also lost some of the acclaim which their predecessors had enjoyed. Mothers were the victims of a cruel ambivalence: in some ways their job was more demanding than ever before, given their newly perceived responsibilities in such difficult areas as their children's psychological development. Yet their success in these areas of parenting were much harder to assess than those of mothers in earlier times, who were seen to have triumphantly fed, clothed and housed their children, often in the face of great hardships.

Fathering

In the earlier study it would have been wrong simply to describe fathers as patriarchal. Indeed, in matriarchal families it was often the father who was the 'soft' parent, providing treats, soothing words and mediation between embattled mothers and children. There were, too, the minority of fathers who were tyrannical, dispensing little but punishment to their children, inspiring fear but no affection. Both types of fathers are to be found in the present study, but so too are fathers with rather more involvement with their children's lives than previously recorded. There does not appear to be any one explanation for this development, although it is noted by several contemporary observers.[29] Before the First World War the working week had been fifty-six hours, and much longer for those working shifts.[30] The shorter working week of forty hours after the Second World War gave fathers who did not do overtime more time to be with their children. Those whose wives worked an evening shift clearly had sole charge of their children at teatime and bedtime.

Rather more difficult to assess than these effects of changing work patterns for both men and women was the changing social climate which 'allowed' men to be seen caring for and playing with their children, without being regarded as 'cissy' or 'unmanly'. In this area there was some blurring of gender roles during the inter-war period. Mothers appear to have welcomed this increased involvement of fathers in the lives of their children. Some more 'traditional' women may have rejected, and indeed resented, men's involvement in housework (as was seen in chapter 2); however, there are no recorded instances of resentment about fathers being involved with their children, either among the older respondents or among respondents of any age who retained more traditional views of a woman's place being in the home. The changing position of some fathers appeared to have accorded well with increased expectations of more sharing and of doing things together. These expectations may have been not realized as far as marital relationships went, but in some families they were fulfilled in the father–child relationship. Mothers may well have been losing their traditional role as the most influential and powerful parent but there was no oral evidence to suggest that they were aware of this trend.

However, absolute generalizations about fathers' roles are impossible and there were a few fathers who bullied and dominated their families. The two respondents who were accused by close relatives of abusing their wives appear to have had relationships with their children which were based almost entirely on the father's concepts of discipline, and his expectation of total obedience. There was no mention of fun, affection or pride in their children's achievements. Mr Needham had three daughters and one step-daughter:

> I used to drum it on to them, the same as I was told. When I had a meal at the table, 'Please may I leave the table?' But you see, I got them doing that until I got into trouble with my wife. She said I'd been too stringent with them. So of course that went by the board.
> Would you say that you and your wife were strict with your children?
> I think I was. I was classed as a 'bad 'un', quite honestly.
> You were more strict than your wife?
> Yes, I'm fully convinced of that, being so dominant and adamant in my ways. And I get mad with them because they just won't listen to sense – what I think is sense.
> What kind of rules did you have for them?
> They had to be in at a time. No shenanagins, they had to be in, no lateness . . . I never laid a finger on them . . . but I've chastised them. I've told them straight and shouted at them and frightened them, oh yes.[31]

But, even in a family like that of Mr Needham's, the children were indulged with gifts to an extent which would have been both unthinkable and indeed financially impossible in Mr Needham's own childhood. The Needhams claimed to have never been in debt in their married lives but said with pride that they had paid into a Christmas Club for their children. Mrs Needham said, with her husband expressing his approval,

> I paid so much a week for the kiddies' toys, to £10. We always made sure our kiddies had a good Christmas. We always had a big Christmas tree and they had a sackful of toys because £10 went a long way in them days.[32]

Fathers like Mr Needham were, however, uncommon; the trend was for fathers to be more involved with their children than their predecessors had been. They still might not have played a major part in childcare, but they positively enjoyed their children and were happy to express tender feelings towards them. While it is difficult to identify companionate marriages, it is not difficult to find companionable relationships, not only between mothers and children, but also between fathers and children. In an analysis of the 'affluent worker' it was stated that 'Work . . . tended to be devalued in other than its economic aspects; the family rather than the work was, for these men, their central life interest.'[33] There is, unfortunately, no room in this book for an analysis of men's attitude to work, but certainly the majority of men, unskilled as well as skilled, would have agreed with this statement. Close relationships between fathers and children often began when the child was quite young. Mr Kennedy was a docker and the father of six sons:

> I found it very relaxing when you had finished work to be able to sit in the chair, and if the missus had other jobs to do I'd say, 'Give me the baby and I'll feed him.' It's relaxing you know.[34]

As has been seen, some women chose to work an evening shift, leaving their husbands to look after the children. Clearly, these men did rather more for their children than simply play with them. Mr Norton, the father of four, played a definite part in their upbringing, as his wife often worked in the evening:

> I think of the joy the kids give you. There are certain things in your life where your memory is never going to fade, and one of those is when the kids had been bathed and were ready for bed. And there is only kids who shine like that when they have been bathed. They have a bloom that nobody else is entitled to. They came downstairs and they stood in a row . . . and that is the nearest I've been to God. To look at my children glowing like that, full of innocence and going to bed to sleep the sleep of the innocent. It's as simple as that.[35]

Some fathers were anxious actively to promote their children's educational development. Mr Stephenson, also the father of four, saw education starting when the child was very young. He also believed it should be fun:

> Sunday mornings, it was a ritual. I used to get them out of the wife's hair. I used to pile them in the car, and we went all over the place. I've still got some of the books ['News Books' written by the children at school]. I delight in reading them. And a lot of the spelling is bad, but it is comical the things they have put in. 'My dad we went here; my dad took me here; my dad took me there.' One of the teachers at open day said, 'You must have one heck of an imagination, Mr Stephenson.' I took them to Blackpool; and I said to one of the girls, 'Oh look, there's the King of Blackpool!' when we were passing that big hotel, it's like a castle. And one said, 'I can't see him,' and of course when you've got children one will always say, 'Well, I can.' And they were waving like mad to the King of Blackpool, and they put that in their little story.

When asked if any of his children went to playgroup, Mr Stephenson replied, 'No, I was their playgroup.'[36]

Conclusion

In the evidence of some respondents, especially mothers, there was an undercurrent of anxiety, a lack of self-confidence about the handling of their children. There was an ever-increasing reliance on professional help and advice. But, despite these worries about their children's development, most mothers and fathers positively enjoyed caring for their off-spring. They found parenting to be a rewarding and enriching experience. Fewer children, rising incomes and, for some families, more time free from work meant that families could devote more attention to their children whose needs and interests were seen as having a high priority.

9

Attitudes to Social Conditioning and Education

Parents did not reject or abandon the standards of behaviour under which they had been brought up, but they were rather less strict in enforcing those standards and in punishing breaches of them. While there was still widespread agreement about the standards which should be aimed for, there was little consensus about the importance of formal education. While more and more working-class parents wanted their children to enjoy a 'good' education, others continued to believe that it was irrelevant either to their children's happiness or to their future job opportunities.

It would indeed be extraordinary if parents had wholeheartedly, spontaneously and suddenly abandoned their old ways of bringing up children and adopted new methods and ideas. It is therefore not surprising to find many of the older standards and attitudes of parents towards children surviving in the period 1940–70.

In the previous study there were, of course, individual differences and emphases, but it was possible to discern a strong pattern of similarities in the conduct of working-class parents and in their expectations for and of their children. Parents had had a somewhat limited view of their role: they hoped their children would survive childhood and grieved when they did not; they were very anxious adequately to feed, clothe and house their young; they were determined that they should learn the difference between right and wrong. There seemed to have been little doubt as to what these right standards of behaviour were. The mores of the time required children to be honest, to be respectful to those in authority, to obey their parents, to work hard, and to consider the needs of the family before their own.

A small but growing minority of parents had been ambitious for their children and sent them to grammar schools, but the large majority saw education as a process through which their children passed as the law required, and one which was useful in giving them the basic skills of reading, writing and arithmetic. They had expected, however, that the process of education should last for as short a time as possible, as their children's primary task was to earn as much money as they could as quickly as possible.

Setting Norms of Behaviour

As has been seen in chapter 8, some mothers became very anxious about the psychological well-being of their children. Some worried about their own mental health. But it must be stressed that these women were in a small minority before 1970; no fathers were found who shared these apprehensions. The majority of parents continued to have clear ideas of how they wanted their children to behave and seemed to worry very little about whether or not conforming to these standards might be psychologically damaging.

It is a myth that working-class parents in the earlier part of the century systematically beat their children. Respondents in the earlier studies, who had grown up before the First World War, were unanimous that their parents were very strict about such matters as honesty, obedience, respectability, being in on time at night, and so on. Some transgressors may have been beaten but many were not. Some claimed that a word, or even a look, was sufficient to ensure obedience.[1]

Children brought up in the inter-war and the post-Second World War period remember being expected to conform to similar norms. They were to do as their parents told them; they were to be honest and respectable; they were not to bring shame on their families by getting into any kind of trouble. The majority of parents continued to regard the churches in general, and the Sunday schools in particular, as important agents in the moral education of their children. Most of the respondents went to Sunday school, as had their forebears. There was little parental compulsion, however, and many young people stopped going when they became adolescents. Parents were generally of the opinion that they had done their duty and that at some point their children had to 'choose for themselves'.

However, although some of the norms which children learnt were similar to those acquired by their predecessors, there were, as already been indicated, changes in parental attitudes to discipline. Parents were becoming softer, more lenient and, as rules became less strictly enforced, they began to lose some of their authority; affection was more openly expressed. All the respondents, with only two exceptions (Mr and Mrs Warwick), claimed to be more lenient with their children than their own parents had been. Punishments, especially physical ones, were less severe and rules were more relaxed, most notably the ones relating to the time children and young people came in at night.

These developments were paralleled by changing attitudes in education, which in turn resulted from 'modern' theories about child development. Not only was the maintenance of standards less strictly enforced by parents than had previously been the case, but the wider system of adults establishing, maintaining and enforcing norms was being eroded. Neighbours, the police and teachers were losing their former powers to impose sanctions on children and ensure that they obeyed the rules. There was, of course, some disagreement about what the rules were, but what became more problematical during this time were the rights of enforcement possessed by adults outside the family. The rights of parents to discipline their own children were becoming paramount. There was little discussion among them as to whether they were in fact able to do this without the reinforcement provided by a wider social network.

Mrs Peel was one of the older respondents. She had four children between 1942 and 1959: 'Well, we were strict with them; but I wouldn't say we was as strict as my parents were with me.' She listed the things she was strict about. This list was very similar to the one given by parents from earlier in the century: 'Behaviour at the table, manners when they were speaking to people older than themselves, being in on time, being at the meal table on time.'[2]

Mrs Burrell had three children born between the mid-1950s and the mid-1960s. Her standards were remarkably like those of parents of an earlier generation: 'They had to do what they were told. They had to be in at certain times and we told them the difference between right and wrong but we weren't strict with them really, no. They did more or less their own thing.'[3] (Here again is the often-repeated phrase which appears to have replaced the cliché of an earlier generation: 'It was the thing to do.')

Over and over again the oral evidence indicates, not so much a change in the standards which parents set, but a greater laxity in seeing that the standards were kept, and a marked reluctance to punish breaches of the rules as severely as their parents and grandparents had done. Even parents who regarded themselves as strict were less severe than their own parents had been. Mr Norton, growing up in the 1930s and 1940s, had had a very strict father, a powerful paternal grandmother and a severe mother to contend with:

Grandma really was a very hard person. You didn't get away with anything. She still thought a great deal about you; the love was there, but by God it was disguised. I'm trying to explain, the love of a family was there but by God the strictness and the discipline and the fact that you had to do as you were told! You didn't question the authority, you accepted it. But now and again a small sliver of sunlight crept through and you knew that you were loved. You'd got to be well-mannered, you'd got to be presentable. We hadn't got much money, but that was no excuse for not using soap and water. My dad, oh my God, you've no idea. You wouldn't believe it, but yes he was strict, oh my God, yes. To get a good hiding was really a good hiding. To get a good hiding to the point where you couldn't walk to school the following day. You couldn't move.

He gave the following list of misdemeanours which resulted in such punishment: 'Stopping out late, late was nine o'clock. Not telling him where I'd been, not telling him what I'd been doing, not doing what he said.' Mr Norton described himself as a strict father:

Probably a bit too strict really. They had always to respect their elders and they had to do as they were told. They hadn't to tell lies. Yes, I was pretty strict and I believed in smacking if it was necessary. I didn't like doing it but if it was necessary.

You were smacked as a child?

No, I was beaten, there's a hell of a difference. I never did to my children the way I was beaten. In fact, I relied on a punishment not open to parents of a previous generation, deprivation of television![4]

These respondents who claimed that as parents they had been softer than their own forebears had been were, of course, speaking from a parental perspective. Children's perceptions of parental authority can be rather different, as was seen in chapter 3.

Evidence of continuing harsh discipline in the home can still be found. Alongside the experience of the children of Mrs Peel, Mrs Burrell and Mr Norton can be put the testimony of Mrs Lonsdale, also a child in the 1950s. She was illegitimate; her mother took a common-law husband whom Mrs Lonsdale disliked. She did not have a good relationship with her mother either; she was as strict as any mother encountered either in the present study or in the earlier ones: 'Don't give cheek. If anyone was in, sit there, be seen and not heard; be in at certain times. You had to do little jobs around the house because she was working. Generally keep the place tidy, you know.' Punishment was severe if the rules were broken:

You were given a good hiding. She used to lock me in the coal house. I hated that . . . I was only little and she used to shove me in this coal house and lock the door. And I used to scream. It seemed like hours. It probably wasn't but it seemed like hours, yes. She used to chase me round the street: 'I'm giving you away . . . I'm giving you to the children's home.' I would be charging round the lamp post, all the neighbours coming out to watch, and she'd be trying to whack me.[5]

This threat to give her away was particularly frightening, as the mother had given for adoption a second baby, who had been much loved by the respondent.

Authority Figures

Earlier in the century children had been well-behaved, not only because their parents had set down the rules, but also because they had perceived their lives as being controlled by an interlocking chain of authoritarian figures: neighbours, teachers, clergymen and policemen. All too often this terrifying group of adults acted in concert, applying the same standards of behaviour and the same punishments. One could not be played off against another; they presented a united authoritarian adult front against the young offender, even if the offence was quite trivial.

Mr Warwick went to Sunday school until 1945 when he was fourteen:

I went to St Thomas's. Mr Jones was one of the teachers. I missed Sunday school once, you know, and I thought we'd got away with it. Me and all the lasses. And I think my mother was scrubbing the step, and he came and said, 'Do you know that George didn't go to Sunday school this morning?' I heard him, I was in the bloody kitchen. I thought, 'I've had it.' So that was it, a clout. We had all gone on the canal bank. I never liked him after that, reporting me.[6]

The Police

Older respondents, especially those growing up before the Second World War, remember this authoritarian atmosphere well. Mr Lodge, like most of his contemporaries, was afraid of the police:

I was jumping off this wall into a sandpit and the policeman came who was patrolling. He said, 'You shouldn't be doing that.' And he got his gloves and he just hit me on this ear and then on that ear. I screamed out and he said to a woman who was passing, 'Now you see how soft they are. Just hitting him with one of my woollen gloves.' In the fingers of their gloves there was stuffed marbles, we knew that. The police didn't use to run you in for anything, they sorted it out there and then.[7]

Not all children growing up before the Second World War had personal encounters with the police, but they were still afraid of them. Mrs Peel expressed the views of many when she said: 'As children we were terrified of the policeman. I think because we were threatened by parents, "If you do this the policeman will have you." And we were afraid of them. You had that respect for authority.'[8] Children who did get into trouble with the police knew that there was very little point in complaining about it at home.

Mr Boswell had interesting views on the police:

We used to run, the enemy of all small boys. They used to hit you about the head, it did you the world of good. There were very few police court cases. They used to catch you in the street and correct the misdemeanour by taking their belt off and flaying you round the street. And then when you went

Figure 9.1 The friendly policeman teaching a toddlers' group their kerb drill in London in 1957
(Photo courtesy of Popperfoto)

home and told mam and dad, they would give you another hell of a belt for what you had done, and it worked a treat.[9]

There are very few references to police hitting children after the war; the latest incident recorded by respondents was in about 1948.[10] Increasingly parents encouraged children to regard policemen as their friends, an attitude which appears to have been encouraged by the police themselves. Mrs Thornbarrow, who was born in 1949, had a markedly different view of the police compared to that of the immediately preceding generation:

> The most contact I had with the police was the nice policeman at the corner to take you across the road, and the one who came and told you about road safety . . . The only brush I had with the police was one time we were coming back from school and we started climbing on some railway wagons and one came and told us off.[11]

In the 1950s and 1960s there was a marked diminution in the fear which children had of the police.

Neighbours

Neighbours chastised the children of the neighbourhood less and less frequently (as will be seen in chapter 11), because more and more parents objected to their children being the object of what they considered to be either physical or verbal abuse. A reprimand from a neighbour came to be seen as the cause of a dispute rather than the means of ensuring neighbourhood discipline and order. The balance between individual rights and group norms tipped in favour of the former.

School Teachers

Historically, working-class parents tended to leave schools and teachers very much alone. Only a very small number ventured into the school, either to question a teacher's judgement or the justice of a punishment given to a child. Indeed, confrontations between parents and teachers were not common by 1970, but they were increasing and were perhaps only the tip of the iceberg as far as changing parental attitudes to teachers were concerned. Peculiar ambivalences developed.

A striking example of ambivalence occurs in the evidence of Mr Trickett, who left school before the Second World War, but whose experiences can be said to be harbingers of the future for some members of the working class. Mr Trickett had very pronounced views on what he saw as the lack of discipline in schools and in society as a whole in the late 1980s. He did not see that incidents, like the one he describes below, when repeated on a wide scale, might well have contributed to the problem he so abhorred. One may well have sympathy for Mr Trickett and his family, who suffered dreadful poverty, and the school can rightly be criticized for insensitivity. This incident, which took place in 1938, demonstrated that, on this occasion at least, the authority figures of parents and teachers were quite clearly not united and were indeed very hostile to one other:

> We were doing gym and I had no galoshes and so I couldn't do it. And if you didn't do PT you didn't go to football. Well, I wanted to go to football and I told my mother, and she said, 'You go to football.' So of course mother was the boss, so I fell in with the class to go. This lad came down and said, 'You've got to come in, Mr Simms wants you.' So I said, 'No, I'm not coming.' He [Mr Simms] dragged me all the way up the steps by the ear. And then he got the cane out and I had six of the best. There was no hanky-panky like there is now. You see, we have taken the power out of the parents' hands and the schoolteachers' hands. Well, my mother went back to school. I didn't tell her, she found out off another source. You didn't come home and tell your parents if you got the cane because we knew that you got it again off your mother. 'Serves you right' attitude. Anyway, she found out and she went to school the next day and she got hold of the teacher and she hit him. Yes, and she had my baby sister by the hand. She hit him in the classroom, everybody seen it, the lads. And then the argument and the teacher in the next classroom had to come and help out . . . You see, now they run wild, there's no discipline. Education has gone to the wall.[12]

Apparently this was the only visit Mrs Trickett senior made to her son's school.

Thirty years later Mrs Hutton was having endless battles with schools on behalf of her three sons:

> They just didn't like school, none of them liked school. They weren't particularly good scholars and they just hated it. And I hated them going, because I was forever going to school about things I didn't agree with. I don't like teachers. I think they are a damned nuisance.

On one occasion one of the boys encountered a woodwork master whom he did not like, although he liked the subject:

I never used to show up at parents' evenings, but I did do on this particular occasion and I particularly asked to see this woodwork teacher. And I said, 'You needn't look like that. You are looking as if you don't like him. He doesn't like you either. If you were a nice person and a nice teacher all your pupils would be star woodwork pupils. My lad really liked woodwork, but you are that damned nasty, no wonder they go off you.' And so I used to have barneys like that.[13]

Although there are only a few reports of confrontations such as these, they are symbolic of the erosion of the unity between various authority figures which was taking place throughout the period. Children's attitudes to authority were changing, but this would appear to be in response to radical shifts in those of adults themselves. The increasing private nature of the family, the emphasis on individual rights and the erosion of a commonly accepted system of values regarding social behaviour, all contributed to adult uncertainty about the best way to deal with other people's children. It could be argued that this uncertainty finally affected parents' relationships with their own children, but that appears to have occurred mainly after 1970. Josephine Klein, writing of the post-war changes in working-class life, said, 'Ours is not the age of authority.'[14]

Changes in Educational Opportunity

Parents exhibited a wide range of attitudes to formal education, choice being made possible because of changes both in government policy and in levels of prosperity. In the post-war period, changes in educational legislation, notably in the 1944 Education Act which introduced free secondary education for all, the provision of grants for such items as uniforms, and greatly improved real wages and housing conditions, made it much more possible for working-class parents to see that their children were better educated and for a longer period than they had been. All three towns in the survey maintained selective secondary education, with grammar and secondary modern schools, until 1970 and beyond; Barrow also had a secondary technical school.

In the earlier part of the century very many working-class parents had not had this choice and had been unable to afford either secondary or further education for their children. They had struggled with grossly inadequate incomes, so that even if their children passed the scholarship examination to go on to grammar schools, they could not afford the uniforms or the books, nor could they afford to delay until the age of sixteen their children's entry into the world of work. Overcrowded home conditions meant that doing homework was difficult, and parents, preoccupied with worries about feeding clothing and housing their families, were not too anxious about their children's academic and intellectual development. It is to their eternal credit that so many working-class parents managed to provide their children with a good education.

Greater opportunities and improved economic conditions in the post-war world did not necessarily lead either to better education for working-class children, or to their achieving 'better' jobs in adult life. The Oxford Social Mobility Project showed that, nationally, boys (the project sadly did not examine girls' education) who were born after the First World War continued to enjoy a large expansion of selective state education. These first-generation grammar school boys from 'uneducated' homes received a 'superior' education but, because of their comparatively less-advantaged backgrounds, did not enjoy the improved life chances they might have had if they had come from a middle-class home.[15]

Parental Attitudes to Formal Education

Many children did not, of course, progress even as far as gaining entry to a grammar school. Officially this was because they did not pass their eleven-plus examination, which selected children either for academic grammar schools or non-academic secondary modern schools. However, it is reasonable to assume that parental attitudes affected the performance of many children, not only in the examination itself but in their whole primary school career.[16] Some parents continued in the old tradition of sending children to school only because the law demanded it. Education was seen as the teachers' job and basically as a means of helping their children to get jobs. They did not regard education as being intrinsically important.

Mr Hinchcliffe failed his eleven-plus exam in 1958: 'My mother did not take much interest in my education. It wasn't really an issue; they just accepted it.' There was no help with his homework:

> No interest at all. I can bring you my school reports; some weren't even signed by my mother. But it wasn't their fault. They just thought that that part of life was to do with the state. In those days if you were a good mum you would look after your kids. You would ring the doctor on every occasion. I'm not getting at my mum or my gran, but that was a part that would be

delegated completely, would be the school, in the working class. But you
would look after your kids and tell them right from wrong.[17]

Evidence like that of Mr Hinchcliffe could be interpreted as contradicting
the suggestion, made in the previous chapter, that working-class parents
were lacking in confidence and relied more and more on the advice of
professionals. Clearly, if Mr Hinchcliffe's mother had heeded the advice of
the school she might have encouraged his education rather more. However,
his evidence can be also seen as an example of a parent relying totally on the
'experts', to the extent of virtually abandoning all responsibility for her
son's education. The linking of the comments about school with mention
of consulting the doctor on every occasion would reinforce this point.

Some parents continued to have financial difficulties, especially those
with large families. Mr Monkhouse was one of eight children; the family
always had a struggle to make ends meet. He too, like Mr Hinchcliffe, failed
his eleven-plus exam and went to a secondary modern school in 1959. He
would have liked to stay on at school (he later trained to be a nurse) but his
parents did not feel that this was an option:

> It wasn't presented as a choice at all. They did sit down and talk to me. And
> I felt such a sense of duty towards my family that I didn't fight against it too
> hard. It was the greater good against what I felt was a selfish thing![18]

Some parents would perhaps have valued education more if their children
had been more academic. As it was, they saw it as a waste of time. Mrs
Turnbull was a caring but unambitious mother of four children who were
born in the 1950s and early 1960s. Commenting on the fact that her
youngest daughter had had to stay on at school until she was sixteen when
her older children had been able to leave at fifteen, she remarked: 'They stay
on longer and longer, don't they?' When asked if she thought that this was
a bad thing she replied:

> Well, I suppose it is in a way. I suppose it's how your brains are. If you've
> got a good brain, well fair enough, it gets you somewhere. But I think it's a
> bit of a waste of time. You could get a job. But they mess about at school. I
> think it is a waste of time. Two of our three older ones have been factory
> workers and one is a hairdresser. The youngest one is a childminder.[19]

Other mothers were opposed to 'pushing' children and some families felt
that all the children should be treated the same, regardless of their abilities.
Mrs Boyle had five children in the 1950s and 1960s.

> One of them, Ann, was very clever at school and we were told to encourage
> her to stay on and I said she had to do but Barry [the father] said she hadn't

to because the others had had the chance of leaving and she wanted to leave. But they said that she had possibilities of going a long way. She always said she wanted to be an accountant. And they said that if she stayed on and went in for 'O' levels she would have done it. But like Barry said, we didn't push the others so we didn't push her.

Mrs Boyle gave as the reasons for her daughter wanting to leave school: 'Well, like the others, just keen to get away, go in a job and get money.'[20] (Ann became a factory worker, she did not marry.)

Ambitious Parents

Some respondents were, like Mr Hinchcliffe and Mr Monkhouse, understanding and tolerant of their parents' views on education; others had a very different attitude. They believed they had been deprived of the education to which they were rightfully entitled and, as adults, they were very resentful. This resentment fuelled their determination that their own children should have the benefits of a good education. They joined the ever-growing number of working-class parents, some of whom had had a good education themselves, who valued education and sought the best possible for their children. Academic success was increasingly seen as the way to a successful career and also carried its own prestige and status. These parents realized that if children were to 'do well' then they had to have full parental support. Fathers were more involved than before in their children's education and are, for example, recorded visiting schools for parents' evenings. However, in most families it still tended to be the mothers' attitudes which determined the type and quality of education received by the children. Parental support could take various forms: some parents deliberately taught their children some basic lessons before they went to school. Other ways in which parents helped were by playing educational games with their children, taking them on educational outings, encouraging them with homework, reading with and to them, assiduously attending functions at school, providing them with whatever 'extras' were deemed to be necessary at whatever cost to the parents, preferring children to study rather than help with household tasks, and perhaps most importantly, discussing many different topics with them.

The following extracts are illustrative of the actions and attitudes of the parents who sought educational achievements for their children. Some were following in a family tradition but many were making a conscious break with the past, deliberately trying to bring up their children in a way different from the one they themselves had experienced. None of the 'achievers' or their parents commented on Mr Monkhouse's interesting remark about his pursuit of education as being 'selfish'.

Mr Stephenson had had very little formal education and regretted it:

> None of my family were educated, they'd sign a contract with the shake of a hand. Well, I think that has been the failing of our family. When it came to my sons I rectified it in a way. When the eldest went to school, I know I got in a bit of lumber because he could say his tables up to twelve when he started school [1954]. And one of the teachers said I was teaching him the wrong way. We had a bit of a falling out job because they had a system of teaching.[21]

Mrs Burrell went to the grammar school in 1942:

> I was quite good, I was always top of the class. I wanted to go to the grammar school. My parents didn't want me to go. My dad wasn't interested. My mother was bothered about the expense of the uniform. She had quite a struggle. While I went through grammar school I didn't have the things that the other girls had. I didn't have a tennis racket of my own, a hockey stick of my own. I had nothing. I never had hockey boots. She found it very difficult, you know, to keep me there; and I left school before School Certificate. I had been off school quite a few months and the head teacher called mother up to school and mother always went, father never went near school. She asked if she would be willing to let me stay on for an extra year to do the extra work, but she said, 'No.' They wanted me out to get work, a bit of extra money coming in. So that was it. I had no backing at all while I was at school.[22]

In a later interview, when speaking of her own sons, Mrs Burrell said:

> I wanted them to go to the grammar school. I wanted them to have the best. I knew they were both clever boys and they had all the backing off us. Really, I think neither my husband nor I had the backing when we were young with our schooling. So we wanted to do the best, you know.[23]

Mrs Lewthwaite grew up in the inter-war period. She had a happy childhood but received little encouragement educationally. Although intelligent, she did not go to a grammar school; indeed, it does not appear to have been thought of. Her parents were preoccupied with the problems of making ends meet. Father was unemployed for long spells and mother worked very hard in a variety of cleaning jobs. Mrs Lewthwaite married a painter and decorator and their only son was born in the 1950s, and she devoted herself to him:

When he was at school he was a great reader. Well, as I say, family life was different to what it is now. We used to play a lot with him, you know, and read a lot. Even when he came home from school at dinner time, we used to read to him before he went back. And we always went out a lot. We got our first old second- hand car when he was about four and we went picnicking, we've always been great picnickers.[24]

Mrs Lewthwaite's son went to grammar school and on to university.

Mrs Critchley was the youngest child in a very poor family, her father was a labourer on the railway. In 1937 she was the first person in her family ever to go to grammar school. Her mother, who was then almost fifty years old, had to return to work in the mill to pay for the extra expense incurred by her daughter's education (she was interviewed in the 1970s and was very proud of her daughter's achievement). Mrs Critchley married a policeman and had three sons; she was determined that their lives should be different to hers:

I've told you that I felt very much indebted to my parents for letting me go to the grammar school and I used to dread having to ask my mum for money for books. And I thought, 'If I have kids, they'll have every chance, they'll go to university if they are clever enough and there will be none of this.' I have never said, 'We've had to do this for you and you're lucky to be going,' and all that. If they needed anything that was it, they had it. If there was a holiday abroad from school they went. If there was anything, I never said, 'We can't afford it.' They always went. We never had any holidays abroad but we weren't bothered. But we made sure that they all had one each while they were at school. And this was the big thing, because I had suffered when I was young and I didn't want this for my kids. It's putting a lot of onus on them. I thought they will have every chance and my husband felt the same way. That's why I never wanted to go to work when my children were little, because when I was at the grammar school and my mum got a job, I used to have to come straight home from school. I couldn't play hockey. I couldn't be in the team because I couldn't stay behind for a practice. I'd always to get home, get the fire on and the tea started. Saturday I used to have to go shopping, do all the jobs. I always had a lot to do, that was alright, I'm not grumbling. I think it stood me in good stead, because when I was married I knew how to keep house. I didn't regret it but I wanted better for my children.[25]

All three of Mrs Critchley's sons went to university. But she added a sad postscript to her story: none of her sons lives near her, whereas she had, as an adult, lived close to her mother: 'People whose children don't go to university and who work locally have a better life really. Their families don't get broken up.' [26]

Mrs Jenkins also came from a very poor family; her father worked as a railway labourer and her mother was a cleaner. Although clever, she did not manage to go the grammar school, and at the age of fourteen, in 1945, she started work as a living-in domestic servant. She, too, was determined that her three children, born in the late 1950s, should have more opportunities than she had had:

> I always remember when I was little, if I asked a question and people were talking, they used to say, 'Oh little girls should be seen and not heard.' I always felt that I should answer every question that my children asked and that's what I did. And I bought books to do it. I like to think I was closer to them than I was to mam and dad. I mean, mam and dad were working most of my life. I didn't work those first few years and I used to take them out every day. We went out every afternoon; and when they started school I used to meet them and take them out. And I always regret starting work because my son does not speak very clearly and I blame myself. My daughter says I shouldn't. I made a career out of bringing up my children and I just used common sense.[27]

Mrs Jenkins's three children all went to university.

Mrs Lodge also came from a very poor family and, like Mrs Jenkins, did domestic work. She had four children and it was not always easy to make ends meet on her husband's wages as an unskilled labourer. Her children, however, had every encouragement to learn and to do well at school:

> I intended them to think for themselves and not to be smothered with what other people thought. You know, to be free thinking and make their own decisions. And never once as they got older to ask if they had been to church.

Mrs Lodge was a devoted and devout Catholic. All of her children entered a profession.[28]

It is fitting that the final word should be given to one of the children of parents with great enthusiasm for education. She was born after the war; her father was a skilled manual worker and both parents were very ambitious for her:

> What did 'bettering yourself' mean?
>
> Well, it meant to do well at school and I think my dad had in mind something like being a teacher rather than getting married and not having a career. To have a career was important. And with not having a son all his ambitions fell on my shoulders. It didn't feel like a burden or pressure

because in the evenings everything was made into a game. I don't know whether they thought, 'Well, we've got to put away the tea things and find time to teach some extra things she hasn't learned at school.' I don't think they thought like that, but I don't think they ever bought me a toy which wasn't educational. I learned to count at a very early age from playing 'Snakes and Ladders', I still think of rows of ten blocks when I think of addition and subtraction under a hundred. They taught me to read at home.

Her mother took her on educational visits and to the theatre and museums. At home she did not want her daughter's help:

I know that my school work was extremely important to her. So long as I did that and got good reports from school I think she felt that that was her reward for making sure I didn't do a lot of skivvying. And she was extremely ambitious for me to better myself and not have the same sort of life she had had.[29]

The respondent went to the grammar school and on to university.

A very wide range of attitudes to the value of formal education was revealed in the survey. A few parents were overtly hostile to the whole system, many were indifferent, and a growing minority very enthusiastic. This enthusiasm for education had hardly been noticeable in the earlier studies. Attitudes were clearly changing but so too were opportunities and family incomes. Enthusiasm for a good education is not enough if the family budget cannot support a child long enough for him or her to achieve full potential. There was a clear and unsurprising correlation between parental aspirations and children's academic achievements. A growing trend was observable in the study: that of children from working-class homes going to grammar schools in increasing numbers, and from there on to university or some other institute of higher education. Out of the 170 respondents interviewed in the earlier studies only two went to university (and they were among the younger respondents). Out of the ninety-eight respondents in this study, thirteen went to some form of higher education, six of these still being in higher education in 1970. They were mirroring a national trend. Among the men born between 1922 and 1927, 3.3 per cent went to university, compared to 10.4 per cent of men born in the years 1947–52.[30] The great post-war expansion in university education is indicated in the figures of both students and institutions. In 1950 there were 85,000 students in twenty-six institutions. By 1970 the figures had increased to 460,000 students in forty-four institutions. It is a moot point whether these academically successful people, however 'working-class' their background, can continue to be so described themselves. Respondents are ambivalent and unsure on this point and certainly not in agreement with each other.[31]

Conclusion

There were many variations in the way children were brought up during this period. Parental attitudes were not uniform, but it is possible to describe the large majority of the families as child-centred. In this regard they conformed to a trend, written about by contemporary observers in various parts of the country. Zweig wrote of men with little ambition for themselves but a lot for their children, and reported a common view as being 'We want to give them a better chance than we had.'[32] Young and Wilmott quoted one respondent as saying, 'When I was a child dad had everything. Now it is the children who have the best of it. If there is one pork chop left the kiddy gets it.'[33]

The devotion of parents, and especially mothers, to their children cannot be doubted, but the wisdom of adopting a very child-centred approach to family life was already, during the period, being questioned. Fletcher, in his book on the family published in 1962, wrote:

> We may be bringing into being a generation of young people who are self-centred and uncooperative, who are intensely aware of their own rights and what they can demand of society but not so sensitively aware of their duties.[34]

In 1968 Dr Spock also sounded a warning. Although he was addressing an American audience, his remarks were not without relevance for British parents and children. He criticized the child-centred nature of American culture and recommended that children be brought up 'with a feeling that they are in the world, not for their own satisfaction, but primarily to serve others'.[35] No parent who was interviewed expressed this view, but ironically it would not have been an unacceptable precept to parents of an earlier generation. This is another ambiguity of progress.

10

The Extended Family

There were changes in the nature of the extended family during this period but also strong evidence of continuity. The extended family continued to offer practical help and emotional support to many individuals. This chapter examines the problems concerning membership of the extended family, changes and continuities in co-residence and the reason for it. It is always important to remember that much help for kin was not only dependent upon relations living in the same house, much assistance being rendered by members of the family living nearby. The reasons behind help given to, and received by, kin are often difficult to disentangle, and clearly there was often a variety of motives. Some respondents expressed irritation with, and even resentment of, relatives, but these feelings did not necessarily lead to an abandonment of long-established norms regarding obligations to help kin. Some of the ways in which families gave and received help are examined: grandparents caring for grandchildren, parents accommodating their married off-spring, care of the sick and elderly, and more mundane day-to-day help and support.

Who Was Included in the Extended Family?

Kin, or extended family, is a term loosely used to describe relations, whether by blood or by marriage, outside the nuclear family of parents and dependent children. Kin is the term which sociologists would use to describe relations, but respondents used the word family. Both terms are vague and have different interpretations in different situations.[1]

A study of families over more than one generation shows that one set of extended-family relationships may evolve into a new pattern as children become adults and, in their own phrase, 'start a family'; although, in effect, they are continuing one. Siblings, parents and in-laws become part of the extended family. These were generally the most important members of the kinship group in the perceptions of the respondents; but some families maintained close ties with cousins and other more distantly related kin. It is in fact difficult to give an exact definition of kin as families tended to make their own. It cannot be stressed too strongly that any generalizations about kin cover a wide range of differences. Help and support were not given to everyone claiming kinship, however distant, nor was it universally expected. Some respondents and their relations, indeed the majority, saw kinship support as a first line of defence, but others regarded it as a safety net, when all else failed. Individual personalities, choices and circumstances, which included past relationships, were very important and could affect the quality and amount of the care offered and also accepted.

Demographic changes from before the Second World War had already affected the size and structure of the extended family. Women had fewer children, and smaller nuclear families meant smaller extended families. The period of time during which women bore and raised children was shortened (the average woman in the 1970s had finished childbearing by the age of 28). At the same time there was an increasing proportion of older people in the population, some of whom needed help and support. Michael Anderson suggests that these changes would mean more and more women returning to work after childrearing and that they would be unavailable to help with grandchildren. Similarly, older grandmothers would be unable to seek support from their daughters and daughters-in-law, as they would be employed in full-time work: 'The possibilities of reciprocity of the kind found in "traditional" working-class communities had disappeared by the 1970s.'[2] Anderson was concerned with the future implications of demographic change, a debate which continues to interest sociologists, policy-makers and others concerned with the family. It is interesting to see how far extended family relationships had changed in this region by 1970. It is impossible not to accept the implication of Anderson's argument; clearly, it was women who were the principal carers. This is suggested both by other studies and by the oral evidence.[3] It is rather more difficult, as will be seen, to suggest that women were neglecting their kin in favour of paid work. As in the case of childcare, women tried very hard to accommodate family care as well as the demands of the workplace.

Were links with the wife's family more important than those with the husband's? Klein argued that families tended to be matrilocal: 'A newly married couple is more likely to be living close to the wife's family than near to the husband's.'[4] When, however, both bride and groom came from the same area, as was often the case in this study, they clearly lived near both families.

In general it is possible to see the help offered to relatives as being gender-linked. Men gave assistance with tasks which had usually been regarded as 'men's work' – gardening, household repairs and home maintenance. Women were more likely to help with such things as washing (both personal and household), cooking and cleaning. But, as will be seen, there was no clear and absolute gendered difference to the help offered to relatives.

Not all kin were seen as being as important as others, and thus did not qualify for the same degree of support and help as did 'closer' kin. Conversely, more distant kin could not reasonably be called upon to help out, nor were they likely to offer help themselves. Clearly, relationships between parents and adult children were most important, followed in order of decreasing importance by those between grandparents and grandchildren, adult siblings, aunts and uncles, nieces and nephews and cousins. Relationships between cousins were often rather tenuous, and restricted to family occasions such as weddings and funerals.

Co-residence

It is clear that there was a close relationship between co-residence and gender. In our study it was almost twice as likely for the co-resident kin to be related to the wife and mother than to the husband and father.

There were some changes in co-residence over time. Although this book is primarily concerned with the years 1940–70, references have frequently been made, for the sake of comparison, to the earlier part of the century. It is clear that patterns of co-residence changed during the life-time of our older respondents. This study suggests some decline in co-residence. Evidence for this may be seen if respondents are divided into two equal groups: those born before 1935 and those born between 1935 and 1950. In the former group 54 per cent had spent part of their childhood co-resident with members of their extended family (with or without parents); in the latter group this figure had fallen to 36 per cent. There was also a slight reduction in the incidence of newly married couples living with older relatives (usually parents). Of the twenty-nine couples who were married before 1955, twelve (41 per cent) lived with in-laws for some period of time. Of the twenty-nine couples married between 1955 and 1970, eight (27 per cent) were co-resident with relatives when newly married.

There were also changes in the length of time young couples remained co-resident. Of the twelve couples married before 1955, five stayed with relatives for less than one year, four stayed between one and five years and three stayed for longer periods (six, fifteen and thirty years, respectively). Of the co-resident couples married after 1955, four stayed under a year, three for one to five years and only one for longer – ten years. Improving housing conditions and increasing prosperity undoubtedly affected these changes in patterns of co-residence.

The forms which characterized co-residence, that is, who lived with whom, are exceedingly complex. Out of the total of twenty-one newly married couples, seven lived with relatives on the male side of the family, while twelve lived with relatives on the female side. Two couples alternated between the two sides of the family.

During the period 1940–70 many respondents lived with an elderly relative. Nine respondents as adults did so, while seventeen recalled a co-resident elderly relative when they were children or young adults. Eleven of those lived with aged relatives from the male side of the family while fifteen lived with relatives from the female side.

There were various other patterns of co-residence. There were six co-resident bachelor uncles living with respondents when they were children; two lived with their brothers' families and four with those of their sisters. Two respondents lived with adult siblings until their marriages. Six children spent substantial parts of their childhood with relatives other than their parents (four on the female side of the family, two on the male). Three couples shared accommodation with adult siblings on a short term basis; three had much longer-term arrangements. Three respondents remembered, as children, married siblings sharing the home for a while. It is interesting to note that in the ninety-eight cases of co-residence recorded, twelve respondents appear more than once; that is, they had lived with different relatives at different times.

Some examples of co-residence indicate the variety of these arrangements. Mrs Marley[5] was brought up in the 1920s and 1930s in a household owned and run by her aunt and mother who had both been left widows, each with one child, at the end of the First World War. Mrs Fleming[6] shared her married sister's home after her own marriage in 1941 and continued to do so for thirty years. Mrs Rowlandson,[7] for part of her childhood in the 1950s and 1960s, shared a house with her parents, her aunt, uncle and grandmother; it was purchased jointly. Mrs Christy,[8] as a child in the late 1940s and early 1950s, had no less than four periods of co-residence. At various times the household included a maternal and a paternal grandparent, a married brother and his wife, and a married sister and her husband.

This pattern of co-residence, indeed even the custom of living close to relatives, appears not to have been usual among middle-class families. Firth, in his study of kin in London, wrote: 'Living near kin was not a very common practice among middle-class families.'[9]

There were various reasons for co-residence, most of which were fairly obvious: elderly relatives requiring help; newly married couples wanting temporary accommodation before moving into their own homes; children sometimes having to be cared for away from their own nuclear families. Earlier in the century there had been many orphans; happily, there was only one orphan in the present study, but some youngsters continued to spend considerable periods of their childhood with relatives.

In the early years of the war several respondents were evacuated from Barrow, some with officially organized groups, some because of a privately made arrangement. While the official evacuees usually returned home within a year, children living with relatives could stay considerably longer. Mrs Webster was four years old when she was sent in 1940 to live with a childless aunt in Ulverston, eight miles away, leaving her parents and a newly born sister behind. She said she was there for years. Far from being distressed by this separation she appeared to have had the time of her life:

> It was home from home. I was made very welcome, probably very spoiled because I was like an only child. Right through school I was thought of as an only child. They were very surprised when I said I had a sister.[10]

It is, of course, impossible to generalize about the effects on children of being sent to stay with relations. Mrs Rowlandson was three years old in 1948 when her sister was born. Sadly, the new baby was very ill and Mrs Rowlandson was sent to stay with her paternal grandmother who was very strict and believed that children should be seen and not heard: 'That's my earliest recollection. Because I ran away, but I knew my name and address and I told a policeman where I lived and he brought me back.' In a later interview Mrs Rowlandson returned to what had clearly been a distressing experience:

> When my sister was born I was kind of pushed out. It didn't work out with my granny, so I was kind of pushed on to other relatives. From pillar to post you know, nobody wanted me. When I came back I started stammering and I carried on stammering for years and years. And my mum wanted me to see a specialist and my dad said, no I was putting it on.[11]

There are many other examples of co-residence given throughout this chapter, but it is unwise to dwell unduly on this as many respondents were in close contact with kin who were not living with them but who lived in reasonably close proximity.

Reasons for Helping Kin

The motives for helping kin tended to be the same whether or not they were co-resident. It is, of course, always difficult to assess people's motives; their reasons for behaving as they did towards relatives were complex. Generally, one can speak of individuals acting from a mixture of love, duty, affection and obligation; but clearly individuals emphasized some feelings more than others; many did not discuss their feelings at all. Relatives were cared for because it was assumed that that was what one did. It is interesting that, in a period when certain traditional working-class norms were weakening, especially in relation to neighbours, for many people they appeared to be strong where kin was concerned. 'Blood is thicker than water' remained an important axiom. Relations were cared for because 'it was the thing to do'. As in other areas of social behaviour, a desire 'to do the right thing' was sometimes reinforced by a fear of gossip and social disapproval if an 'incorrect' course of action was taken. It is also likely that some individuals cared for relatives because there appeared to be no viable alternative; but this was not a problem which was discussed; their conviction that they were 'doing the right thing' was reason enough.

It is possible that there were regional differences in the strength of kinship ties. Firth's conclusions about London have already been mentioned.[12] Gorer, in 1958, argued that 'the break up of the extended family has proceeded much further in the South of England than in the Midlands or the North'.[13] On the other hand, this study could well share the conclusions in a study of a working-class area of London, which was made in 1982. Jocelyn Cornwell wrote:

> Some relationships are based upon shared skills and practical activities and this is all. Others involved some degree of emotional intimacy and the mothers and daughters are each others' confidants. Still other are based simply on family loyalty and a sense of duty.[14]

Obligation

A strong sense of obligation could lead to considerable self-sacrifice on the part of some relations. Sadly, accompanying it in some cases were strong feelings of resentment.[15] Obligation might result in co-residence, even when personal relationships were not good. Mrs Britton's parents were married in the mid-1930s and immediately went to live with the husband's parents, who kept a public house. It was intended that the husband would carry on with his own job but that he and his wife would also work in the pub. The wife was not happy with this arrangement and, just before the war, persuaded her husband to move out:

> They probably lived in that little house for four years. She said that was the happiest time of her married life because she had her own home and her own front door and her own kitchen and was free to do as she wanted. She was very unhappy when they moved back.

From that time onwards Mrs Britton's mother was a very frustrated woman, feeling that she had little control over her life. Mrs Britton continued:

> My grandmother refused to look after me; she said it was my mother's place to stay at home and do the cooking and cleaning and not go out to work. They didn't get on at all but they lived together. My mother's marriage was very unhappy from that point of view because this went on for years and years and years. They never hit it off. My mother and father had terrible rows. They were devoted to each other, but at the same time the frustrations and illnesses they both had and the overwork and the fact that my mother was continually begging my father to leave this place and tell my grandmother that they'd got to live a civilized life. My grandmother wouldn't agree because she wanted the income, and my father was torn between the two of them. They had terrible rows. I used to lie in bed at night absolutely frightened to death because they were arguing and quarrelling. They never hit each other. They would never be violent, but it used to be terrible and my mother used to threaten regularly to leave, and I used to be terrified that she would leave me behind.[16]

It is clear from the rest of the interview that Mrs Britton's father was totally dominated by his mother and that the obligation he felt to help and support her was stronger than his feelings for his wife.

Affection

It is also clear that relatives loved each other and that affection in most cases, but not all, was the primary reason for their caring. While Mr Ingham was very unusual in being a man who took sole charge of an elderly relative, his devotion to his mother was similar to that shown by many other respondents. His mother had been living alone, but by 1970 was showing clear signs of senile dementia, so Mr Ingham decided to have her to live with him and his twelve-year-old daughter. He and his wife had been divorced two years before.

> She had always suffered from bronchitis so I bought her a great big sheepskin coat, gloves, hat and boots. And then my mother used to walk and she never had bronchitis again. Looked after my mum a lot. Having really good meals, steaks and things. The dementia, the main thing is they get very irritable, but if you irritate someone by retaliating you bring out the aggression in them. So what you have to do is to be very calm and gentle with them. I used to bath my mother. I never thought I would bath my mother but I did. She used to have on half a dozen singlets, three or four bras. God knows how many pairs of pants and jumpers and dresses all on top of each other. That was her idea of changing her dress.[17]

Eventually Mr Ingham asked for help with his mother's bathing, but on the first occasion that two young women came his mother punched one of them and laid her out on the bathroom floor. Mr Ingham resumed the bathing. He cared for his mother for two years until she had a stroke and had to go into hospital.

Instrumentality and Reciprocity

What of other motives? Sociologists and anthropologists have discussed the existence of instrumentality (self-interest) and reciprocity (the need for help to be given in return) within the context of kin relationships. It is, however, very difficult to unravel relationships solely in terms of instrumentality or reciprocity. For example, in certain cases of co-residence with elderly parents it could be argued that younger relatives were acting from motives of self-interest: getting their relatives to sell their houses so that a larger, 'grander' one could be purchased for their co-residence. But it could also be argued that the agreement was one of mutual interest, indeed one of reciprocity, the house being in exchange for the care of the elderly person. However, where in certain cases this care was required for many years, it then becomes debatable whether the younger relations continued to act out of self-interest or in a spirit of reciprocity. It would be more accurate to say that they were acting in a spirit of self-sacrifice.

Mr Winterburn and his wife decided to sell their house in the late 1950s when it became clear that Mr Winterburn's seventy-year-old father was unable to look after himself. He also sold his father's house, and the combined proceeds from these sales purchased a large, attractive house in a desirable area. A bald account of this arrangement, without hearing from the family, might suggest that here was an example of self-interest at work. The truth was rather different. The father lived with the family for twenty years, a period during which Mr and Mrs Winterburn were bringing up their three children. Mr Winterburn described his father as Victorian, as indeed he was, being forty years old when his son was born in 1925.

Mrs Winterburn said:

> He wasn't an easy man to get on with. It wasn't just because he was with a daughter-in-law, he wasn't an easy man. We coped, the house being the size it is helped, because you weren't on top of each other. He loved them all, but he was a rather rough sort of man, he wasn't the cuddly sort of grandfather. He used to quite often think we weren't bringing them up correctly, but it wasn't easy socially.

Mr Winterburn added:

> We didn't always agree with what he did; for instance, if they walked in front of him he would rap their ankles with a walking stick. We had to stop him doing that. He didn't realize the weight of those sticks. [He had had his leg amputated ten years before his death.] And when he died the bond of affection and love there'd been between them really showed itself. They were terribly upset, all of them.

There was a serious problem about holidays in this particular family:

> My father was interested in Blackpool, so we had one or two Blackpool holidays. And we also had one in the Isle of Man, and I think those were the only major holidays we had.
>
> But you took your dad with you?
>
> Yes, yes, he went with us, because at that time he was still mobile. When he became incapacitated this was another thing. Holidays for us virtually stopped. He was used to the house, he couldn't manage, you see. So we couldn't do it. We did try latterly leaving the children in charge and getting away for a week or so; but unfortunately it didn't work because he being the type of man he was, he wasn't going to take orders from his grandchildren. There'd been a certain amount of friction and trouble and a strike was declared on both sides! And I remember one occasion when the doctor came and he said, 'You really must let these people have a holiday, because they need a holiday. Will you go into a home?' And my father said he would. And

the doctor went out through the door and he said, 'I'm not going you know.
I only said that to get rid of him!'[18]

It is easier to find examples of reciprocity between adult children and
their parents who were not in need of care and attention. Young married
couples who lived with parents paid a rent and in return received lodgings
and possibly board. It is fair to say, however, that most parents providing
this service acted out of a spirit of altruism, desiring to help their children
rather than make money out of them.

In the cases of co-resident aunts and uncles there also may have been an
element of reciprocity, an extra wage coming into a house in return for
board and lodging could have been a useful arrangement to both parties.
But some of these arrangements had a clear element of altruism too. Mr
Parkinson said:

> My mother's brother had been in the RAF and he'd been invalided out with
> TB. So father had always wanted a shop. Uncle was out of work and favoured
> having a go as well, so he moved in with us and worked the shop, although
> technically it was mother's and father's. It didn't really work out, and after a
> short spell my mother had to do a bit more and more and more, and
> eventually it was too much for her. So they sold it.[19]

Mr Watkinson, like Mr Parkinson, was growing up in Barrow just after
the Second World War:

> My uncle, that was my father's brother, was living with us and they worked
> the allotment together. He was a single man, he suffered from Parkinson's
> disease and he just lived with us as a matter of course. He lived with us for
> seventeen years.[20]

Exploitation

It is difficult to write about the exploitation of kin by kin, as no clear
definition of what constitutes exploitation exists; moreover, the perceptions
of an observer may well be different to those of a participant in the family
drama. Mr Adderley, born in 1926, came from a poor family. He told his
story quite directly and without reflection on his relatives' motives. There
are no clear answers to questions like, 'Were the relatives trying to help his
parents or were they acting in their own best interests? Were they helping
Mr Adderley or exploiting him?'

Well, my mother had a cousin who was married to a farmer. What they were trying to do, they couldn't have children of their own. They were trying to talk my mother and father into letting my brother and myself go up to the farm, live there for a few weeks and they could choose which one they wanted to adopt. Anyhow, my mother and father wouldn't agree to it, but what they did agree was that I could go and live with them as soon as I left school when I was fourteen [in 1940].

Later in his interview Mr Adderley returned to his life on the farm:

I lived with them and I lived in and my pay was one shilling a day, seven shillings a week. So being seven shillings I had to work seven days. In those days you were only paid twice a year; every six months. So you could get your wages and come home and give it to your mother, and she'd give you back what she thought was correct for spending money. After the first six months I worked I spent two shillings and that were for a new cap.[21]

Among the respondents, Mrs Yardley appeared to suffer most from the unreasonable demands of someone who was not even closely related, although Mrs Yardley herself did not see things in quite that way. She was married in 1947, and a year later found herself living with her new baby in a bed-sitting room. Her mother's cousin asked her if she would look after the cousin's mother, Mrs Yardley's great-aunt. The daughter would buy a house and Mrs Yardley could have it at a reduced rent in return for looking after the old woman, who was blind. This arrangement lasted for sixteen years, during which time a second child was born. The house had only two bedrooms, one of which was occupied by the old aunt. There was no bathroom and the aunt had a bucket for a lavatory, sometimes kicking it over because she could not see. She insisted on cooking on the open fire in her room and Mrs Yardley was continually worried about the dangers of this. Worst of all, from Mrs Yardley's point of view, was the old woman's pointedly praising one child and continually criticizing the other. Mrs Yardley did not, however, feel exploited. When asked if she and her husband had considered putting the aunt into a home she replied: 'Well, we couldn't do. It was their house.' When further asked if she had considered leaving the house in order to force the daughter to make other arrangements she said: 'I wouldn't have done that. You see, we had been brought up to look after each other.' She did have some regrets, though. Her husband died six months before her great-aunt, 'So we never really had any married life or anything on our own.'[22]

Attitudes Towards Kin

Feelings for and about kin were closely connected to people's motives in helping their relatives. Affection, as in the case of Mr Ingham, may have been the most important reason for choosing to care for a relative. Other respondents may have had different motives, but it is not difficult to find many feelings of affection between relatives, whether resident or not.

On the other hand, it is also quite easy to find many negative feelings. Many expressed feelings of resentment towards relatives. An example of this has already been mentioned in Mrs Britton's evidence. Sometimes resentment was felt on their own behalf but it is also noticeable that younger respondents were angry on behalf of an older relative, possibly indicating a change between generations in expectations about such matters as privacy and personal autonomy.

Mrs Wheaton grew up with her parents, a brother and a grandmother in a small terraced house. She believed that being evacuated in 1940, when she was seven years old, made her very independent; she was certainly very critical of her father's and grandmother's attitudes especially towards her mother:

> My grandmother looked like a retired headmistress, she behaved like one and she ruled with a rod. She ruled my dad, I mean her word went and that was it. I objected to what she said, because you couldn't have the radio on only for the news. And she didn't hold with going in neighbours' houses so my mother wouldn't stand a chance. I think my mother would have done. She used to talk the hind leg off a donkey. My mother got allotted jobs; one of them was dusting and my mother hated it. I always got the impression that my mother was told. I couldn't have stood it.[23]

There were sometimes acute strains between young adults and their in-laws. Mr Simpkins, a widow cleaner, was married in 1953 when he was twenty-one; his wife worked in an office. He spent the first four years of his marriage with his in-laws in a council house:

> When we got back from our honeymoon I just happened to say to my wife, 'At the end of the month we will be able to open a joint account and start saving.' My mother-in-law was in the process of lighting the fire and was down on her hands and knees scraping out the ashes. She turned to me and said, 'You're not taking her money. If you think I've worked all these years to give her a good education for you to take her money, you've another think coming!' Well, my retort was, 'You'll mind your own business, she's my wife

now and keep out of our affairs!' Whereupon my wife burst into tears so I felt
a rat. And it's a no-win situation. No, I didn't back down. If I was contributing and saving, so should she![24]

There were also quarrels and feelings of resentment among non-resident
kin. Mr Ingham, who cared so devotedly for his mother, was involved in
several disputes with his brothers and sisters. None of them would look
after his mother on a full-time basis and he refused to allow her to divide
her time between her various children: 'I was not having my mother living
out of a suitcase.' When he was having trouble bathing her he asked for
help, but his siblings replied, 'Oh we haven't time to come and help,' and
he said, 'I went off them a little at that because I thought it was the least
they could do.'[25] These periodic discussions among the adult children of
Mrs Ingham senior is one of the examples of a family consciously attempt-
ing to talk through a problem and negotiate a settlement; this attempt
failed. This kind of family discussion is not often reported, although they
must frequently have taken place. Individuals, in choosing to take on the
care of a relative, must have had at least an internal debate about the most
appropriate course of action. But the overwhelming impression which the
respondents gave was that they acted out of a feeling that it was 'the thing
to do'. Finch suggested that explicit round-the-table negotiations do not
always take place; it is sometimes just 'understood' that a particular person
will take responsibility for a relative. This understanding may develop
gradually over time.[26]

Some families had lost the habit of easy sociability which had characterized so many kin social relationships in earlier times. There was resentment that social relationships resulted from a feeling of obligation rather
than from enjoyment of each others' company. Several women who were
married in the late 1950s and early 1960s felt trapped into entertaining or
visiting their relatives regularly, especially on Sundays. Mrs Hunter said:

> Mother-in-law. Well, we used to go every other Sunday. It was taken for granted
> that they would come down to us one Sunday and we would go up there the
> next. With me seeing my mum every day during the week she was sort of
> out at the weekends. I used to go to my mum's for my dinner every day.

When asked about the tea she provided on Sundays she replied:

> Well, I wouldn't say it *had* to be, but I felt it *ought* to be home-made cakes.
> I used to be up at six o'clock in the morning baking Victoria sponges and
> scones, and I used to resent it. I wouldn't do it now. I used to think, 'I'm so
> tired I want to stop in bed!' But my mother-in-law seemed to expect it. If we

ever wanted to go out it had to be arranged around their coming. And it got worse when my father-in-law died, she used to come every Tuesday for tea. I'd be working all day and I had to come home and you always fuss your mother-in-law and I had to make tea after a day's work. I used to resent her coming. And there was one time she started coming down twice a week. It was a big bind, it was a great hassle to me, but it seemed to be the expected thing.[27]

For Mrs Hunter and those who expressed similar resentments, the sense of obligation remained stronger than the feeling of being put upon, and the socializing continued.

As has already been mentioned in chapters 6 and 7, there were strains and tensions between some young mothers and their mothers and mothers-in-law over the matter of baby-sitting. Some grandmothers not only refused to mind their grandchildren while their mothers worked, but they also refused to sit when parents wanted to go out socially. This refusal tended to engender feelings of resentment. Mrs Webster said:

Well, my mother had her own interests, my mother-in-law had her own interests, so you just tend to get on with your own life.

She rarely saw her mother when her children were small, although she lived nearby:

My mum has always lived a life of her own. She has gone to coffee mornings, she has played outdoor bowls, she played badminton until she was sixty. After lunch she used to get dressed up and off out and most off out in an evening.[28]

(The coffee-mornings referred to were public occasions organized by churches, charities or similar organizations; they were not noticeably middle-class events.) These conflicts over tea parties and baby-sitting appear to encapsulate the conflict between ideas of family solidarity and concepts of individual freedom and autonomy.

Other Help for Kin: Grandparents and Grandchildren

Whatever the motives and whatever the feelings, it is clear that there continued to be a very considerable amount of help for both co-resident and non-resident relations throughout the period. And there were many happy memories as well as feelings of resentment.

Some children who lived with grandparents, unlike those already described, remembered their experiences with fondness. Mrs Lodge, who was born in 1921, was brought up in a household which comprised her maternal grandparents, an unmarried uncle, her brother, and her mother who was in full time work:

> I had a very loving mother and she taught me love, and my grandmother too. I have been very well blessed. I've had only love.
>   Were they strict with you?
>   My grandmother was. She wouldn't let me go bathing. She was Irish and a bit old-fashioned, but very loving. She used to sit; in the winter, when I was a child, apart from going to the pictures occasionally, there wasn't much to do, you know. And she used to tell us ghost stories, and stories about Ireland. She was adamantly Irish; so very, very proud of being Irish.[29]

Mr Hinchcliffe was twenty-five years younger than Mrs Lodge, of a different generation, but, like her, he grew up in his grandparents' home. His mother married three times and it is clear that his grandmother was the reliable rock on which his life was founded:

> My infant life was based on my grandmother. I was very close to my grandmother, that's why I am still there. There's no bond between me and my mother, to be quite honest.

For several years, when he was a little boy, his grandmother took him to a Butlin's holiday camp. During the course of the interviews Mr Hinchcliffe's grandmother died. He said simply, 'I wept buckets for my gran.'[30]

Young Couples and In-laws

Some children lived with grandparents because their young parents continued to have problems in buying or renting a home of their own, and consequently shared that of *their* parents. In the period after 1940, as has been seen, many young couples began their married lives with relatives. The shortest stay was six weeks, the longest thirty years! The success or otherwise of these arrangements varied enormously. Mr Simpkins, who had had the argument about his financial affairs, quoted earlier, obviously had a negative experience. Mrs Leighton was eighteen when she married in 1959; she worked in an office and her husband was an electrician:

> We never thought about renting. I don't know. Because my husband was an only child we were offered accommodation there if we wished. But what

happened was, there was only me left at home and so we used to spend the
week at my parents and at weekends at my husband's parents. But it was all
right, it worked out all right, although I would have liked to have bought a
house sooner, but my husband was quite keen on keep changing the car. We
did buy one, but actually it was four years later that we bought this house.[31]

Mr and Mrs Fleming were married in 1941. They lived with Mrs Fleming's much older sister and her husband and also her elderly parents. The
Flemings subsequently had six children, but they continued to live in the
same four-bedroomed house until they finally had a home of their own in
1969: 'I suppose we should have tried to get somewhere. But time went on,
and of course we had the three older folk to look after.' Her brother-in-law
was fifteen years older than her sister and became seriously ill with some
kind of cancerous growths on his face:

He went to Christies [in Manchester] then. It was terrible having them taken
off and he never recovered. He had a kind of stroke. Oh, it's really rotten to
talk about it. He used to do his business, and he would have it in his pocket.
And you would have to clean him up. Terrible. For the last eighteen months
he only breathed. She wouldn't let him go away. She was working, so she
looked after him when she came home at nights, but it was up to me.
Shocking it was. Washing, and I had no washing machine. I was washing for
twelve.[32]

But Mrs Fleming expressed no resentment at this situation, simply recording it as a terrible time. Later, in the mid-1950s, when the youngest of her
children had started school, she returned to work as a domestic in a local
hospital. This time she benefited from living with so many relatives as her
sister, now retired, cared for the children in her absence. When asked on
several occasions why she went to work, she was clear that she needed the
money to clothe the family. There was no hint that she worked to escape the
extended family.

Care of the Elderly

As can be seen throughout this chapter, there is a recurring theme of the
care of the elderly, either in their own or in their children's homes. The
most obvious reason for co-residence with the elderly was old people's need
of care, but there were sometimes other factors, such as emotional and
affective ties. Mr Kirkby and his wife lived with his mother, who was in

excellent health, for a total of seven years. Finally, he recognized that his wife needed a home of her own, so they moved into the house which had, in fact, been bought in the year of their marriage and had been rented out.[33]

Contacts between non-resident kin were very important. It was quite possible to help old people in their own homes, and many elderly folk preferred this, because they were able to retain a degree of independence. Townsend, in his study of elderly people in Bethnal Green, described attitudes which were also found in this area:

> When old people lose their husbands or wives it seems that many of them go on living alone. What causes them to do this? Do children neglect them, or do they choose to live alone? The short answer is, on the basis of the interviews carried out, that most of them choose to.[34]

Independence, or a degree of it, was particularly easy when several relatives lived in close proximity. Different generations in a family could all enjoy this situation. Mrs Brayshaw grew up in the 1950s and 1960s, and felt that she had at least two homes:

> We had relatives living next door, my mother's cousin and her husband. My grandmother and her sister lived next door but one. When I was a small child I remember having two breakfasts most days. I use to have one at home, and then shuffle off to next door to have porridge with masses of syrup on it.

The combined efforts of the family meant that grandmother was able to stay in her own home for many years; it was only necessary for her to move in with her daughter for the last year of her life.[35]

There was, very often, a particularly strong bond between a mother and her married daughter. This bond was commented upon by many observers.[36] Sometimes non-resident kin, and especially daughters, were able to do more for the elderly than those living under the same roof. In the late 1950s Mrs Kennedy's mother was unable to look after herself, but her daughter was not able to accommodate her as she and her husband and their two boys were already overcrowded in a little two-up-two-down house:

> She was too ill to look after herself. She went to live with my brother; he only lived in the next street to me. So when they went to work, she used to come round to me all day, and then go back to them when she had had her tea. That was for about eighteen months before she died. She was no trouble at all. The boys used to play with her and if I wanted to go to the shops, she would look after them for me.[37]

Mrs Turnbull's grandmother lived across the street and her daughter was able to do as much for her as if she had lived with her. When Mrs Turnbull was fourteen in 1946 her grandmother had an accident:

> She had a fall; it was snowing and she slipped and broke her femur. She was in hospital a few months and home a couple. She never got out of bed again. My mother looked after her. My brother was born on New Year's Eve and my grandmother had this fall in February. My mother used to go across to sit. She would take the baby in the pram and sit all night. My father was home in the evenings, but for about three months she sat day and night with her, did my mother.[38]

Help for Non-resident Kin

There was a variety of other practical help for relatives. The sick were visited, shopping was fetched, and washing and housework shared out. These tasks were mostly carried out by women. Men used to 'speak for each other', that is, recommend relatives for job vacancies at work, although this seems to have been less common than earlier in the century, probably because it was somewhat easier to find a job during this period. Many respondents spoke about leaving a job on Friday and starting another one the following Monday. Margaret Grieco argued strongly for the continuing importance of kin networks in helping relatives to find work: 'Kin networks represent the most effective channels of information transfer, and they provide employers with the possibilities of social control over individual workers.'[39] But her work relates to a later period when full employment no longer existed. In this study, kin were more usually a source of information about job opportunities, although they were still sometimes able to play a major role in the securing of work for a relative.

Mr and Mrs Grimshaw offered interesting examples of continuity in family traditions. Mr Grimshaw's father (who was interviewed in an earlier study), having left school for the cotton mill, worked in succession for an aunt, a cousin and then his father. Mr Grimshaw junior, forty years later, left school in 1956:

> I actually went to work for my uncle. I'd applied for a few jobs, but then my uncle saw my dad and said if I wanted a job I could go with him as an apprentice. My eldest brother, again he went to work for some relative of my dad, making chip ranges. And then my sister got a job at Horrockses and she got that through my dad.

Mrs Grimshaw also had family help: 'My uncle put in a word in for both me and my sister, because we both worked at the same place and he was a boss there.'[40]

The most common form of contact between relatives were those which provided social activity and psychological support. Women who were not in full-time work tended to see a lot of their female relatives and did not complain of loneliness. Again, the bond between mothers and married daughters was significant.[41]

Mrs Warwick was married in 1959. Her husband, an electrician moving from contract to contract, was often away from home:

> You weren't lonely at home?
> No, When the children were little, I used to go down to my mother's a lot, most days. And we used to go for walks.

She also met her sister once a week.[42]

Mrs Whiteside was only seventeen when she married and had her first baby in 1960. At first she lived with her parents-in-law, but after six months she and her husband and baby moved into their own council house. She continued to enjoy her relatives' company, visiting both her mother and mother-in-law, who lived opposite each other, at least four times a week. In the summer holidays her routine changed a little:

> My sister-in-law had three children, and we always went to Morecambe or Heysham, nearly every day, from them being small up to the age of about nine or ten. We'd be off at ten in the morning, and six o'clock in the evening back, and they were straight in bed, you know![43]

The life experiences of Mrs Owen illustrate the importance of a neighbourhood kinship network for friendship and support. Mrs Owen's reservations about her mother's medical remedies have already been noted (chapter 8), but that did not mean that she did not value her family's nearness, and the frequent contacts she had with them. When she was married in 1940 she had, living within a small group of streets near her home: her mother, four aunts, two sisters, an uncle, a cousin, two grandparents and a mother-in-law. When she was interviewed she was widowed but was still living in the same house. Sadly, both her sisters, who had also lived in the neighbourhood after their marriages, had died, but her mother and an aunt still survived nearby. Living across the road were Mrs Owen's only daughter with her husband and three children. The family continued to drop in on one another on a very regular basis. Indeed, Mrs Owen and her daughter still spent much of their day together, that is, when Mrs Owen was not visiting her own mother. Looking back on her life in the period 1940–70 Mrs Owen said of her mother: 'I saw her most days. I always used to say I was going home. My husband used to say to me, "Well, what's this?" ' Her mother-in-law also lived close by and she went blind; 'She used to come more than my mum really.' Mrs Owen offered help to relatives in need, and in turn received assistance from those able to give it. When she first married she was particularly close to one of her aunts, who was fourteen years older than her:

> My auntie lived down the street. If I didn't know how to cook anything; and especially when I was having the baby; I mean I knew nothing. My mum never told me the facts and I being nosey used to go and ask Auntie Mary.

This closeness was long-standing. Years before, when she was a girl, Mrs Owen often went to sleep at her grandmother's for a 'treat' and there she shared a bed with her aunt, who was as yet unmarried:

> Well, when I started my periods I was sleeping with my Auntie Mary, and I came from the toilet, and I was crying and she asked me what was the matter, and I told her I was bleeding, and it was her that told me all about it. I used to go and ask my auntie everything.[44]

Sometimes there was a degree of reliance on a relative which seemed excessive to other members of the family. Mrs Grimshaw gave this account, which relates to 1950s and 1960s:

> The auntie who started coming every night was on my dad's side. When her husband died she came every night at about seven o'clock and she'd go about ten o'clock. She came every night for twenty years; it must have been twenty odd years. She said she couldn't stay in the house by herself.

The brother and sister-in-law even took her on holiday with them sometimes. Mrs Grimshaw understandably felt that 'there must have been a lot of arguments about that'. But she offered no evidence to support this supposition, and the arrangement continued for a very long time.[45]

Mrs York's refusal to buy a house after the war has been mentioned in chapter 2. It is very possible that another reason for her refusal to move was her dread of leaving her sister, who lived only a five-minutes walk from her existing house:

> Never a day went by. Because her husband had been called up and I was expecting, and she had a little girl and we were always together. In fact that was the only thing that made any trouble when we were first married. My

husband used to come home and I wouldn't always be in, and he'd say, 'You're always at Rita's. Do you not like your own little home?' I'd say 'Yes' but when I'd tidied up in the morning, I had nobody and there was nothing to do. Well, I'd go down to my sister's and we'd go into town and I used to bathe the baby and play with her. There was nothing in my house when he was at work and he used to say, 'You're married to me now, you shouldn't be so close to your sister.' I said to him, 'Look, don't even try to come between me and Rita, because you would be the first to go.' So I really thought more of my sister than I did of my husband.[46]

Family Occasions

Some extended families went on holiday together and there are happy memories of aunts and uncles and hordes of cousins playing on the beach.[47] Some kin only appeared at important events in the life of the extended family, notably weddings and funerals. These were seen as times for renewing family bonds, exchanging news and, where appropriate, jokes. Both these events were undergoing changes. As has been seen in chapter 4, weddings were becoming larger, but funerals were decreasing in size and grandness, although for some they continued to represent an epic event in

Figure 10.1   Families relaxing on Biggar Bank, Walney, in the 1950s.
(Photo courtesy of *North Western Evening Mail*)

the life of an extended family. The only example of an Irish wake in this
study was given by Mrs Whiteside. Her father died in 1964 and his Irish
relations, with whom the English branch of the family had had very little
contact, descended on Lancaster. Their presence does not seem to have been
appreciated:

> Well, my dad was Irish, but my mum seemed to be frightened of his family.
> And when my dad died she wouldn't have him taken away, even though we
> were relatively young. He died on the Monday, they came from Ireland on
> the Wednesday, and they just knelt in the bedroom for Wednesday and the
> whole of Thursday, just prayed and prayed round the bed. And they were all
> weeping and making terrible noises. And we were kneeling at the top of the
> stairs saying the rosary. And in the bedroom they had two candles and a cross
> and the holy water. It was awful. And one of dad's sisters was spraying the
> house, because she had the smell of death. And round the graveside they were
> all crying and awful, awful noises. And they were all in black from head to
> foot. We got back home and I'll never forget it. I mean after all that weeping
> and wailing. Uncle Mike and the men started off in the pub and Auntie
> Sarah, who had been in deepest mourning, within half an hour of coming
> home she was dressed in a canary yellow outfit! All the food and all the beer
> and all the reminiscing. And we have never seen them since![48]

Mr and Mrs Whiteside did not appreciate all the fuss and the emotion,
feeling that it did not help the immediate family of the dead man. Clearly,
they felt that there was something artificial about the grief of the Irish
relatives. With the passing of the years, however, they did enjoy the
humour of the event.

Conclusion

Is it possible to speak of any diminution of kinship support and friendship
during this period, as compared to earlier times? This is very difficult to
answer since it is virtually impossible to quantify these things. Even if one
could, there would remain the insuperable difficulty of estimating the
quality of such help. Some things can be enumerated, of course; for instance,
as has been seen, there was some decline in co-residence. However, this
decline, as witnessed by our respondents, does not necessarily imply any
lowering of standards of care for relatives nor a loosening of the bonds of
kinship.

There was no evidence to suggest that elderly relatives were being 'deposited' in old people's homes. Those requiring hospital care received it, but the rest were cared for in their own or their relatives' homes. In a study published in 1977, Michael Anderson suggested that fewer than 1 per cent of old people with living children were in institutions. This can be compared with the figure in 1908 when about 1 per cent of elderly people with close surviving relatives were in institutions.[49] Although there are no comparable local statistics, it would appear that our evidence would support these findings.

In her brilliant analysis of contemporary family relationships, Janet Finch examines such concepts as rules, obligations and duties. She suggests that families take into account many factors before giving assistance to a relative. These include their genealogical relationship, the history of the relationship, and whether the assistance being considered will be the right thing both for the giver and the receiver at this particular time of their lives.[50] Clearly, those in our study did not give help to just anyone claiming kinship. Although there were exceptions, as with adults living in a sibling's family home, the most usual help was given up and down a straight genealogical line of grandparents, parents and children. While it is clear that respondents were aware of rules and obligations governing their relationships with kin, it is much less apparent that they consciously assessed the various considerations identified in studies of rather more recent relationships. Family discussions on the subject of what to do about helping or not helping relatives are rarely mentioned. As with their forebears, respondents appeared to possess norms which had long been internalized. Respondents generally acted as they did towards kin because 'it was the thing to do'.

It should be stressed, however, that some respondents, looking back from the perspective of the late 1980s, were critical of what they felt to be impositions made on their families by kin. Others, even within the period of the study, felt and expressed feelings of resentment about their kin. This would appear to indicate a change over time, because, although such feelings may have been experienced, they are voiced very rarely in our studies of the earlier part of the century.

Only a very small minority of respondents had few contacts with their relatives, having lost touch through quarrels or through migration. The great majority continued to be 'close' to their kin, or at least to some of them. Given the empirical evidence, it is difficult to discern any serious weakening in the attachment between, and the help and support given to, relatives during the period 1940–70 when compared to the earlier decades of the century. There is no evidence of women putting their jobs before the care of their relations; those who worked sought to balance demands of job and kin. The extended family continued to be, as it had been earlier in the century, a major source of help, support and companionship throughout the period.

11

Neighbours and Neighbourhoods

The various functions of the older, closely knit neighbourhoods which were experienced by the overwhelming majority of respondents and their families at the beginning of the period are first examined in this chapter. As the period progressed we see these experiences becoming increasingly less common, either because respondents moved away from the district or, more probably, because the social relationships between those within working-class neighbourhoods underwent significant change.

Introduction

Josephine Klein, in her analysis of working-class neighbourhoods in the 1950s and 1960s, wrote of some being 'traditional'.[1] This is a useful short-hand term which will also be adopted in the chapter. Its use does not imply that 'traditional' neighbourhoods in their twentieth-century form had existed from time immemorial. They had been in existence in this geographical area from at least the 1890s and were described in *A Woman's Place*.[2] They continued into the period studied in this book, 1940–70. They were characterized by the provision of mutual practical help and social support.

In times of trouble, despite the arrival of the welfare state, many poorer people's second line of defence, after their immediate families, was the neighbourhood. Neighbours could still provide vital assistance when there was a birth, a death or sickness in the house, and a helping hand in the more mundane problems of everyday life.

The close-knit neighbourhood also continued to act as an agent of social control, with its own methods of establishing and enforcing standards of cleanliness, respectability and good behaviour.

It is not easy to define a neighbourhood at this time except in terms of its functions. Physically it could be one street, or more usually a small group of streets. Although some people were well aware of living in a certain area, or on an estate, these larger groupings tended not to operate in any meaningful sense as a community. What was of primary importance in practical terms was the street in which you lived and your immediate neighbours.

Among the respondents were those who were moving away from working-class districts. In the three towns surveyed, small terraced houses were regarded as essentially working-class property until well after 1970. Increasing prosperity meant that more could afford to become owner-occupiers in semi-detached houses with gardens. In 1940 over 90 per cent of respondents (or their families, in the case of those yet to be born) lived in working-class neighbourhoods, either in council houses or small – sometimes very small – terraced houses; of the remaining 10 per cent, four respondents moved into the area well after 1940 and their earlier lives were not recorded, and three were children of respondents in the earlier studies who had left working-class areas in the inter-war period. By 1970 those living in such areas had fallen to 60 per cent. Respondents who moved usually, but not always, developed an attitude to their new neighbours which was described by Gorer as one of 'distant cordiality'.[3] They 'kept themselves to themselves' and 'minded their own business'. Not all those who moved adopted such an attitude but they tended to encounter it among their new neighbours and were inevitably influenced by it.

Those who remained in working-class districts also experienced many changes, basically resulting from widening social differences and changing social attitudes within the working class. The stability of some areas was disturbed by the increase in numbers of those buying houses which had previously been rented. Ownership of these small houses was seen as the first rung on the property market ladder and their occupants tended to move on quickly. Elsewhere some council estate dwellers increasingly suffered from disorder, vandalism and rising minor crime. In almost all areas there were people who appeared to be unsure about ways of establishing good relationships with their neighbours, some adopting a attitude of distancing, others becoming over-familiar.

There had always been some problems about how best to get on with one's neighbours; the period 1940–70 saw an increase in the scale and frequency of breakdown in relationships. Individuals increasingly saw themselves in the role of neighbours without necessarily being part of a neighbourhood. They like to be considered 'good neighbours' although the definition of the term underwent noticeable revision, but they opted out of the obligations and the sociability of the neighbourhood.

There was also a new development, still only observable in a small minority of areas: neighbours' property was abused and rights ignored. Neighbours were regarded with neither 'distant cordiality' nor 'effortless sociability'[4] but with outright hostility. The neighbour was now the enemy. Such a situation had not been reported by respondents in the pre-war period.

Mutual Help

Neighbourliness and neighbourhoods were strongest in the poorest areas. This accorded with Klein's findings: 'We find that the lower down the social scale we go the more close-knit the network, and by inference the more traditional the way of life.'[5]

Mrs Boyle was an important witness about the way in which old neighbourhoods functioned. She was one of the poorest of our respondents; her husband was unskilled and frequently out of work. In the second half of the 1950s she lived with her husband and a growing number of children in a tiny house in a small street in the centre of Preston. The street was demolished in 1961 when Mrs Boyle and her neighbours were dispersed to various council estates. Life was never quite the same again for Mrs Boyle. Her evidence is supported by other witnesses who lived in similar streets:

> Everybody looked after one another. I couldn't have had better friends than Mary and Janet. When I was having Helen, Janet used to come across and they would do your errands and they would take the nappies. They would come across and give you a meal during the day because you used to stay in bed seven days. And when I was having Christine, Mary would take Helen for me; come for her in the morning and have her all day. Janet came across and brought me my breakfast and stayed until the midwife came. Do all my nappies; they were absolutely great.[6]

There was also an exchange of goods and services on a more mundane day-to-day basis. Mrs Boyle was not only a recipient of help, she also provided it:

> There was a lot of old people as well, so you wouldn't hesitate like. There was Uncle John [no relation] next door. I used to go in in the morning and shout, 'Uncle John, are you alright?' and he would be sat there. But nobody did owt for Uncle John. He did all his own washing and cleaning, but you could run errands for them and if they wanted the doctor you could ring for them and

go and get their prescriptions, go and draw their pensions. You would help one another that way.

The neighbour on the other side was Susan: 'She was the best! "Have you half a carrot, Dorothy? Have you half an onion?" And how on earth anybody got half an onion or half a carrot!'[7]

Living on a council estate did not necessarily mean that there was no neighbourliness. Mr Whitaker was brought up by his grandparents on an inter-war Preston council estate. His grandmother died in 1970 and the neighbours remained supportive and friendly to the end.

> Well, Mrs Rhodes used to come in quite often when grandma was in her later years; come in and talk to her, make her something to eat, make her a drink of tea. And other neighbours would come and do the same. Mrs Brown and Mrs Thomas came in every night to play dominoes.[8]

Social Life

The neighbourhood also provided a place where people, and more especially women and children, could socialize. It was, indeed, where the people with whom it was customary to socialize came from. Women from these areas continued to talk of friendly neighbours, or neighbours who were friendly. They mention rather less frequently friends who lived elsewhere. It has been suggested that the conscious selection of friends was indicative of the kind of social confidence not usually found in these poorer areas and that this led to the uncritical acceptance of neighbours as friends.[9]

Much of the social life of poorer women and children took place on the street, with people from the street. Not only were the interiors of terraced houses rather small for social gatherings, but more importantly it was easier to control both the length and the depth of an encounter made in the street. Either party could walk away when she liked. Traditional working-class people appear to have sought 'effortless sociability' and the street provided ample opportunity for this. It was not necessary to make an appointment, no special arrangements nor the provision of hospitality was needed. For men, the pub provided a comparable venue.

Historians are wont to describe women as occupying the private sphere of the home; but women who lived in small overcrowded houses tended to lead much of their lives publicly and communally. Children, too, when not in school, spent a large part of their lives on the street with their friends.

Figure 11.1   A VE Day party on the Ryelands Estate, Lancaster
(Photo courtesy of Lancaster City Museum)

These were usually their contemporaries, but younger children were often under the watchful eye of neighbouring adults. Mrs Boyle said: 'Janet would say, "Do keep an eye on them. I'm going to do such a thing. Are you alright?" "Yes, go." So you'd keep an eye on everybody.' Mrs Boyle's street was, in effect, an informal mother and toddler group:

> You know, you would all go together. There might be four mothers with a load of kids; we'd all go together to Moor Park; let them play in the park with balls and things like that.[10]

Women appear to have had recognized times for socializing. The mornings were regarded as a time for housework, so it was really only acceptable to chat to neighbours when apparently working; for instance, while 'doing the front' or hanging out the washing in the back yard, or when visiting the local shop. The afternoons were the time for talking, but certainly not beyond the time when the husband was due home for his tea. That was *his* time. In the evenings wives only seemed to have met together if their husbands were out at the pub, or if couples joined together for some social activity. Mrs Boyle said:

> I was never one for going out. Barry would go for a drink. I always had Mary or Janet to keep me company. Always, you know. If it was summer we sat on

my step with a brew, and two of us smoked. There was always fag ends. We had to sweep them up the morning after. We sat on the step while half past ten; but so did everybody. Old ladies used to be sat out on their chairs or on their little stools. You would hear everybody coming home from the pub and we used to say, 'Pubs are loose, we are going in.'[11]

Going in at this time was a move calculated both to avoid having a domestic fracas with one's husband on the doorstep in front of the neighbours, and also to spare one's neighbours the embarrassment of witnessing their altercations. It was well known that husbands could often be at best argumentative and at worst violent after an evening at the pub. Earlier in the century domestic battles had sometimes been fought in the street, cheered on by the neighbours, but those days had largely passed and now disputes took place behind closed doors.

In a minority of streets large-scale social events were organized. They celebrated victory at the end of the Second World War, the Coronation in 1953 and, in Preston, the Guild of 1952. (Preston Guild is held every twenty years, except in wartime.) Mr Whitaker remembered the street party of 1952: 'People just made things. We had raffles, bought toys for the kiddies. We played games, racing in the street, hopping races, races round the block. We had tea, pop, trifle, sandwiches, sing-songs.'[12] Not surprisingly, Mr Whitaker had no precise memories of the organization of this party, but its existence indicates the ability of members of the working-class neighbourhoods to co-operate and arrange quite an ambitious event.[13]

Bereavements

Neighbours had traditionally been of great support to a bereaved family. One woman in each neighbourhood proffered the specialized help of laying out the dead, a service for which they were not usually paid but for which they may have accepted a gift. Mrs Whiteside's father was laid out by a neighbour when he died in 1964. This appears to have been the last time in the respondent's memory that a neighbour undertook this duty. Others offered more general help and support. They visited the bereaved family and paid their 'last respects' to the dead by viewing the body. They drew their curtains on the day of the funeral and came out to stand silently while the hearse set off to the church or cemetery. They then prepared the funeral tea in readiness for the mourners' return.

Although 'laying out' may have ended by 1970, other customs remained. Events in the life of Mr Whitaker illustrate this continuity. In his experience the deceased were taken home if they had not died at home and were then visited by neighbours. He stated this as if it was a general rule. His sister was tragically burned to death in 1945, when she was five and he was six:

> I saw my sister. We had her on a gate-leg table. The coffin was on a gate-leg table in front of the window. And I went to my friend's sister's funeral in 1955. I went to see her in her coffin and then I sang in the young people's choir at the funeral. It was an accepted thing in those days that all the neighbours in the street used to close their blinds and come out and bow their heads as the hearse was passing. I still do it.[14]

Mr Whitaker's mother-in-law, with whom he and his wife had lived, died in 1967:

> We brought her home. The neighbours were very respectable people. They were the old-fashioned type. Nothing was too good if somebody had a bereavement; everybody cared. The neighbours collected for a wreath, and Edna, a neighbour, made the funeral tea.[15]

These various small rituals, in themselves, may not have been very significant, but they gave comfort and support to the bereaved.

The Continuing Ethos of Traditional Neighbourhoods

What factors produced these close-knit communities? The ethos of helping one's neighbour was largely unspoken but widely acted upon, as had been the case earlier in the century. For many it remained the norm – 'the thing to do'. For some respondents it was their practical response to the religious instruction to 'love your neighbour'. Poverty also bound people together; neighbours provided goods and services which the more prosperous could buy but which they could not themselves afford. One reason for the continuing power of this ethic was that children learned it when young, partly by observing their parents' behaviour and also because they were expected to be of service to their neighbours, usually by running errands for them. Some children acted because it was their perceived duty to do so, others felt encouraged by the prospect of a small reward.

Mrs Morrison, in a very simple account, indicated some of the complexities and obligations which existed in neighbourly relations in a small working-class street in the 1950s. She said:

I used to shop for the lady next door. She had a bad leg. I used to go and get groceries, that was at the corner shop which was just two streets away. And she used to get me to go to the chemists to get ointment for her bad leg. And she always seemed to come and knock when I was going to have my tea.

Could you say, 'Wait until I have had my tea'?

No. I used to go because it was only round the corner. It was funny, if I was about to sit down to my tea, she would just give a little knock. But then, her son was good, he was much older before he got married. I used to play the piano and he enjoyed me playing the piano, and he had an allotment where he grew flowers, and he was always bringing me flowers. So we always had lovely big bunches of flowers, because he appreciated listening to me playing the piano. So that was very nice.[16]

Earlier in the century some respondents remembered being forbidden by their parents to accept any reward for running an errand for neighbours. This prohibition was mentioned less frequently by younger respondents, and this may have had some significance in the history of neighbourliness. Mr Grimshaw grew up in the 1950s and 1960s on an inter-war council estate in Preston. When asked about running errands for neighbours and whether it was possible to refuse to do so, he replied, 'No, you did it. I mean you were always "tret", whether by sweets or coppers.'[17]

Children learned a lot about neighbourhood solidarity by playing out on the street from an early age. Sometimes youngsters were incorporated into a single-sex group, sometimes a mixed one. It is not possible to make any generalizations about this as it seemed to depend on who was available at the time, but with sub-teenage children there was a preference for single-sex grouping. From these groups children learned lessons about co-operation, about the importance of consensus, conformity, conflict resolution, fitting in and following group rules. This was especially true of children who played team games in the street, and particularly true of boys who belonged to street gangs. They may not have been practising socially reponsible behaviour, but they had first-hand experience of group solidarity.

Mr Kennedy, referring to the end of the 1930s, said:

We had street gangs. There was the Aqueduct Street gang, and my brother was the leader of that gang. And there was the Byron Street mob. They used to come down; same as November, you would be laying your bonfire and they would pinch your bonfire stuff, and you would go up and pinch theirs. And you would have dustbin lids and sticks and you would be throwing stones at each other. All that kind of stuff went on; people accepted it more.[18]

Mr Kennedy's remark about 'people accepting it more' is an interesting one, and may not mean quite what it seems. Possibly he thought that it was right to support one's neighbourhood against others. However, in the light of what he said later, it probably meant that, in his view, neighbours were more likely to deal with problems of misbehaving youths themselves, rather than seek police intervention. Certainly, there is a considerable amount of evidence that many aspects of children's behaviour were not approved of by adults in the neighbourhood. Cheekiness, attacks on property, practical jokes, ball-games in backyards, excessive noise are all mentioned as being unacceptable. Having an unwritten, yet widely understood, set of rules strengthened children's identification with their neighbourhood, increased their feelings of solidarity with their friends and reinforced standards laid down by parents at home. Enforcing the rules also ensured some degree of public order and gave adults a feeling of 'ownership' over public spaces. They perceived themselves as being in control of what happened in their own neighbourhood.

Mr Kennedy continued his account of childhood activities as follows:

> I think there is more tendency to bring in the police to kids today. Most of the parents would come and if you were giving a load of lip to anybody, or doing anything wrong, 'Eh, alright', and they would clip your earhole. They would chase you down the street and kick you up the backside. You'd run away. You didn't dare go home in case they told your mum and dad. They would give you another one for doing it, you know.[19]

Mr Whitaker was ten years younger than Mr Kennedy, but he told a similar story about his upbringing in the late 1940s on a council estate which had been built in the inter-war years. Of his neighbours he said:

> . . . not only tell us off. They were allowed to clip us round the earhole, for want of a better word. Oh yes, and there were no questions asked. If you went in and said, 'Mr So-and-so has just told us off, he's been hitting us', 'You deserved it, don't do it again.' It was the accepted thing and it didn't do us any harm. It learned you to respect your neighbours; it learned you to respect your friends' parents.[20]

Gossip

It could be said that the solidarity of a neighbourhood was, to a large extent, maintained through gossip; especially, though not exclusively through that of women. To some respondents the word 'gossip' was a pejorative term, but it played a vital role in the life of a neighbourhood and the lives of individuals. This was true of many communities throughout the country, as Klein observes:

> The members' activities are known to all; none can escape the sanctions of gossip and public opinion. In these circumstances people tend to reach a consensus on norms and exert a consistent informal pressure on each other to conform.[21]

In more traditional working-class areas gossiping was an integral part of women's lives; it confirmed their feeling of belonging to a social group with a common history, common traditions and shared standards of behaviour. It helped those experiencing difficulties in their lives.

Gossip was also feared; it could ruin reputations. Individuals took care not to become the objects of gossip by conforming to the accepted norms, the neighbourhood rules of the time. These may well have encompassed such diverse topics, from the way in which the front of the house was kept clean through to questions of sexual morality. There was inevitably gossip when a girl became pre-maritally pregnant. Obviously, for that girl gossip could not change the course of events, but it could bring shame to her as punishment for breaking the rules. The gossip was also intended to act as deterrent to any future sexual 'deviance' in the community.

Mr Monkhouse was one of the youngest respondents, having been born in 1948. His memories relate to the 1950s, growing up on a council estate built between the wars. He was asked about attitudes to girls who became pregnant before marriage:

> Oh, a matter of great shame. It was very much talked about. She was considered a hussy. People would distance themselves from it. I can actually remember seeing people whispering behind their hands, and it was obvious that this person was being shunned. The shock was appalling, and she was a very quiet, shy, sensitive girl. That must have been an appalling thing. It was known throughout the local community; and in good families it was looked on with great shame. Having your daughter going and doing that and letting down the family name. When someone got married at short notice there would be a great nodding and winking. 'And when is the baby due?' It was really very gossipy. And if someone married at short notice, regardless of the circumstances, speculation would be absolutely rife; an awful lot of gossiping. If it was a registry office wedding . . . Whoo! That was seen as confirmation; you must be pregnant. 'She's not going down the aisle in white, she must be pregnant.'[22]

Figure 11.2   Neighbours talking in a back street, *c*.1950
(Hulton Deutsch Collection)

Gossip had a more positive role in the context of the neighbourhood support system. Without gossip it was difficult to know who was ill or who needed some kind of assistance. Gossip was the only way in which informal rotas of helpers were arranged. Without gossip neighbourhoods could not have functioned as such caring, helpful communities.

Well into the 1960s the working-class street provided the ideal physical location for the exchange of gossip. Some women continued to make several visits each day to the corner shop and many went more than once. Mrs Grimshaw, who grew up in the 1950s and 1960s, when asked how often her mother went to the local shop replied, 'Two or three times a day. I think people did. It sold everything. And you found out all the gossip. The lady who owned the shop knew everything about everybody.'[23]

The ritual donkey-stoning of the front door-step also provided an opportunity for women in the street to exchange gossip. Mr Stephenson was married in the late 1940s and lived until 1960 in a street of small terraced houses in the centre of Preston. He saw the daily donkey-stoning routine both as a time for exchanging news and as a method of shaming those women who were not keeping their 'fronts' clean:

> If anyone had been dirty in the street, what would have happened to them?
> Well, it just didn't happen. The first thing they did was donkey-stoning, and they were all out, you know. And if the step wasn't done, the neighbours would go in and see if she was ill. And probably they were someone who didn't want to do the donkey-stoning. Because everybody did it; and they would say, 'Are you ill?'[24]

Mr Monkhouse remembered the women on his council estate:

> It wasn't unusual, on a Monday morning, to see at nearly every door-step various ladies' bottoms moving up and down as they donkey-stoned the step. They used to hold up their nylons with elastic bands. It wasn't very dignified; rather large, rotund old ladies with long bloomers on! But you just accepted that was the nature of things. They would all be out doing the steps.
> Would you be talked about if you didn't do it?
> Oh yes – sloppy woman![25]

There was often a back street where the washing was hung out, and this was another feature of the household routine which afforded the opportunity for gossip with one's neighbours.

Men gossiped less on the streets, their day being spent at their place of work. However, in the pub in the evenings their gossip had the same effect as that of their womenfolk; it reinforced group solidarity and helped maintain certain standards. Mr Norton spent most of his childhood and young adult life in the 1930s and 1940s on a council estate, and was asked about the keeping of gardens:

There was the odd one that neglected them, but it was the odd one. There was a sense of pride really and a sense of shame if it wasn't done. Even the group who didn't want to look after the gardens made an effort. I think possibly because of the local pub. Their names would be mentioned; I think that was enough then. No pressure as such, but a man's own pride wouldn't let him neglect.[26]

Among many men and women was a dread of losing their reputation – of 'getting a bad name' amongst their neighbours. Having a 'good' name meant having neighbourhood respect, being able 'to hold up your head'. Losing this could mean 'being looked down on', not respected, sometimes being ostracized and occasionally verbally abused.

Changing Neighbourhoods

Inevitably, over the thirty-year period covered by this study, changes were taking place. The great majority of respondents who were interviewed in the earlier study remembered living in close-knit, supportive yet stifling inquisitive streets, for at least part of their lives. In the present survey, although, as has been seen, the majority of respondents continued to live in working-class areas, only a minority still experienced in 1970 the social atmosphere of what has been described as the 'traditional' neighbourhood.

Moving away

The topography of some respondents' neighbourhoods changed as they moved away from streets of small terraced houses. Sometimes this was a matter of choice, sometimes one of necessity. In Preston a massive programme of demolition carried out by the council in the 1950s and 1960s cleared away thousands of homes.[27] Some respondents who were re-housed commented that their 'better' homes had gardens which not only provided a physical space between them and their neighbours, but also created a psychological distancing.

Those who chose to move to a house with a garden did not, of course, thereby move into the middle class overnight. Mrs Webster's parents had spent all their married life in a street of small terraced houses in central Barrow. Her father, a shop assistant, was a keen gardener and the council wanted his allotment for building land:

We lived in a terraced house until I was twenty-two [1958] then we moved
to a semi-detached; but it wasn't the same spirit. Everybody had their garden
and kept themselves to themselves.[28]

Mr Kennedy was a docker; after years of saving he and his family moved
to a semi-detached house in 1970. He remarked, 'The terraced houses round
here are a lot friendlier. You get these semi-detached houses and you cut
yourselves off in some ways.'[29]

The existence of sizeable gardens, coupled with the growing volume of
traffic, meant that children tended to play in their own territory and
became detached from the street life of their peer group. It was clearly a
different socializing experience to mix with a small, carefully selected group
of friends on family property than with a much larger group of assorted
children in the no-man's-land of the street.

Mrs Lewthwaite, whose husband was a painter and decorator, moved in
the late 1950s from a small terraced house to a bungalow with a garden,
where she brought up her son. When asked where he played, she replied:

> Not in the street. I can't remember him playing in the street, no. He always
> used to enjoy playing in the back. He had a tent up and his friends used to
> come to play.
>   What is the biggest number you remember coming to play?
>   Oh, only four, I would say.[30]

But the physical distance between neighbours in the newer houses was
not the main factor in creating less friendly neighbourhoods. As has been
seen, the inter-war council estates with their gardens continued to function
in the manner of the old terraced communities. More important than the
physical changes to the environment were people's changing attitudes both
to neighbours and neighbourliness.

Keeping One's Distance

There were many factors which tended to produce a more private family and
a less closely knit neighbourhood. There were 'pull' factors such as gardening and the television, which caused people to spend more time in their own
homes. There were also the 'push' factors which made people want to have
less contact with their neighbours. Some wanted to avoid the gossip, some
sought to guard their independence, and an increasing number could afford
not to rely on neighbours' help any longer. Some resented the invasion of

their privacy which they believed would result from too close a contact with their neighbours. These attitudes were not new but, as the century progressed, more and more people adopted them.

Neighbours spoke of 'keeping themselves to themselves' and 'minding their own business'. Those likely to have made such remarks earlier in the century were generally from the most respectable members of the working class. Their increasing desire for privacy was closely linked to their devotion to respectability. They appear to have believed that the less their neighbours knew about their business the less there would be to gossip about. For obvious reasons the respectable dreaded being the subject of gossip.

In our study the great majority of respondents could be described as 'respectable', probably only four being 'rough'. This was also the case in the earlier studies where the 'rough' constituted only a small minority. It is not possible to argue that this study involved respondents who were more respectable than those interviewed previously, nor can it be said that the current group became more respectable over the period under review. What appears to have changed is that whereas, earlier in the century, only the *most* respectable, a minority, of the working class adopted attitudes of 'distancing', throughout the period 1940–70 an increasing number of the respectable became 'distantly cordial' rather than 'effortlessly sociable'.

Such changes of attitude were accompanied by increasing material prosperity which meant that the need for practical help from neighbours decreased. It was no longer necessary to 'borrow' food or household goods; the more affluent people became the less need they had of the mutual support on which poorer people had relied earlier in the century.

The respectable feared too close an involvement with neighbours who could in any way be regarded as 'rough' or 'common', in case this association tarnished their own respectability. Mrs Winder was interviewed in the 1970s and spoke of her childhood during the First World War and after. Although the family lived in a working-class street, her father worked as a clerk and her mother prided herself on her respectability.

> Well, mother never encouraged neighbours in and out. I know my sister went to this family on the side street. They were a family of girls and they all worked in the mill. My sister went an awful lot. She went to the pictures with them. But I've seen at times my mother has clamped down. 'Now, you're to stop going.' Perhaps some little thing had come back from somewhere else. We had a bit of a 'nosey parker' next door, and she would repeat what she had heard. My mother didn't like gossip, and she didn't like this running in and out and people knowing your business.[31]

After the Second World War this desire for privacy and 'keeping to oneself' can be found in poorer areas as well as among the more upwardly aspiring. The passion for privacy did not necessarily mean total isolation from one's neighbours; rather, the careful drawing of boundaries and the selection of those with whom one associated. Mrs Sykes's mother was distant but cordial with her neighbours, but her close relationships were with friends with whom she socialized by arrangement. The person she sat with lived several streets away and could not be described as a neighbour. She appears to have made the same transition as many other women: from having friendly neighbours – or neighbours who were friends – to a position where she had made friends with those who were not her neighbours:

> Well, when it was nice we were always out in the garden, and you used to shout over to your neighbour and they were always passing my mother strawberries and things out of their garden. They were always very friendly. My mother, when she had blackcurrants, she used to pass them back, and one time she had eggs and she used to swop eggs. Oh yes, they were very friendly.
>
> Did you pop in and visit each other?
>
> Not a lot, because my mother did not like that, people popping in all the time, she didn't let many in. She used to have special friends who came on a Tuesday morning for a coffee, and then she would go to their house, but neighbours, no.
>
> Do you remember your mother helping anyone?
>
> My mother was always helping someone. She used to sit sometimes at night with people. I remember a lady in Harrison Street who was very ill, and she went two or three nights a week and sat all night.[32]

Mrs Sykes's father was an unskilled labourer and the family could in no way be described as 'middle class', which makes the reference to the coffee mornings interesting.

Many respondents asserted that they themselves were, and that they had always had, 'good neighbours'; but is clear that their concepts of good neighbourliness differed from those of the previous generation. They were unable to flesh out generalities with specific examples of neighbourly behaviour. Mrs Lewthwaite's mother was interviewed in the 1970s and her experiences suggest that distancing, even between neighbours who were extremely poor, already existed in the earlier part of the century. She spoke movingly about the dreadful poverty experienced by her family in the Depression of the 1920s when Barrow's economy collapsed. Her husband was long-term unemployed and at one point she had tried to supplement the family income by doing some cleaning while also drawing Poor Relief. For this she was reported by an anonymous neighbour and was in considerable difficulties. This incident must have influenced her attitude towards her neighbours, although her daughter did not accept this.

On more than one occasion Mrs Lewthwaite, speaking about her mother, said, 'She was friendly with everyone really, she was liked wherever she went and she would do anything for anybody. But she didn't like to be running in and out of houses, you know.'

Mrs Lewthwaite could never specify help given by neighbours to her mother or vice versa, and confined heself to generalities such as: 'They were all in the same boat. They couldn't really give.' In the late 1930s her mother was seriously ill, but when asked if the neighbours had helped she replied:

> Well, they were very friendly, they would have done anything, you know, but they weren't actually in the house doing anything. Of course, I was sixteen and I used to look after the house.
> So you managed without the neighbours?
> Oh yes.

When asked again about neighbourly help in a later interview, this time referring to her own neighbours in her adult life, she said:

> They always knew if they wanted anything, you would help them and that sort of thing.
> You don't remember any examples of the help they used to give?
> No, not really, no.

She moved to her present house in the late 1950s and said simply of her neighbours, 'We see them in the garden. I go and have a talk with them in the gardens.'[33] Another example of 'distant cordiality' rather than 'effortless sociability'.

Although gardens did not create the changing attitudes to neighbours, they can be seen as a symbol for the growing distance between working-class neighbours. In earlier times, when terraced houses did not have gardens, those who wanted to cultivate plants, whether from expediency as a means of supplementing the family diet or for personal satisfaction, had an allotment on a public site. These were invariably cared for by the menfolk, providing a meeting place where they could exchange gossip as well as surplus garden produce. The acquisition of the private garden behind the house increased the potential for aesthetic enjoyment, and many respondents gave the desire for a garden as their reason for moving into a different area. However, the private garden, frequently surrounded by a hedge or fence, encouraged social isolation from the neighbourhood as a whole while providing the possibility of private contact over the fence with one's immediate neighbours. In some neighbourhoods, as will be seen, the garden was both the cause and focus of tension and bad feeling.

Some Recollections of Changing Neighbourhoods

There are difficulties in comparing the recollections of children with those of adults. Children's perspectives are different and they are more likely to have had more frequent contact with their neighbourhood peer group than did their parents. Given these reservations, it is nevertheless interesting to look at the evidence of two respondents who, as adults, returned to live in the street where they had grown up. They found that the neighbourhood had changed, and so had they.

Mrs Adderley grew up in a rented terraced house in Lancaster. She left in 1951, having spent the first two years of her married life looking after her mother who was frequently ill. She and her husband moved to a council house in a town about eight miles away, where they lived for some years before returning to buy a house in the same Lancaster street in 1957. When asked about the kind of help given by neighbours when she was young she replied:

> Well, anything; they'd do anything for you. If my mum wasn't well, the lady across the road would come and get all the washing and wash it for us, another would come and do the ironing; there was no limit. And if anyone else was sick my mum would go and help. It was quite a lot of neighbours, not just one or two, it was really friendly. At Christmas they would come in and have a piece of cake and a drink; but if anyone came in the kettle was always on to make drinks, and if you went in anyone else's they did the same.

Mrs Adderley returned to her old street because she missed her mother and the old neighbours:

> I was used to going out and seeing everybody and shouting 'Hello' and everybody saying 'Hello' to me. It didn't matter how many times you saw them [that is, the people in the town to which she temporarily moved] they wouldn't speak to you; they just used to treat you like a foreigner.

However, things were not as they had been when she returned home:

> It had changed, because a lot of the older people had died and the younger ones, they didn't mix the same as the older ones did. It was still friendly, but not like it used to be, you know.

She was asked if the neighbours would still help, and she replied:

> Well, I suppose they would, but not like they did before. They just used to
> come in and take over before, whereas you would have to ask them; before
> you didn't have to ask them.[34]

It appears that people no longer had clear rules about their relationships
with neighbours, or perhaps it is more accurate to say that perceptions of
what was meant by being a 'good neighbour' varied from person to person
and were not always compatible. Klein, writing about newly settled
neighbourhoods, said, 'Because no conventions are generally established,
everyone worries about the proper type and the proper amount of interac-
tion or friendliness between neighbours, of visiting, of borrowing and
lending.'[35]

Although these problems may be more pronounced on a new estate, they
were not confined to them. People in older areas increasingly appear to have
been unsure how to behave towards their neighbours. Those who were most
certain and secure were the older women, but as they died or moved away
so those remaining lost their certainties. Indeed, a recurring theme of this
study has been the decline in confidence about rules of behaviour.

Some women displayed very ambivalent attitudes towards neighbours,
and there was sometimes a clear disparity between what they said and how
they acted. Mrs Adderley's account of declining friendliness and decreasing
levels of help and support in the community is apparently straightforward.
But she had another story to tell which added another dimension. She was
asked why she had decided to go back to work, not long after returning to
Lancaster:

> Well, to be quite honest, it was a neighbour across the road. I had befriended
> her as she was lonely. I said, 'If you get lonely, just come across for a chat.' It
> turned out that she was in nearly as much as I was. I didn't want to offend
> her, so I thought if I could get a little job, just to get out of the way for a
> while. She was coming across as soon as the kiddies went to school at nine
> and she didn't go until they came home in the afternoon.[36]

This anecdote seems to encapsulate some of the problems of being a
neighbour in the late 1950s and throughout the 1960s. The neighbour did
not understand the rules about how long one stayed on a visit, and Mrs
Adderley could find no simple means of telling her neighbour to go home.
She wanted to be friendly, but other considerations proved to be more
pressing in the long run. She became afraid that her life would be taken over
by the neighbour if too close a relationship was established.

There had always been the possibility of neighbours overstaying their welcome, but the likelihood of this occurring was greater in the post-war period. The reasons are not difficult to discern: with the arrival of more labour-saving devices women had less to do in the home than previously, and there were far fewer children to care for. Coinciding with these general trends was the more particular one which affected some families: migration of kin, which left women without their traditional friendship and support systems. Mrs Adderley mentioned that her neighbour was especially lonely because all her relatives were in Canada. Migration had been a feature of life in this area for generations but historically whole families had migrated together. Migration continued after the Second World War, usually to Commonwealth countries or the USA, but now this involved single persons or young couples with or without children, not their extended families.

Mrs Adderley's decision to return to work once her children were at school, a decision taken by many other women, also weakened the neighbourhood's support systems because women at work all day were clearly less involved in their neighbours' lives and less able to offer help and comfort.

Mr Trickett grew up in a terraced house in one of the poorest areas of Barrow. After war service and a spell in the Navy he returned in the 1950s, as an unskilled labourer, to the street in which he had been born. Unlike his parents, he and his wife were able to buy their house, but the area remained a poor one. He spoke strongly and warmly of the friendliness of the street when he was a child:

> We had something that nobody will have today, friendship, comradeship. My mother would say, 'Oh, I don't know, there's no tea. Go and ask Mrs Brown for a spoonful of tea to make a brew. Half a cup of milk.' You never locked your front door; you went in anybody's house.[37]

He remembered women taking large groups of children (their own and those of friends) out for picnics. Children's outgrown clothes were passed on, money was collected for wreaths for the dead, neighbours helped with the funeral teas. Neighbours talked on the doorstep in the evening and popped in and out of each other's houses with all the latest street gossip, but observed the niceties by always addressing each other as Mrs—, first names never being used.

But Mr Trickett was aware of another element in the relationships between neighbours, which he feared: he did not like the gossiping that went on. As has been seen, this had a positive function of relaying news about those in need and of maintaining certain standards of behaviour.

However, Mr Trickett was much more aware of the negative aspect of gossip; he found it intrusive and often pernicious:

> In summer they all stood on the doorstep, some would bring their chairs out, and they were pulling Mrs Jones down the road to bloody pieces. I remember that, yes. The coalman, if he dumped three bags of coal at that house, well obviously she hadn't the money to pay for that, she was giving him her body, to be honest. Oh, it went on in those days, you know.[38]

From his evidence it would appear that Mr Trickett believed in the truth of the gossip even if he disapproved of it. Knowing how many bags of coal were being delivered to a neighbour indicates a level of surveillance probably unknown in modern neighbourhoods. Mr Trickett was therefore both enthusiastic and very critical of the neighbourhood of his childhood. He appeared to be quite unaware of the deep ambivalences in his attitudes, ambivalences which became even more apparent when he discussed the same street in his adult experience.

> This house is ours.
> You feel that an Englishman's home is his castle?
> Oh, without a doubt. I'm particular about who I invite in here. At work fellas would tell you, 'You'll never get into Trickett's place.' This is mine. I haven't got a lot but, by Christ, it's ours. I remember just after the war, and I was working on the Corporation, and we had a woman across the road from us, and she was a nosey bitch. She always wanted to know what was on the table. And she came in every dinner-time, and I said, 'Mam, tell her not to come in between twelve and one.' 'Oh, it's alright.' And I said, 'No, it's not, mam, she's only wanting to come and see what we've got on the table.' Anyhow, my mother wouldn't tell her. So she came in the next day and I said, 'Eh, missus, do you mind leaving this house.' 'What?' 'Do you mind leaving this house while we are having a meal, I think it is very bad manners to come here every dinner-time. If you like I will write it down on a piece of paper and push it through your door.' Oh, she went out of the house in a flipping huff. And my mother went to clout me, and I was twenty-three, twenty-four years old, and she went to clout me because I had insulted her friend.[39]

When Mr Trickett returned to the street in the 1950s, he found few of the old neighbours remained. In view of his attitudes it is interesting to find him complaining about the unfriendliness of the new neighbours!

> They just seemed to want to come home and close the door.
> Did they pop in for a chat?

No, there was none of that like there had been before the war.
Did you pop in and see them?
Well, you never got any encouragement off them.[40]

He felt that young people were too busy earning money, keeping themselves to themselves, and moving on as soon as they could afford to. Mr Trickett resented the fact that, from about the mid-1950s, young couples did not regard his street as a place where they wished to stay; it was simply the bottom rung on the housing ladder. This trend is certainly observable in the housing histories of many of our respondents. Twenty-two young couples among those interviewed bought such a house when first married. Of these five had subsequently moved to 'better' houses before 1970 and another nine moved on after that date. A previously stable population in rented accommodation was replaced by a transient upwardly mobile group of home-owners who were unlikely to create a strong neighbourhood community.

We do not know what social class these new owner-occupiers belonged to, but it is quite possible that they would have been working class. In Barrow there was a long tradition of working-class families buying their own houses. At the beginning of the century the local Trades Council had run a campaign encouraging workers to buy houses, pointing out that repaying a loan was cheaper than paying rent. Our earlier study identified a small group of families, where the father was an unskilled labourer, who had purchased houses – almost always on the initiative of the wife. In the post-war period this tradition continued and, as has been seen in chapter 2, there was a considerable increase in the number of working-class house-owners. Furthermore there was a greatly increased tendency, as they became more prosperous, to move on to larger houses as soon as they could be afforded.

These couples were not only transitory, but very often the wives worked full time in an effort to raise the money for the 'better' house. They tended to have few contacts with the neighbours. Some couples bought houses in areas where they had grown up, but a note of resentment sometimes enters into their comments about their old neighbours. Mrs Hunter was married in 1956 and she and her husband bought a small terraced house in central Preston. She worked full time until the birth of her child in 1964. Being very house-proud, and having no help from her husband, she seemed to be under permanent pressure:

I mean, it was a ritual to scrub my front step every Saturday, and it was very time-consuming, because with being actually on the road with no garden, loads of people that I knew used to come, and most of the time was spent talking. It took about an hour, just to do the front.[41]

Changes in Housework and Increasing Social Isolation

Changing attitudes towards housework and different methods of household management also affected neighbourhood relationships. An increasing number of young wives in the 1950s were rejecting the tradition of donkey-stoning. Mrs Britton was married in 1954:

> Front steps, they were always doing those, they used to whiten them with a donkey-stone. I got married and I said, 'I'm not going to spend my life scrubbing front steps.' It was absolutely ridiculous and I refused to do it. My mother came and did mine. She wouldn't let the neighbours see that I had a front step that hadn't been done. So then I had to do it myself, to stop my mother coming and doing it, and I was very resentful.

She was finally able to stop when her mother died: 'I gave it up then, as there was no threat of her coming round and doing it any more. But I couldn't see her doing it, I had to do it, it was like a moral blackmail.'[42]

Rationally, women's decision to abandon the donkey-stoning ritual was understandable, but there was a social cost. Gradually, then rapidly after the mid-1950s, an opportunity for women to communicate with one another on a regular basis was lost. Other 'sensible' solutions to housekeeping problems also resulted in a weakening of neighbourhood relationships. The arrival of supermarkets in the 1960s was welcomed by most women, their goods were cheaper than those in the corner shop and it made more sense to buy a larger number of items less frequently. Inevitably, the decline of the corner shop resulted, and with it another venue where women could socialize informally was lost.

By the end of the 1960s no alternative meeting places for women had emerged, although the school gate provided a gathering point for young mothers. Women who abandoned old customs such as chatting on the doorstep were unwilling to join organizations. There was the old reluctance to 'put yourself forward' and a fear of 'letting yourself in for things'.[43] Playgroups were becoming well established by the 1970s but only a minority of women were involved. Respondents who increasingly felt lonely were more likely to attempt to solve the problem by going out to work than by joining a neighbourhood group.

Figure 11.3 A woman donkey-stoning her doorstep

A few, like Mrs Owen,[44] were determined to go on living in an area where they believed the old neighbourhood closeness still existed. Others had rather a bleak existence. Mr Kirkby and his wife and young child spent some time in another northern town where Mrs Kirkby seems to have been very lonely in a neighbourhood without any familiar social landmarks:

> Was there anything your wife could join?
>
> Not really, no. We lived on our own. We were not local. We'd no relatives, no babysitters, and we just didn't go out very much.[45]

Figure 11.4   A corner shop in Lancaster in 1965. (It has since been demolished.)
(Photo courtesy of Lancaster City Museum)

The Acquisition of Labour-saving Equipment

The rapid rationalization and mechanization of housework during this period may have had the beneficial effect of liberating women from some time-consuming and physically demanding tasks, but these processes may also have had a detrimental effect on neighbourhood relationships. In some cases they resulted in rivalry and competition. The advent of the washing machine in the majority of homes by 1970 meant, for example, that there was less need for neighbours to take in washing when a woman was sick or newly delivered. In poorer areas there appears to have been no serious rivalry about possessions. Mrs Leighton, growing up in a council house in the 1950s, said:

> We were all in the same boat, we didn't have much money. There wasn't any 'keeping up with the Joneses' in those days, like there is today. Nobody could afford a holiday, nobody could afford luxuries. I never felt envious of anyone, because everybody had the same.[46]

However, the acquisition by some neighbours of modern labour-saving devices clearly influenced other women into buying them, There are no

Figure 11.5   The official opening of Tesco's supermarket in Barrow in the 1960s
(Photo courtesy of *North Western Evening Mail*)

direct references to the purchase of such items to 'keep up with the Joneses', but the fact that so many respondents seemed to acquire vacuum cleaners, fridges and washing machines within such a relatively short period (see chapter 2) suggests that they were to some extent being influenced by the example of neighbours.

In the earlier part of the century, women who could be regarded as the leaders of their community offered advice and services to their neighbours. They shared information about bargains in the shops, recipes, treatments for common ailments, advice on how to deal with officialdom, and many other topics. Their help and advice cost their neighbours nothing but it did much to improve the quality of their lives. There are signs that, by the end of the 1950s, these capable women were leading the way in the acquisition of house-hold equipment, again seeing it as a way of improving the quality of their lives. They may well have helped their neighbours, through their example, to reduce their burden of housework, but not without involving them in considerable expense. Mrs Jenkins had left school at fourteen to become a domestic servant; she was married in 1954, and was ambitious for herself and her children. Five years later she and her husband were able to afford to sell their small terraced house and buy a bigger one:

> I had this washing machine, and they were all a lot older than me and they used to say, 'Oh, we'll not have a washing machine.' And they gradually got one, because my washing was so lovely and clean that it persuaded them. But I would say that I was very . . . I had read a lot. I had three children and I didn't need help from anybody really.[47]

Neighbourhood Hostility

Quarrelling in neighbourhoods was hardly new; throughout the century neighbours had had disputes, very frequently about children and their real or imagined bad behaviour. Such quarrels were mentioned by almost all respondents, but they invariably added that they were not long-lasting. What is observable in this later period is real dislike and even animosity between neighbours; it was not widespread, but where it existed neighbours were perceived as hostile and threatening to one's own family's well-being. Differing standards of behaviour were often commented upon; no longer were respondents and their neighbours perceived as being 'all in the same boat'. Some neighbourhoods were judged by their residents to have deteriorated. Some of the strongest complaints relate to one council estate which had been built to house those from slum dwellings as a result of the 1930 Greenwood Act. This estate had always housed the roughest families, those at the bottom of the social scale. The behaviour of the residents appears to have deteriorated in the 1960s.

No respondent gave the arrival of an immigrant population as an explanation for this trend. Indeed, only Preston had a sizeable ethnic minority, who tended to settle initially in the areas of old terraced houses. The most usual complaints about worsening standards of neighbourhood behaviour referred to council estates where immigrants were not represented.

One cause of increasing disorder was the unchecked behaviour of children and adolescents. As has already been seen, police and neighbours adopted an increasingly 'hands off' attitude to young people.[48] Neighbours were less sure about what standards to enforce and also how the young miscreants and their parents might respond. An increasing number of the latter were much more likely to defend their children against the verbal and physical remonstrations of neighbours than had previously been the case.

Not all the difficulties related to the younger generation; neighbours of

all ages might be seen as threatening. To the outsider some problems appear
to have been serious, other rather trivial. It is possible that in earlier times
these situations may have been resolved by discussion, through a cathartic
row or, more exceptionally, a rapid move of house. It is also possible that
there had previously been a higher level of toleration of some behaviour. But
clearly some respondents could not find a *modus vivendi* with their neighbours, and the resulting tensions led to a deteriorating quality of life.

Mrs Turnbull grew up on a council estate and spoke warmly of her neighbours. She continued to live on various estates after her marriage and all
went well until she moved, about 1960. Her house had an old person's
bungalow attched to it, and Mrs Turnbull found her elderly neighbours
very difficult:

> They made my life hell. She was a funny woman. The little lads used to play
> out, and they had guns, cowboys and that. And she was always at them, yet
> they were always in their own garden, wouldn't go in her garden, you know.
> She was a real pain.

The old neighbour used to rake out her fire at nights; Mrs Turnbull's
husband used to work nights and the noise of the raking frightened her
when she was on her own:

> I used to get into such a state I used to take the children into bed with me. I
> made him put locks on all the doors, I was that frightened. He [the
> neighbour's husband] used to walk up and down outside our house all night.
> I was in a terrible state. I was under a psychiatrist. You see, a lot of people
> don't let you live.[49]

The Decline of the Neighbourhood?

Mr Grimshaw was born on an inter-war estate in Preston which he left on
his marriage in 1969. On return visits to his parents he was aware of a rapid
deterioration in the following four years, before they too moved away:

> It was a different neighbourhood. I think my mother and dad were glad to
> move when they did. Everybody, up to a certain time, looked after their
> gardens really well, but that just went; they were just overgrown. And they
> were rougher, people were a lot rougher. How should I say? The people
> living there were more of a problem. They were shoving people in on the
> estate who had problems; they shoved all the problem people on to the one
> estate and it so happened to be ours.[50]

It should be noted that another respondent in Preston had similar perceptions – but about a completely different estate, one built after the Second World War. It is not possible to say, without detailed examination of council records, whether 'problem' families *were* being moved on to these estates, or whether standards of behaviour were simply declining.

Mr Stephenson moved on to a new council estate from a very overcrowded terraced house in 1960. This house had been in a very poor working-class area of Preston, but in a street which had been very clean and tidy:

> On a council estate they seem to have a system where you get so many good people and you get so many problem families. And the council, in its judgement, put a bad tenant amongst so many good ones, expecting that one to be changed. But in my view it doesn't work. If anything it goes the other way, it possibly turns another one bad.
>
> When you first moved up there how would you describe a bad tenant?
>
> Well, somebody that was inclined to be dirty, the windows were dirty, the house was unkempt. If something dropped out of a dustbin, it would stay there, they just wouldn't move it. And if there were children they would be out late at night.

Mr Stephenson found that the estate children vandalized his garden, stealing fruit and vegetables, and they threw mud at his house.[51] The accounts of Mr Grimshaw and Mr Stephenson are hardly the stuff of headlines, but these apparently small incidents were enough to make them feel uneasy and suspicious and 'not at home' with their neighbours.

Occasionally the behaviour of neighbours caused more than dismay and discomfort. In the early 1960s Mr Whiteside's parents left a council estate where they had been happy to move to another one where close relatives lived. But on this estate they witnessed a tide of roughness and disorder which threatened to carry them away:

> It sort of crept in, it crept in from the other end of the street and it swamped them, it swamped all the nice people on there. It was just the pressure of people who were capable of robbing them. I mean, they got to where they put locks on all the doors; they were reluctant to leave the place, because if 'they' knew there was nobody in, they would be in there. They threw rubbish in the garden, old prams and that. And it wouldn't matter whose garden it was. As they were getting older they couldn't stand it.[52]

The seeds of the disasters which overtook some council estates in the two decades after 1970 appear to have been sown in the 1960s. One of the saddest comments came from Mrs Boyle who had lived on council estates since being re-housed in the early 1960s, at which time her neighbours and her neighbourhood had been very important to her. She said, 'People are too frightened now to bother with one another. All they want to do is get in their house and lock the door.' [53]

It was not only estate dwellers who felt threatened by their neighbours, although complaints about bad behaviour were rare in other areas. Mrs Burrell was married in 1955 and a year later bought a semi-detached house in Barrow. Her husband was away most of the time in the Merchant Navy:

> It was a nice house, the only thing was it was an end house and it was by some old terraced houses and there was quite a lot of rough people living in the terraced houses. And they thought I was a snob because I didn't speak to them very much. And of course I was living on my own. I had quite a bit of trouble with the local louts, throwing things. They filled beer bottles with water and threw them at the gable ends of the house, and pushed things through the letter box. We found out that the previous owners had gone because they had had so much trouble with the people across the way.[54]

No doubt, had the bottle-throwers themselves been interviewed, a different version of the events might have emerged.

Running through some of the evidence is a theme of what appeared to the respondents to be increasing class conflict and antagonism within the working class itself. This does not, of course, account for the collapse of neighbourliness but it is part of the explanation. Mrs Burrell recognized that her neighbours may have thought that she was a snob (although this seemed to be very far from the truth). Mr Trickett, a home owner, deeply resented people from the same background as himself 'getting on' socially and then 'looking down' on him. He once told a foreman who he felt was patronizing him and who had sat next to him at school:

> 'That's the trouble with a lot of you buggers today, you get on and you forget your roots.' The English working man is the biggest bloody snob under the sun. Your own working class – they stink. They get on; they start working; he's working; she's working. Couldn't care less about anyone else, just their own selves. They're snobs, the working class. They are their own worst enemies.
> Do you feel that you were working class when you were a lad?
> Working class? I've been working class all my bloody life.[55]

Mr Hinchcliffe, a plumber, was more temperate in his language, and perhaps more thoughtful; he repeatedly offered 'theoretical' explanations for changes in social life. He was also twenty-five years younger than Mr Trickett, and a Socialist, as opposed to a Conservative supporter. He said, 'It's hard for me to say, being on the hard Left. Once working-class people tend to get something – even if it's a little garden – people tend to divide socially.'[56] There were frequent reminders of a brief comment made by an elderly respondent in the early 1970s about life in his neighbourhood between the wars: 'Help; there was a lot of it, but it was gradually dying out. It somehow died away as you got richer.'[57]

Some people were so involved in their own individual lives (or 'doing their own thing', as respondents so often described it) that neighbours were seen only as obstacles in the way of the attainment of their own satisfactions and gratifications. Mrs Hutton described her neighbours in the early 1970s: 'The two either side of me, a pain in the arse. I'm talking about the ten years when my children were teenagers.' The neighbours might possibly have had the same opinion of the Hutton household as she went on to recall that 'there were motor-bikes and cars and the general rowdiness of teenagers – playing loud music and stuff like that'.[58]

Conclusion

It would be misleading to conclude on such a negative note, for neighbour-liness was still a recognizable feature of community life in 1970. Mrs Hocking said:

> On one side I used to take in her breakfast every morning and see to her up and dressed. Then on the other side I'd take her her meal in when I used to make my meal; give her a bit of this and a bit of that. This went on for about ten years, but the two were very good neighbours. They were good to me when they were able. So I was able to return the compliment when they weren't able.[59]

Mr Whiteside's relations, whose bad experiences living on a coucil estate have been recorded above, subsequently moved to another estate where they settled happily. He himself had lived, since his marriage in 1960, in the same council flat where he and his wife enjoyed friendly and close relations with their neighbours. For tenants such as these the standard of their neighbours' behaviour was more important than the physical environment of the estate.

Mr Kennedy lived in a very run-down part of Preston from 1966 to 1971:

> We had some terrific neighbours, some of the finest I've ever had. When the
> missus was in hospital, the hardest job was who was going to look after the
> children. Somebody would look after them one night, when I went to see her,
> and the following night, if I didn't give them to them, they were sulking
> because they thought that they had done something wrong. But there were
> that many that wanted to look after the younger end. They were great
> neighbours. The house itself – horrible.[60]

With considerable effort Mr Kennedy and his wife saved up, as did so many
other couples, to buy a better house, into which they moved in 1971.

In the final analysis the aspiration towards better accommodation for themselves and their families was stronger than their attachment to a friendly and
supportive neighbourhood. It is, however, doubtful that they were consciously making this choice at the time, only retrospectively were they able
to attempt to balance the gains and losses consequent upon the move.

Mr Whiteside, again, recalled his own childhood living in a little courtyard in central Lancaster, near the market, where his father worked on a fish
stall. The family were resettled in the early 1950s when their house was
demolished:

> My parents were delighted. I think they had waited seventeen years for a
> council house, so they enjoyed moving, like. It was different; a different sort
> of house.
>   Did you think it was better?
>   I did at the time. I thought it was better myself. My thoughts are a little
> bit different now; but it was certainly better.
>   What did you miss about the old house?
>   Well, we were surrounded with our own people. My nana used to live next
> door to us; my nana and my grandad. My great-uncle lived with them. They
> had my dad's brother and wife, and my cousin lived in there too.

Mr Whiteside then listed all the families living in the courtyard, with a few
biographical details, and concluded by saying, 'You was just like a family,
you know, just an extension of cousins, without having the blood tie.'[61]

Mogey concluded his study of the 'traditional' area of St Ebbs, in central
Oxford, and of Barton, an Oxford council estate built just before and after
the Second World War, with this optimistic view:

> The absence of any commonly accepted standards of belief and action distin-
> guishes Barton from the community of St Ebbs. Barton is, in fact, not a
> localised society nor do its inhabitants feel loyal to an isolating set of social

customs. They have lost their ties to a neighbourhood and gained, in return, citizenship in the wider and freer atmosphere of the varied associational life of a city.[62]

This could not be used as a concluding paragraph of a study of neighbourhoods in this area of Lancashire. Those who moved on to new estates, whether privately or publicly owned, were all pleased with the improved quality of accommodation; no one looked back with nostalgia to the houses without bathrooms or other modern facilities. However, few believed that, by moving, they had improved the social climate within which they lived. None appear to have been aware of Mogey's 'wider and freer atmosphere' and the 'varied associational life of the city'. With hindsight, they were far more aware of the 'life we have lost'.

12
Conclusion

Change and Continuity

Historians are concerned with both change and continuity. This study of working-class women and their families has shown, not surprisingly, that both elements were manifest in their lives during the period 1940–70. It was still possible in 1970 to describe a typical family as one with both parents living at home, father being the chief wage-earner and mother being responsible for the housework and childrearing. Adult children continued to live at home until they were married. Close ties were maintained with the extended family, although, as had always been the case, not with all members of it. Within some neighbourhoods, the immediate community setting for the family, there were also continuities. In the poorest neighbourhoods it was possible to find many examples of the old working-class mores being observed. On the positive side there was solidarity, support, sociability and security. Rather more negatively, there was interference, inquisitiveness, intolerance and an indifference to new ideas.

Alongside these elements of continuity, the oral evidence also suggests that notable changes were taking place during this period. This partly resulted from material and physical factors, such as greatly increased prosperity, new housing and improved health care. Other developments stemmed from evolving social and moral attitudes which emphasized the importance of individual rights and self-fulfilment. These wide-ranging economic and social changes had a significant effect on women, their families and the communities in which they lived.

Local communities lost much of their cohesion, mainly because of changing attitudes towards neighbours. Physical and psychological closeness with neighbours was replaced by distancing and, in a few cases, outright hostility. Increased levels of home ownership, and the growing importance of the home and its contents, led both to an increase in time spent within the house rather than out in the neighbourhood and also to greater social and physical mobility in working-class areas. Neighbourhoods which had had relatively stable communities now found that they had a more transient population. Changes in methods of housework, different shopping habits, and the growing isolation of some children from their neighbourhood because of pressures of homework and fear of increased road traffic, all contributed to changing neighbourhood relationships.

Women at Home

There were marked inter-generational differences between the women in this study and those described in *A Woman's Place*. Older women, with the exception of textile workers, had been firmly rooted in the home. There the majority had enjoyed a fair degree of power, controlling the family budget, making many major decisions about the family and its members and determining the family's moral tone. They were esteemed for their managerial skills and their ability to cope with many difficulties, not least those caused by poverty. Some of the older women in the present study were also the dominant figures in the home and family; but women's power, position and status were clearly changing.

Women were increasingly freed from the drudgery of such household tasks as scrubbing floors and coping with huge loads of washing with only primitive equipment. On the other hand, they were trapped into doing more and more housework to achieve ever-increasing standards of household maintainance and cleanliness. Changes in household routines all too often cut them off from their neighbours. They also had a growing number of possessions to care for and frequently a larger house than their parents' to look after; they also believed it right to spend more time with their children. Women welcomed and enjoyed their improved housing conditions but all too often realized that they had lost the closeness of the old neighbourhoods.

Within the home, women's traditional skills of managing, making something out of nothing and budgeting all gradually became less valued, as a consequence of the ending of war-time rationing, the availability of more and more consumer goods, and above all the increased ability of families to afford such items. The pressures to earn more, spend more and consume more were becoming irresistible. In real terms women had more money to spend than had their mothers or grandmothers, and this development may be seen as empowering. However, the percentage of the family budget over which they maintained control decreased. Some couples, influenced by ideas of companionate marriage, decided to share the management of the family finances. In other marriages husbands were determined to have more control of their wages than had their fathers. Wages were increasingly seen as the property of those who earned them and less frequently as belonging to the whole family.

Some women quite consciously rejected the role models presented to them by their mothers and grandmothers. They were critical of the older women in their families whom they regarded as bossy, dictatorial, unfair to men and unfeminine. Women such as these were able to live out the domestic ideology so beloved by the Victorian middle classes, an ideology long aspired to by some sections of the working class but one which had not been financially attainable in the earlier years of the century.

These changes had an effect on women's relationships with their husbands. The clear delineation of gender roles which had been observable earlier in the century was becoming increasingly blurred. Husbands became more involved in matters of family finance, they shared some of the house-work, at least in the early days of marriage, and they were more likely to take some part in looking after their children than had their predecessors. However, the fundamental separation of roles in marriage remained. Women continued to be chiefly responsible for housework, childcare and childrearing while their husbands continued to be the major wage-earners. As some women increased the amount of paid work they undertook outside the home, there was little evidence of a corresponding increase in the amount of work their menfolk did around the house.

After the arrival of children, husbands and wives tended to lead separate social lives. Some families continued to have gendered living spaces; only in retirement did some couples find real companionship. In view of women's loss of power in the home, their lack of equality with men and the separate social lives of husbands and wives, it is indeed difficult to discern many marriages which could be described as companionate, if the criteria of sharing, companionship and equality are adopted.

Women Outside the Home

An increasing number of women turned away from a life centred almost entirely in the home and entered the world of wage-earning work. Changing social attitudes which now approved of women working outside the home, the demands of the labour market and women's own preferences combined to produce this trend; moreover, many found personal satisfaction and fulfilment in the world of work. Working-class women had always earned money: it was estimated that between 40 and 50 per cent of women in the earlier study earned some money at some point in their married life. (Much of this was not recorded in official statistics.) The great difference was that, earlier in the century, most married women (with the exception of textile workers) who earned money, did so in their own or someone else's home.

In the post-war world the increasing number of women who worked outside the home were not able to replace the power and status they had lost in the home with equivalent power and status in the workplace. Their work was low-paid, mostly unskilled, and they did not aspire to promotion or positions of responsibility. While it was true that women did not enjoy the protection of equal pay legislation in this period and employers had clear assumptions about the gendered nature of women's work, it was also true that women preferred to have casual, part-time work because that enabled them to put the needs of their children first. Working women's perceptions were that whereas it was acceptable – indeed desirable – to earn money on their own account, it was not 'right' to have a job which demanded long hours of work and the taking of responsibilities which would leave them too tired, both physically and emotionally, to care 'properly' for their families. Besides, who was to look after the children? There was inadequate childcare provision; but even had it been better, it is not certain that many women would have used it. It was assumed that children should be cared for within the family. No respondent complained about her low wages – particularly low when compared to those of her husband. Women's wages were regarded as being for 'extras' while men's wages were for essentials. Earlier in the century women earned only small amounts, but very often this money was significant in that it raised the family above the poverty line. Women's wage-earning work in the post-war world tended to be marginalized. They had entered the world of men's work but they were not equal in it.

Parents and Children

Relationships changed between parents and children. Earlier in the century, parents had perceived their role as limited to trying to ensure, to the best of their ability, the physical well-being of their children and their correct behaviour. There was usually some distance between parents and children:

they rarely played together and parents' word was law. In the post-war world families became much more child-centred; parents were on the whole closer to their children, less authoritarian than their own parents and less feared; with some exceptions, children were punished less severely. Individual children probably received more parental attention than had any previous generation; parents were much more likely to spend leisure time with them. Children and young people were required to do less work around the house.

Consumerism affected relationships between parents and children; generally higher standards of living meant that children could be indulged materially to an extent hitherto unknown in working-class families; they had more toys than ever before, with the result that some became 'spoilt' and developed unrealistic expectations about material possessions. Older children, after the war, were almost always allowed to keep their part-time earnings while they were at school, and as young wage-earners they retained a larger part of their money than had previous generations. One result of this was that youngsters failed to acquire the degree of self-respect which had been enjoyed by their predecessors, who spoke proudly of the contribution they had been able to make to the family, either in work or in money; a contribution which they and their parents saw as being invaluable. Now married women replaced children as the earners of extra family income.

An increasing number of parents – especially mothers – were conscious of the need to further their children's development in as many ways as possible. Far more children than formerly were helped and encouraged with their education. All children had an extra year of schooling following the 1944 Education Act, and an ever-increasing number stayed at school beyond the age of fifteen and went on to higher education. These wholly desirable developments for some individuals had hidden costs for others. In earlier times an individual's failure to profit from secondary and higher education was largely attributable to financial hardships. As prosperity increased there was a tendency to regard those who did not go to grammar school and then on to higher education as failures, rather than victims of poverty. Academically able children from the working class were increasingly isolated, not only from their communities, but also from their families. As has been seen, those going to colleges and universities were the least likely to return home to live and work as young adults.

Future historians may well be tempted to look back to this period as the 'golden age' of the nuclear family, with its small number of children and its two married parents. Divorce, separation and illegitimacy affected only a very small percentage of the respondents before 1970.[1] There have, of course, been dramatic changes in the family since that date, both nationally and in the experience of our respondents. For example, in the 1970s only 7 per cent of couples cohabited before marriage; by 1990 it was estimated that 50 per cent did so. Two out of five cohabiting couples had children in that year, which is one of the main reasons for 25 per cent of children being born outside marriage.[2] It may be too soon to find explanations for these changes which have affected many counties in Western Europe; it is perhaps not too soon to express doubts about the validity of the period 1940–70 as a golden age for the family.

Working Class or Working Classes?

In the earlier part of the century it was easier to speak of 'the working class', although of course it was never totally homogeneous. There were differences in status and income between the skilled and the unskilled; there were differences in behaviour between the majority who were respectable and the minority who were rough. All political persuasions could be found within their ranks. But all the different groups had more in common to unite them than differences to divide them, and it is possible both to discern and to describe a working-class culture. In the post-war world it became increasingly difficult to define 'the working class'. There was an increasing differentiation between groups in attitudes towards such matters as education and home ownership. There are some examples of class hostility manifesting itself within the working class. Few respondents agreed on what was meant by being 'working-class'; perhaps this was not surprising, given the movement of so many children of working-class parents out of the working class altogether via the educational ladder, especially after 1970. Greatly increased social mobility was not conductive to class solidarity.

Some Ambiguities of 'Progress'

The empirical evidence raises some interesting questions about the nature of 'progress' in society. All the respondents, with the possible exception of Mr and Mrs Boyle, were materially better off than their parents; they lived in much better housing conditions, they had more income in real terms and they were able to purchase a wider range of consumer goods. They benefited from the welfare state and most especially from the National Health Service. This was of particular value to women and children, who were less likely than men to have had health insurance before the war. They also benefited from huge advances in medical treatment. This important development has hardly been referred to in the book as it would require more space than is available. (It is hoped that this will be the subject of a later study by Dr Beier.) The consequent improvement in the quality of life is clearly evident from both the oral evidence and that of the official records. This can only be counted as a very definite gain.

However, many of the changes in the lives of women and their families are full of paradox and ambiguities. These changes represent both progress and decline. There were gains and losses for almost all women and children. Even the improvements in health care had implications for women's power: as the influence of professional health workers increased, so the confidence of women to decide how best to care for and treat their own children declined.

Working-class people were moving from a communally based life to one which was centred more on the home and the nuclear family. Privacy and individualism were increasingly prized and sought. Few respondents commented upon the cost of the family becoming more private and of the individual acquiring more rights. Neighbourhoods in general were weaker social units than earlier in the century but individuals were still anchored in their extended families.

It was still possible to conclude that families, both nuclear and extended, at the end of the period were still able to take care of their members and socialize their children. However, while the state continued to provide so much welfare assistance, the informal social framework within which each family operated carried less authority and became less supportive. Those who asked in the late 1980s, 'What went wrong?', were the people who felt most strongly the loss of community and collective values.

As individual rights became more important many families found it increasingly difficult to balance the demands of their individual members. This problem was rarely referred to directly in the interviews, but it is a thread running through many of them. Who, for example, was entitled to spend wages? The individual who earned them, or the woman on behalf of the family as a whole? It can be argued that women, who were at the centre of the family, played a crucial role in making many of the decisions about family matters. It is an irony that, in a time when there was a growing interest in individual rights, women continued to place others' interests before their own, whether it was those of their husbands, their parents or their children. The interesting exception to this generalization was a group of grandmothers for whom personal interests and pleasures were more important than family obligations.

In a period when the taxation system, the Health Service, the welfare state, the unions and many other institutions had concentrated on diminishing the inequalities between social classes, little was consciously done to attack the inequalities between genders. The women in this study were apparently not conscious of gender inequality. They were not interested in the women's movement which was becoming more vocal and active towards the end of this period, but which still seemed to be confined to intellectual circles. Very few respondents, by 1970, had asserted their own rights and had developed a career or taken and kept a job with prospects of advancement, responsibility and promotion. Indeed, the great majority, like so many other working-class women, expressed no wish to do so.[3] Although a woman's place was no longer seen to be exclusively in the home, home and family nevertheless remained the dominant concerns in women's lives.

About the Respondents

Further Notes on the Interview Group

Some information about the people interviewed for this study appears in chapter 1. People willing to be interviewed were found in a variety of ways. Some came in response to an article in the local press; some employers and trade unions were contacted, as were organizers of schemes for unemployed people and for teaching literacy to adults. Personal recommendations, especially those made by other respondents, were followed up.

Eleven of the respondents were children of people interviewed in earlier studies; these are marked thus* in the biographical notes below.

Twenty couples were interviewed; only in the case of two couples was there felt to be a problem in interviewing both husband and wife together. In both cases the interviewer had been told by other relatives that there had been incidents of wife abuse. However, neither couple, who refused to be interviewed separately – mentioned this problem – understandably. The great majority of couples chose to be interviewed as individuals and their spouses' evidence was not referred to by the interviewer. A small group of couples chose to sit in on each others' interviews but, as far as we could tell, this did not apparently influence the respondents' evidence.

Six respondents were single; at the time of interview eight were widows or widowers and four were divorced. However, as will be seen from the section on marriage breakdown in chapter 6, a larger number than this had been divorced but had subsequently remarried before the late 1980s.

The tapes of the interviews were transcribed and indexed. They are available for use by students and researchers in the Centre for North West Regional Studies and the Library of Lancaster University.

Biographical Notes of Respondents Quoted in the Book

When interviewed each respondent was asked if he or she wanted to remain anonymous; most wished to do so. Some wanted their name to be used and therefore their names were placed on their transcripts. However, it was decided for various reasons that, for the purposes of this book, everyone should be given a pseudonym. The only exception to this is Mrs X, who expressed unease about the accuracy of some of our transcriptions. We were satisfied that they were accurate, but to safeguard Mrs X her transcripts are not on public access; there are no details about her in these biographical notes and the extracts we use in the text are edited to make any recognition of her identity impossible. We remain convinced that her evidence was valuable.

The biographical details below relate only to the respondents quoted in the text. They also, in general, relate only to their lives up to 1970.

In each entry details of a respondent's parents and family are in italics, preceding the full stop; the respondent's own details follow the full stop. The complexities of women's employment patterns often cannot be conveyed in such a brief note; individual histories appear in the main text.

The interviews carried out by Lucinda McCray Beier are marked L. B.; and those conducted by Elizabeth Roberts, E. R.

Barrow

Mrs B. 2. B. b. 1931. *Father a welder; mother no paid work after marriage; two children.* A shop assistant; after marriage, part-time shop assistant and later part-time secretary; husband a fitter; three children. (L. B.)

Mrs B. 3. B. b. 1928. *Father a plater in the shipyard but frequently unemployed, killed in works accident 1935; mother a teacher before marriage, had a lodger when widowed and taught during the war; one child.* A teacher before and after marriage; husband a teacher; three children. (L. B.)

Mr B. 4. B. b. 1920. *Father a fitter, away working for long periods; mother a munitions worker in the First World War, no paid occupation after marriage; seven children.* A fitter; wife a munitions worker in the Second World War; three children. (L. B.)

Mrs J. 1. B. b. 1932. *Father a railway labourer; mother helped at home before marriage, after marriage a cleaner, laundry worker and bus conductress; two children.* A domestic servant, shop assistant and bookkeeper; after marriage a clerk; husband a joiner; three children. (E. R.)

Mrs L. 3. B. b. 1920. *Father unemployed for long periods in the inter-war period, then a storeman; mother* domestic work before and after marriage; one child.* A domestic servant, shop assistant, munitions worker in the Second World War, shop work; continued work after marriage until birth of child; husband a painter and decorator; one child. (E. R.)

Mrs L. 5. B. b. 1943. *Father a draughtsman; mother a shop assistant before marriage; no paid work after marriage; three children.* A teacher before and after marriage, first husband a chemist, died four years after marriage; one child. Later married to Mr L. 5. B. (L. B.)

Mr L. 5. B. b. 1950. *Father a blast-furnaceman; mother a laundry worker, seamstress after marriage; two children.* A draughtsman, merchant seaman. Married to Mrs L. 5. B. (L. B.)

Mrs M. 11. B. b. 1914. *Father killed in the First World War; mother a confectioner before marriage, a Blackpool landlady after marriage; one child.* A clerk before and after marriage; a market trader; husband a plasterer, a sailor and a clerk of works; two children. (E. R.)

Mr M. 12. B.* b. 1933. *Father* a joiner; mother* a professional musician before and after marriage; one child.* Worked in an accounts office; wife (Mrs M. 12. B.) an accounting machine operator; two children. (E. R.)

Mrs M. 12. B.* b. 1936. *Father a shunter; mother* a tailoress before marriage and some outwork after marriage; four children.* An accounting machine operator; husband (Mr M. 12. B.) in an accounts office; two children. (E. R.)

Mrs O. 1. B.* b. 1916. *Father died 1921; step-father a crane driver; mother* a cook before marriage, occasional part-time work as cook after marriage, domestic work after 1945; six children (only three survived childhood).* A shop assistant, no paid work after marriage, husband a driller's burner; one child. (E. R.)

Mr P. 5. B. b. 1950. *Father a fitter; mother an office worker before and eventually after marriage; two children.* A fitter; married after 1970 to Mrs P. 5. B. (L. B.)

Mrs P. 5. B. b. 1950. *Father a borer; mother worked part-time in shop; three children.* Mrs P. in higher education in 1970; (later married to Mr P. 5. B. and had five children). (L. B.)

Mrs P. 6. B. b. 1921. *Father a post office worker; mother worked in a pub before marriage, when widowed ran a boarding house; two children.* A shop assistant, at times after marriage a shop assistant, publican; married three times, (1) a seaman/shipyard worker, (2) a rugby player, (3) a retired welder; four children. (L. B.)

Mrs R. 4. B.* b. 1936. *Father a draughtsman, later a manager; mother* a secretary before marriage, no paid work after; one child.* A teacher before and after marriage, husband a teacher; two children. (E. R. and L. B.)

Mrs S. 3. B. b. 1927. *Father an electrician's mate; mother a shop assistant before marriage, no paid work after; three children.* A shop assistant, clerk (until birth of first child); husband a packer; two children. (E. R.)

Mr T. 4. B. b. 1949. *Father a butcher, storeman; mother after marriage helped in shop, trained as a nurse; one child.* Mr T. in higher education in 1970. Later married Mrs T. 4. B. (E. R.)

Mrs T. 4. B. b. 1948. *Father a shipwright; mother, before and after marriage, a shop assistant, two children.* Mrs T. in higher education in 1970. Later married Mr T. 4. B. (E. R.)

Mr T. 5. B. b. 1923. *Father a street vendor, left the family 1930; mother a munitions worker before marriage; took in washing after husband left, four children.* A sailor in Royal and Merchant Navies; shipwright's mate; wife's work before marriage not given, no paid work after marriage; no children. (E. R.)

Mr W. 4. B. b. 1923. *Father a tackler in cotton mill; mother's work not given, one child.* An engineer; wife a clerk before and after marriage until birth of first child; three children. (E. R.)

Mrs W. 5. B. b. 1933. *Father a fitter; mother a factory worker before marriage, no paid work after; two children.* A clerk before marriage; no paid work after; husband a clerk; two children. (E. R.)

Mrs W. 6. B. b. 1936. *Father an assistant in a grocer's shop; mother domestic work before marriage, no paid work after; two children.* A typist before and after marriage until birth of first child; husband a gardener, meter collector; two children. (E. R.)

Mr W. 7. B. b. 1945. *Father a machinist; mother a machinist before marriage, a midwife after; two children.* A fitter, a policeman; wife a nurse, no paid work after children were born; two children. (L. B.)

Lancaster

Mrs A. 3. L. b. 1944. *Father a farm worker, shop keeper; mother a mill worker before marriage, helped on farm and in shop after marriage; three children.* A nursery nurse before marriage; telephonist after; husband an engineer; two children. (L. B.)

Mr A. 4. L. b. 1926. *Father a labourer; mother an usherette before marriage, munitions worker in Second World War, sewing at home; eight children.* A farm worker, war service, factory work, a 'rep', publican; wife (Mrs A. 4. L.) a clerk before marriage, shop assistant, later worked in pub; three children. (L. B.)

Mrs A. 4. L. b. 1932. *Father a farm worker; mother a mill worker before marriage, no paid work after; two children.* A shop assistant, clerk; after marriage (to Mr A. 4. L.) shop assistant, pub landlady; three children. (L. B.)

Mrs B. 4. L. b. 1936. *Father a fitter, helped in family pub; mother a secretary before marriage, later helped in family-run pub; one child.* No job before marriage; later part-time garage job; husband a labourer; one child. (L. B.)

Mrs C. 7. L.* b. 1926. *Father a labourer; mother* a weaver before and after marriage; five children.* Clerk before and after marriage until birth of first child; husband a policeman; three children. (E. R.)

Mrs C. 8. L. b. 1942. Mrs C's early life was spent out of the area and most of it was not recorded. *Mother was a mill worker before and after marriage.* A mill worker before and after marriage, part-time cleaning; husband a mechanic; two children. (E. R.)

Mrs F. 1. L. b. 1921. *Father a railway worker; mother in domestic service before marriage, no paid work after; four children.* A baker, after marriage a munitions worker, part-time domestic work; husband a butcher; six children. (L. B.)

Mr F. 2. L. b. 1946. *Father a butcher; mother in domestic work; six children.* A mechanic, wife had occasional part-time work; three children. (L. B.)

Mr G. 3. L. b. 1937. *Father a labourer; mother a domestic servant before marriage, later did occasional cleaning and took in lodgers; five children.* A storekeeper; wife a shop assistant before marriage; two children. (E. R.)

Mrs H. 5. L. b. 1931. *Father a bus conductor, later shop work; mother a shop assistant before marriage, part-time war work as clerk, later hospital work; seven children.* Worked in an office very briefly and then factory work before and after marriage until birth of first child; husband a painter and decorator; three children. (L. B.)

Mrs H. 6. L. b. 1933. *Father a tailor, war service, did not return to family to live afterwards; mother had no paid work before marriage, a proof-reader after husband left; two children.* A key-punch operator, telephonist, no paid work after marriage; husband an electrician, a 'rep'; three children. (L. B.)

Mr H. 7. L. b. 1947. *Father and mother divorced when he was a small child, mother married three times; mother a mill worker before marriage, a cleaner after; one child.* A plumber. (L. B.)

Mr I. 2. L. b. 1930. *Father a bookmaker, café proprietor; mother a teacher before marriage, no paid work after; seven children.* An electrician; wife before and after marriage a shorthand typist; one child. (L. B.)

Mrs L. 2. L. b. 1941. *Father a dental technician; mother a shop assistant, returned to work when children at primary school; three children.* Office work before and after marriage; husband an electrician; two children. (L. B.)

Mrs L. 3. L. b. 1947. *Father unknown; mother a mill worker; three children.* Factory and mill worker before and after marriage; husband an electrician; two children. (L. B.)

Mr M. 10. L. b. 1948. *Father a labourer; mother a mill worker before marriage, part-time cleaning when youngest child at school; eight children.* Office work, shop work, nursing; married, wife office work before and after marriage; two children. (L. B.)

Mr N. 2. L. b. 1931. *Father a labourer (died 1943); mother did munitions work in the Second World War; two children.* A joiner, labourer, plasterer, policeman, printer; wife worked in fish and chip shop before and after marriage; four children. (L. B.)

Mr N. 3. L. b. 1921. *Father a window cleaner; mother a mill worker before marriage, helped in café after; six children.* A labourer before and after war service; wife (Mrs N. 3. L.) in mill work and domestic work before marriage; four children. (L. B.)

Mrs N. 3. L. b. 1919. *Father a labourer; mother a mill worker before marriage, some taking in washing after; seven children.* A mill worker, factory work, cook; husband (Mr N. 3. L.) war service, labourer; four children. (L. B.)

Mrs P. 3. L. b. 1948. *Father a labourer; mother in factory work before and after marriage, later cleaning; two children.* Office work before and after marriage; husband a cook; one child. (L. B.)

Mrs S. 6. L. b. 1948. *Father a labourer; mother after marriage evening factory shift, later nursing; nine children.* In school in 1970, later factory work, nursing. (E. R.)

Mr S. 7. L. b. 1932. *Father a newspaper seller (died 1938); mother worked in family business before having children, as a widow she lived on public assistance; five children.* A weaver, window cleaner, a practitioner of a form of alternative medicine; first wife a clerk, second wife a nurse; three children. (L. B.)

Mrs T. 2. L. b. 1932. *Father died before her birth, step-father a labourer; mother a carder before and after marriage; four children.* A weaver, after marriage home help and nursing; husband a soldier, a labourer; four children. (L. B.)

Mrs W. 4. L. b. 1923. *Father a shop keeper; mother in domestic service before marriage, helped in shop after; two children.* A shop assistant, war work, office work; after marriage opened parlour shop; husband a hospital porter, helped in wife's shop; three children. (L. B.)

Mr W. 5. L. b. 1940. *Father worked on a fish stall; mother in domestic service before marriage, casual cleaning jobs after; six children.* A factory worker; wife (Mrs W. 5. L.) part-time cleaning, clerk after marriage; one child. (E. R.)

Mrs W. 5. L. b. 1943. *No details available about her parents.* Mrs W's interview was mostly about her married life (to Mr W. 5. L.). A part-time cleaner and a clerk; husband a factory worker; one child. (E. R.)

Mr W. 6. L. b. 1931. *Father a labourer before and after war service; mother a mill worker before and part-time after marriage; three children.* An electrician; wife (Mrs W. 6. L.) a bookeeper before marriage, afterwards evening domestic work in hospital, shop work; two children. (E. R.)

Mrs W. 6. L. b. 1937. *Father a merchant seaman; mother a shop assistant before marriage, various war work; three children.* Shop work, bookkeeper; after marriage (to Mr W. 6. L.) evening domestic work in hospital, shop work; husband an electrician; two children. (E. R.)

Mrs Y. 1. L. b. 1927. *Father a labourer before and after war service; mother a munitions worker in the Second World War, no paid work after marriage; seven children.* Factory work before and after marriage, part-time cleaner; husband a soldier, a labourer; two children. (L. B.)

Preston

Mrs B. 10. P b. 1947. *Father a lorry driver, office work; mother a bookkeeper before and after marriage; two children.* In higher education in 1970. (E. R.)

Mr B. 11. P. b. 1937. *Father a labourer; mother a cleaner, factory worker; eight children.* A labourer; wife (Mrs B. 11. P.) a mill worker before marriage, afterwards a childminder, taking in sewing; five children. (L. B.)

Mrs B. 11. P. b. 1936. *Father a riveter; mother in factory work before marriage, afterwards a cleaner; six children.* A factory and mill worker; after marriage (to Mr B. 11. P.) childminding and sewing at home; husband a labourer; five children. (L. B.)

Mrs B. 12. P. b. 1929. *Father a docker; mother a weaver and munitions worker in the First World War, no paid work after marriage; eight children.* A carder 1944–69; husband a millworker; one child. (E. R.)

Mr C. 8. P.* b. 1928. *Father* (when interviewed in the earlier study it was about his life earlier in the century when he had kept a little shop in a poorer area of Preston) an insurance agent, war service, clerk; mother a part-time handicraft teacher; three children.* Chemist; wife (Mrs C. 8. P.) a laboratory assistant; three children. (E. R.)

Mrs C. 8. P.* b. 1940. *Father a laboratory assistant but frequently unemployed; mother* a factory worker before marriage, part-time domestic work after; five children.* Laboratory assistant before marriage (to Mr C. 8. P.) and part-time after; three children. (E. R.)

Mrs E. 2. P. b. 1937. *Father a sprayer; mother a weaver until birth of child; one child.* A factory and mill worker before and after marriage; husband a labourer; two children. (L. B.)

Mrs G. 5. P. b. 1958. *Father a labourer; mother a mill worker before marriage, afterwards childminding and sewing at home; five children.* Still in education in 1970. (L. B.)

Mr G. 6. P.* b. 1945. *Father* a cotton worker, labourer; mother a weaver before marriage, part-time domestic work after; five children.* Clerk, printer. (E. R.)

Mr G. 7. P. b. 1941. *Father a cotton worker, labourer; mother a weaver before marriage, part-time domestic work after; five children.* An engineer; wife (Mrs G. 7. P.) a comptometer operator until birth of first child; two children. (E. R.)

Mrs G. 7. P. b. 1944. *Father a shop assistant; mother a shop assistant before and after marriage; two children.* Comptometer operator until birth of first child; husband (Mr G. 7. P.) an engineer; two children. (E. R.)

Mrs H. 3. P.* b. 1931. *Father a labourer, crane driver; mother* a weaver, factory worker before marriage, afterwards factory work, childminding, shop work; two children.* A secretary before and after marriage; husband a teacher; one child. (E. R.)

Mrs H. 9. P. b. 1945. *Father a market gardener, labourer; mother a weaver before marriage, afterwards helped in market garden, shop work; two children.* A trainee nurse in 1970. (E. R.)

Mr K. 2. P. b. 1930. *Father a docker; mother before marriage in domestic service, after marriage munitions worker 1939–67; three children.* A trawlerman, docker; wife (Mrs K. 2. P.) a spinner before marriage, afterwards part-time evening work in mail-order warehouse; six children.   (E. R.)

Mrs K. 2. P. b. 1936. *Father a docker; mother a weaver and munitions worker in the First World War, no paid work after marriage; eight children.* A spinner, later evening work at mail-order warehouse; husband (Mr K. 2. P.) a docker; six children.   (E. R.)

Mr L. 3. P. b. 1919. *Father a mill worker; mother a weaver before and after marriage; cleaner; two children.* War service, labourer, docker; wife (Mrs L. 3. P.) a munitions worker, domestic work, part-time domestic work after marriage; four children.   (E. R.)

Mrs L. 3. P. b. 1922. *Father unknown; mother a mill worker; two children.* Mill work, domestic work, munitions, domestic work after marriage; husband (Mr L. 3. P.) a labourer, docker; four children.   (E. R.)

Mr M. 7. P. b. 1922. *Father a smallholder in Ireland; mother helped on the land; ten children.* Shop work, agricultural work in the Second World War, docker; wife a factory worker before marriage, in domestic work afterwards; three children.   (E. R.)

Mr R. 1. P. b. 1944. *Father a shop worker, clerk; mother a weaver before marriage, afterwards domestic work, evening work at mail-order warehouse; one child.* An engineer; wife (Mrs R. 1. P.) a factory worker, no paid work after birth of child; one child.   (E. R.)

Mrs R. 1. P. b. 1945. *Father a riveter; mother a cook before marriage, childminder after; two children.* A mill worker, factory worker until birth of child; husband (Mr R. 1. P.) an engineer; one child.   (E. R.)

Mr S. 9. P. b. 1925. *His parents died when he was very young and he was brought up by his aunt and uncle, uncle worked in family business; twelve children.* Merchant Navy seaman, engineer; wife a factory worker before marriage and until birth of first child; four children.   (E. R.)

Mr W. 7. P. b. 1940. *Father a soldier; mother a cotton and munitions worker; brought up by grandparents; one child.* A mill and factory worker, labourer; wife a factory worker before and after marriage, clerk; no children.   (E. R.)

Mrs Y. 1. P. b. 1915. *Father on war service, a mill worker in Preston and New England; mother a mill worker; five children.* A mill worker in New England and Preston, nurse, after marriage NAAFI and munitions work; husband war service, building worker; three children.   (L. B.)

Notes

Chapter 1. The Context

1 Elizabeth Roberts, *A Woman's Place: An Oral History of Working-class Women, 1890–1940* (1984).

2 Elizabeth Wilson, *Only Half-way to Paradise: Women in Post-war Britain, 1945–68* (1980), pp. 41–59, examines attitudes to the interconnected roles of women as mothers and paid workers.

3 This study was carried out between 1987 and 1989 with the financial support of Economic and Social Research Council and under the aegis of the Centre for North West Regional Studies in the University of Lancaster.

4 Paul Thompson, *The Voice of the Past: Oral History* (1978; 2nd rev. edn, 1988); Stephen Humphries, *The Handbook of Oral History: Recording Life Stories* (1984); Trevor Lummis, *Listening to History* (1987).

5 John Singleton, *Lancashire on the Scrapheap: The Cotton Industry, 1945–70* (1991).

6 G. Gorer, *Exploring English Character* (1955).

7 M. Young and P. Wilmott, *Family and Kinship in East London* (1957).

8 P. Jephcott, N. Seear and J. Smith, *Married Women Working* (1962).

9 M. Young and P. Wilmott, *The Symmetrical Family: A Study of Work and Leisure in the London Region* (1973; 2nd rev. edn, 1980).

10 R. Firth, J. Hubert and A. Forge, *Families and their Relatives* (1970).

11 Josephine Klein, *Samples from English Culture* (1965).

12 Wilson, *Only Half-way to Paradise*.

13 Janet Finch and Penny Summerfield, 'Social Reconstruction and Companionate Marriage, 1945–59', in D. Clark (ed.), *Marriage, Domestic Life and Social Change: Writings for Jacqueline Burgoyne* (1991).

14 Registrar General, *Census of Population 1951: County of Lancaster*, p. 1, table T.

15 We followed the usual practice of assigning men to a socio-economic group according to their own occupation. Women and children were classified according to the occupation of their husband or father. See Hilary Graham, *Women, Health and the Family* (1984), p. 42. Also note Gorer, *Exploring English Character*, p. 37: 'It would seem that in England women have to take their class position from their parents and, after their marriage, from their husbands.'

16 Mrs L. 3. B., Mr M. 12. B., Mrs M. 12. B., Mrs O. 1. B., Mrs R. 4. B., Mrs C. 7. L., Mrs H. 3. P., Mr C. 8. P., Mrs C. 8. P., Mr G. 6. P., and Mr G. 7. P. were children of respondents interviewed in the 1970s as part of an earlier study.

17 J. Goldthorpe, D. Lockwood, F. Bechofer and J. Platt, *The Affluent Worker in the Class Structure* (1969), p. 157–95.

18 Gorer, *Exploring English Character*, p. 34.

19 S. B. Rowntree and G. R. Lavers, *Poverty and the Welfare State* (1951), pp. 24–5.

20 There were seven of them: Mr B. 3. B., Mrs R. 4. B., Mrs C. 7. L., Mr H. 3. P., Mrs C. 8. L., Mrs R. 2. P., Mr W. 4. B. Two, Mrs M. 11. B. and Mr M. 7. P., had migrated into the area before 1940.

21 Mr L. 5. B., Mrs L. 5. B., Mr R. 3. B., Mrs A. 3. L., Mr K. 1. B., Mrs B. 3. B., Mrs J. 1. B., Mrs L. 2. L.

22 Mr S. 9. P.

23 See chapter 7.

24 John Burnett, *A Social History of Housing, 1815–1985*, 2nd edn (1988), p. 281.

25 S. Pollard, *The Development of the British Economy, 1914–80*, 3rd edn (1983), p. 322.

26 F. Bedarida, *A Social History of England, 1851–1975* (1976), p. 255.

27 Medical Officers of Health, *Annual Reports for Barrow and Preston* (1960).

28 M. Bruce, *The Coming of the Welfare State*, 4th edn (1968), p. 331–2.

29 J. Lewis, *Women in Britain since 1945* (1992), p. 38.

30 Reports of the Education Committee in *Borough of Barrow in Furness: Annual Accounts*, 1920 and 1935.

31 See chapter 9 for a development of parents' and children's attitudes to education. The *Early Leaving Report* (Central Advisory Council for Education, 1954) documents some of the pressures which made children leave school 'early'.

32 See, for example, R. Hoggart, *The Uses of Literacy* (1959); R. Williams *Culture and Society, 1780–1950* (1958); and A. H. Halsey, *Changes in British Society* (1978).

33 Bedarida, *A Social History of England*, pp. 281 and 284.

34 Ibid., p. 256.

35 See chapter 6, section on marriage breakdown, for changing attitudes in some people to marriage both during and after the war.

36 Klein, *Samples from English Culture*, ch. 5: 'Aspects of Change in Working-class Life', *passim*; one of the themes of this chapter is that of people thinking for themselves.

37 Jeffrey Weeks, *Sex, Politics and Society* (1981), p. 252.

38 J. Goldthorpe and D. Lockwood, 'Affluence and the British Class Structure', *Sociological Review*, vol. 11 no. 2 (1963), p. 152.

39 Quoted in Klein, *Samples from English Culture*, p. 279.

40 Some of the work done on the subject of the privatizing of the nuclear family has been done by scholars on the European mainland; see, for example, G. A.

Kooy (Netherlands), 'Urbanisation and Nuclear Family Individualisation: a Causal Connection?', in C. C. Harris, *Readings in Kinship in Urban Society* (1970); Orvar Lofgren, 'The Sweetness of Home: Class, Culture and Family Life in Sweden', *Ethnologia Europaea*, vol. XIV (1984), pp. 44–64.

41 Klein, *Samples from English Culture*, p. 130.

42 Goldthorpe et al., *The Affluent Worker in the Class Structure*, pp. 96–7; Diana Gittins, *Fair Sex, Family Size and Structure 1900–39* (1982), p. 179. She concludes that the increasing practice of contraception was linked, along with other developments, to 'the privatisation of the family'.

43 Bedarida, *A Social History of England*, p. 256.

44 Pollard, *The Development of the British Economy*, pp. 332–3.

45 Klein, *Samples from English Culture*, p. 95: 'Cognitive poverty describes habits of thinking rigidly and concretely without speculation over a narrow range of interests.'

46 Ibid., p. 130.

47 Émile Durkheim, *Divisions of Labour*, (trans. 1947) and *Suicide* (trans. 1951), quoted in G. Duncan Mitchell (ed.) *A Dictionary of Sociology* (1978), p. 7.

48 Mrs H. 9. P.

49 Angus Calder, *The People's War: Britain, 1939–45* (1969). This is a magnificent survey of the civilians' role in and attitudes to the war. Nella Last, *Nella Last's War* (1981) is a fascinating account of one Barrovian's war, based on her diary which she kept for Mass Observation.

50 Mr A. 4. L., Mr B. 3. B.

51 Mrs L. 3. B.

52 C. C. Harris, *The Family and Industrial Society* (1983), ch. 9.

53 Diana Leonard, in *Sex and Generations* (1980), showed that it was still the norm in the late 1970s for young unmarried women to live at home until marriage. We found that this was also true of young unmarried men.

54 M. Anderson 'The Emergence of the Modern Life-cycle in Britain', *Social History*, vol. 10, no. 1 (1985).

55 A. Myrdal and V. Klein, *Women's Two Roles: Home and Family* (1956), p. 190.

56 Jane Lewis, *Women in Britain since 1945* (1992), p. 2.

Chapter 2.   Homes and Houses

1 Mr L. 3. P., pp. 1–2.

2 Mr N. 1. L., p. 4.

3 The Heating and Ventilating Reconstruction Committee of the Research Board of the Department of Scientific and Industrial Research in Heating and Ventilation of Buildings, no. 17 (1945), p. 133.

4 Medical Officer of Health, *Annual Report for Preston* (1970).

5   Mr B. 11. P., pp. 17–18.

6   Mrs B. 11. P., pp. 36–7.

7   Mr and Mrs K. 2. P., pp. 1, 2.

8   See ch. 11 on 'Neighbours and Neighbourhoods'.

9   *County of Lancaster Census, 1971*, tables 19, 20.

10 John Burnett, *A Social History of Housing, 1815–1985*, (1988), p. 282.

11 *County of Lancaster Census, 1971*, tables 19, 20.

12 Elizabeth Roberts, 'Working-class Housing in Barrow and Lancaster, 1880–1930', *Trans. Hist. Soc. Lancs. Ches.*, vol. 127 (1978), pp. 119–120.

13 Medical Officer of Health, *Annual Report for Preston*, (1939 and 1940).

14 Medical Officer of Health, *Annual Report for Lancaster*, (1940 and 1950).

15 *County of Lancaster, Census 1971*, table 19.

16 *Lancashire Evening Post*, 16 November 1966.

17 Mrs W. 5. B., pp. 65–6.

18 Elizabeth Roberts, *A Woman's Place: An Oral History* (1984), pp. 111–12.

19 Mrs H. 5. L., pp. 88, 89.

20 Mrs Y. 2. P., p. 8.

21 Burnett, *A Social History of Housing*, p. 283.

22 G. Browne, *Patterns of British Life: A Study of Certain Aspects of British People at Home, at Work, at Play, and a Compilation of Some Relevant Statistics* (1950), p. 104, table 23; L. Needleman, 'The Demand for Domestic Appliances', *National Institute Economic Review*, no. 12 (1960), table 2; Electricity Council, *Background Information on Electrical Domestic Appliances, Electrical Heating Systems and the Domestic Uses of Electricity* (1981); C. Davidson, *A Woman's Work Is Never Done: A History of Housework in the British Isles, 1650–1950* (1982), p. 160.

23 Mrs H. 5. L., pp. 20–1.

24 See chapter 8, 'Parents and Children'.

25 Alva Myrdal and Viola Klein, *Women's Two Roles: Home and Work* (1966), p. 37.

26 Myrdal and Klein, *Women's Two Roles*, p. 36.

27 Mrs M. 12. B, pp. 39–40.

28 Myrdal and Klein, *Women's Two Roles*, p. 37.

29 Mr and Mrs K. 2. P., p. 108.

30 Davidson, *A Woman's Work*, p. 163.

31 Mrs H. 5. L., p. 18.

32 Quoted in J. Klein, *Samples from English Culture* (1965), p. 297.

33 Mrs P. 6. B., p. 82.

34 Mrs C. 7. L., p. 70.

35 Mr and Mrs W. 6. L., pp. 61, 85.

36 Ellen Ross, 'Labour and Love: Rediscovering London's Working-class Mothers, 1870–1914' in Jane Lewis (ed.), *Labour and Love: Women's Experience of Home and Family, 1850–1940* (1986), pp. 73–99.

37 Carol Dyhouse, 'Good Wives and Little Mothers: Social Anxieties and the Schoolgirl's Curriculum, 1890–1920', *Oxford Review of Education*, vol. 3, no. 1 (1977); and Roberts, *A Woman's Place*, pp. 30–4.

38 Richard Hoggart believed that this was a commonly held view in Northern England; see Klein, *Samples from English Culture*, p. 165.

39 Mr R. 1. P., pp. 55–6.

40 Mr G. 3. L., p. 26.

41 Mrs J. 1. B., pp. 25–6.

42 Mrs W. 6. B., p. 51.

43 Ann Oakley, *The Sociology of Housework* (1974), pp. 156–7.

44 Roberts, *A Woman's Place*, pp. 110–21.

45 Ibid., p. 118.

46 Oakley, *The Sociology of Housework*, p. 159.

47 Leonard Benson, *Fatherhood: A Sociological Perspective* (1960), pp. 310, 307.

48 M. Young and P. Wilmott, *The Symmetrical Family* (1973), pp. 113, 114, 122.

49 Oakley, *The Sociology of Housework*, p. 137.

50 Jane Lewis, *Women in Britain since 1945*, p. 88.

51 Mr R. 1. P., p. 56.

52 Mrs H. 5. L., p. 95.

53 Myrdal and Klein, *Women's Two Roles*, p. 4.

54 Davidson, *A Woman's Work*, p. 193.

55 Oakley, *The Sociology of Housework*, p. 154.

56 Mr G. 3. L., p. 21.

57 Mr N. 2. L., p. 40.

58 Oakley, *The Sociology of Housework*, p. 154.

59 Mrs O. 1. B., p. 14.

60 Ibid., p. 71.

61 Mr and Mrs W. 6. L., p. 48.

62 Mr N. 2. L., p. 41.

Chapter 3. Growing Up – Relationships with Parents – Getting a Job

1 Elizabeth Roberts, 'The Family', in J. Benson (ed.), *The Working Class in England, 1875–1914* (1985).

2 Mr and Mrs L. 3. P., p. 73.

3 Ibid., p. 22.

4 Mrs B. 12. P., in Mr and Mrs K. 2. P., p. 97.

5 M. Abrams. *Teenage Consumer Spending* (1959), p. 5.

6 Mrs L. 3. L., p. 41.

7 Mrs W. 5. B., pp. 10, 11.

8 Mr and Mrs K. 2. P., p. 59.

9 Mr R. 1. P., p. 48.
10 L. Tilly and J. Scott, *Women, Work and Family* (1987), p. 219.
11 Mrs R. 1. P., p. 59.
12 Mrs H. 9. P., p. 21.
13 Tilly and Scott, *Women, Work and Family*, p. 185.
14 J. Klein, *Samples from English Culture* (1965), p. 146.
15 See ch. 6.
16 Mrs B. 2. B., p. 96.
17 Mrs A. 3. L., p. 44.
18 Mrs P. 6. B., p. 33.
19 Mrs B. 12. P., in Mr and Mrs K. 2. P., p. 100.
20 Mr and Mrs K. 2. P., p. 165.
21 Mrs B. 3. B., p. 24.
22 Mr and Mrs L. 3. P., pp. 12, 13, 14.
23 Mrs J. 1. B., p. 4.
24 Mrs E. 2. P., pp. 32–3.
25 Mrs R. 1. P., pp. 9, 10.
26 Mrs. L. 3. L., pp. 39, 42.
27 Mrs A. 4. L., p. 33.
28 Mrs S. 3. B., p. 16.
29 Mrs N. 3. L., pp. 50–1.
30 Eva Figes, *Patriarchal Attitudes* (1970), p. 171.

Chapter 4.   *The Opposite Sex: Courtship and Weddings*

1 J. Klein, *Samples from English Culture* (1965), p. 146.
2 Mrs H. 5. L., pp. 54–5.
3 Mrs B. 11. P., p. 68.
4 Mrs G. 5. P., pp. 32–3.
5 Mrs M. 10. L., p. 71.
6 Mrs H. 9. P., pp. 22–3.
7 Mrs S. 3. B., p. 70.
8 Mrs C. 7. L., p. 31.
9 Mr and Mrs C. 8. P., p. 113.
10 Mr and Mrs T. 4. B., pp. 88–9.
11 Mr and Mrs T. 4. B., p. 27.
12 G. Gorer, *Exploring English Character* (1955) and *Sex and Marriage in England Today* (1971).
13 Mr M. 10. L., p. 100.
14 Ibid., pp. 24–5.
15 Mr T. 5. B., pp. 15, 17.

16 Mrs L. 3. L., p. 44.
17 Mr T. 5. B., p. 14.
18 Mr H. 7. L., p. 46.
19 Mrs L. 2. L., p. 40.
20 Mrs S. 6. L., p. 30.
21 Mrs L. 3. L., p. 46.
22 See chapter 8 'Neighbours'.
23 Mr M. 10. L., p. 71.
24 Mrs L. 3. L., p. 43.
25 Mrs N. 3. L., p. 12.
26 Mrs E. 2. P., p. 32.
27 Klein, *Samples from English Culture*, p. 153.
28 Mrs J. 1. B., p. 75.
29 Mrs B. 11. P., p. 69.
30 Mrs E. 2. P., pp. 41, 40.
31 Mrs L. 3. L., p. 48.
32 Mrs N. 3. L.
33 Mr and Mrs W. 5. L., p. 92.
34 Barrow Medical Officer of Health, *Annual Report, 1970*.
35 Medical Officer of Health Reports for Barrow, Lancaster and Preston, 1960–70.
36 In the UK the percentages of illegitimate births out of total births were as
    follows: 1961 5.8, 1971 8.4, 1988 25.6; *Social Trends*, 1 (1971) table 13, and
    Social Trends, 18 (1988) table 2.23.
37 Mrs L. 3. L., p. 1.
38 Mrs N. 3. L., pp. 64, 66.
39 Mrs H. 6. B., p. 43.
40 Mrs H. 9. P., pp. 17, 27.
41 Mr R. 1. P., pp. 49, 50.
42 J. Lewis, *Women in England since 1945* (1991), p. 42.
43 *Lancashire Evening Post*, 30 September 1966.
44 John Gillis, *For Better, For Worse: British Marriages 1600 to the Present* (1965),
    p. 289.
45 Rachel Reeve, 'Marriage in the Fifties', *Sociological Review*, new series no. 11
    (1963), p. 219.
46 Gillis, *For Better, For Worse*, pp. 285–6.
47 Ibid., p. 294; D. Leonard, *Sex and Generation: A Study of Courtship and Weddings*
    (1980), pp. 138–9.
48 Mrs S. 2. B., pp. 55–6
49 Mrs M. 12. B, p. 26.
50 Mrs R. 1. P., p. 12.
51 Mr G. 3. L., p. 42.

Chapter 5.   Family Planning and Role Relationships in Marriage

1   R. Fletcher, *The Family and Marriage* (1962), p. 148.
2   Mr and Mrs K. 2. P., p. 115.
3   Mr M. 10. L., p. 64.
4   Mr M. 10. L., p. 30.
5   Jane Lewis, *Women in Britain since 1945*, p. 93.
6   Mrs R. 1. P., p. 53.
7   Mrs W. 4. L., p. 25.
8   Mr M. 12. B., p. 1.
9   Mrs L. 3. L., p. 42.
10   Mrs H. 5. L., p. 42.
11   Mrs J. 1. B., p. 11.
12   Mrs T. 2. L., p. 85.
13   Mrs H. 5. L., pp. 111–15.
14   See Barbara Brookes, *Abortion in England, 1900–1967* (1988) for an examination of conditions before the 1967 Abortion Act.
15   Royal Commission on Populations, *Family Limitation* (1949) vol. 1 Cmd 7695, table 14. The Report stated that, of those married between 1900 and 1944, 12 per cent were actually childless and denied using any form of birth control.
16   Mrs O. 1. B., p. 28.
17   Mrs W. 5. L., pp. 60–1.
18   Mrs P. 6. B., p. 62.
19   Mrs H. 3. P., p. 89.
20   E. Roberts, *A Woman's Place; An Oral History* (1984), ch. 3. The empirical evidence on which this particular chapter is based is totally at variance with the views expressed by some sociologists in the 1970s. Bell and Newby, for example (in 'Husbands and Wives: the Dynamics of the Deferential Dialectic', in Diana Barker and Sheila Allen (eds), *Dependence and Exploitation in Work and Marriage*, 1975), argue that husbands retained their *traditional* power of decision-making. The historical evidence on which this assertion is founded is not quoted.
21   *Inter alia*: Helen Bosanquet, *The Family* (1906); Carl Chinn, *They Worked All Their Lives* (1988); Louise Tilly and Joan Scott, *Women, Work and Family* (1987).
22   J. Klein, *Samples from English Culture* (1965), p. 177.
23   E. Bott, *Family and Social Networks* (1971), p. 60.
24   L. Davidoff and C. Hall, *Family Fortunes: Men and Women of the English Middle Class, 1780–1850* (1987).
25   Mr and Mrs L. 3. P., p. 139.
26   Mrs H. 5. L., p. 11.
27   Mrs N. 3. L., pp. 5–6.

28 J. Sarsby, *Romantic Love and Society* (1983), p. 131.

29 Mrs N. 3. L., p. 17.

30 Mr and Mrs W. 6. L., pp. 22, 126.

31 Ibid., pp. 125, 86.

32 Mrs M. 12. B., p. 69.

33 Mr G. 3. L., p. 59.

34 Jane Lewis, *Women in Britain since 1945* (1992), p. 44. The average age of men at marriage in 1951 was 26.8 and 24.6 for women; in 1971 men's average was 24.6 and women's 22.6.

35 Mr S. 9. P., p. 31.

36 Ibid., pp. 30, 32–3.

37 Tilly and Scott, *Women, Work and Family* (1987), p. 176; Roberts, *A Woman's Place*, pp. 110–13.

38 Mrs L. 2. L., p. 51.

39 Mr M. 7. P., p. 31.

40 Mrs M. 12. B., pp. 51, 52.

41 Mrs A. 3. L., p. 33.

42 Mrs W. 6. B., p. 44.

43 Klein, *Samples from English Culture*, p. 164.

44 Mrs S. 3. B., p. 82.

45 Mrs L. 3. B., p. 57.

46 Mr and Mrs L. 3. P., pp. 79, 43–4.

47 Mrs B. 4. L., p. 58.

Chapter 6.   Marriage: For Better? For Worse?

1 L. Stone, *The Family Sex and Marriage in England, 1500–1800* (1977); see also J. Sarsby, *Romantic Love* (1983), pp. 12–3.

2 J. Lewis, *Women in Britain since 1945* (1992), p. 47.

3 J. Klein, *Samples from English Culture* (1965), *passim*.

4 M. Young and P. Wilmott, *Family and Kinship in East London* (1957), p. 15.

5 Janet Finch and Penny Summerfield, 'Social Reconstruction and the Emergence of Companionate Marriage, 1945–59', in D. Clark (ed.), *Marriage, Domestic Life and Social Change* (1991), p. 7.

6 J. Cornwell, *Hard Earned Lives* (1984), p. 15: 'Public accounts are sets of meanings in common social currency that reproduce and legitimate the assumptions people take for granted about the nature of social reality . . . in sticking to the public account, the person doing the talking can be sure that what they say will be acceptable . . . The private account . . . springs directly from personal experience and from the thoughts and feelings accompanying it.'

7 Mr and Mrs K. 2. P., pp. 10, 18.

8   Mr M. 7. P., p. 17.

9   Mrs W. 6. B., p. 39.

10   Mrs H. 5. L., p. 89.

11   Mrs R. I. P., p. 66.

12   Mrs L. 5. B., p. 9.

13   Extensive surveys have been carried out on the gendered nature of leisure time activities in the 1980s; see E. Wimbush and M. Talbot (eds), *Relative Freedoms: Women and Leisure* (1988).

14   E. Bott, *Family and Social Networks* (1971), *passim*.

15   Wimbush and Talbot, *Relative Freedoms*, p. 134.

16   Mr and Mrs W. 6. L., pp. 110–12.

17   Mr and Mrs W. 5. L., pp. 69, 70, 90.

18   Mrs H. 3. P., pp. 12, 15.

19   Ibid., p. 85.

20   Mrs W. 5. B., p. 36.

21   Mrs W. 6. B., p. 39.

22   Ibid., p. 58.

23   Mr N. 2. L., p. 39.

24   Mr T. 5. B.

25   Finch and Summerfield, 'Companionate Marriage', pp. 30–1.

26   Mrs G. 5. P., p. 16.

27   R. Fletcher, *The Family and Marriage* (1962), p. 142.

28   Roderick Phillips, *Putting Asunder: A History of Divorce in Western Society* (1988), p. 564.

29   Mr T. 5. B.

30   Mr F. 1. L.

31   Mrs W. 4. L.

32   Mrs H. 6. L.

33   Mrs P. 6. B., pp. 50.

34   Mrs P. 5. B., pp. 50–1

35   Mrs P. 6. B., pp. 56.

36   Phillips, *Putting Asunder*, p. 557. There was a national rise in the number of divorces in the post-war period, see p. 553, table 13.2.

37   Mrs L. 2. L., pp. 55–6.

38   Mrs H. 5. L., pp. 105–9.

39   Mrs B. 4. L., pp. 23–4

40   Mr S. 7. l., pp. 26, 27–8

41   Mr I. 2. L., pp. 53–4.

42   Mr N. 2. L., p. 48.

43   Mrs P. 3. L., p. 45.

44   Phillips, *Putting Asunder*, pp. 620–7.

45   Gillis, *For Better, for Worse* (1985), p. 318.

Chapter 7. Married Women's Paid Employment

1 Penny Summerfield, *Women Workers in the Second World War* (1984).

2 Mrs L. 2. B., pp. 7, 22.

3 Royal Commission on Population, *Report* Cmd. 7695 (1949).

4 *Economic Survey for 1947*, Cmd. 7046.

5 Jane Lewis, *Women in Britain since 1945* (1992), p.74.

6 Ronald Fletcher, *The Family and Marriage* (1962), p. 132.

7 A contemporary study made in the 1950s of married women workers in Bermondsey found that just over half the wives (and widows) interviewed worked outside the home for wages. Half of them worked part-time (P. Jephcott, N. Seear and J. Smith, *Married Women Working* (1962), p. 164).

8 R. D. Barron and G. M. Morris, 'Sexual Divisions and the Dual Labour Market', in D. Barker and S. Allen (eds), *Dependence and Exploitation in Work and Marriage* (1976), pp. 46–65.

9 Lewis, *Women in Britain since 1945*, p. 80.

10 *Social Trends, 1976*, p. 99 (table 11).

11 Catherine Hakim, *Occupational Segregation* (1979).

12 Lewis, *Women in Britain since 1945*, p. 81.

13 Ibid., p. 75.

14 Summerfield, *Women Workers in the Second World War*.

15 Royal Commission on Population (1949).

16 Even as late as 1988 a European Community labour force survey indicated that 64 per cent of all women working part-time in the UK gave their reason for so doing that they did not want a full-time job. Only 9 per cent said that they would prefer a full-time job but had failed to find one.

17 Lewis, *Women in Britain since 1945*, p. 74; L. Tilly and J. Scott, *Women, Work and Family* (1987), p. 218.

18 Elizabeth Roberts, 'Working Wives and Their Families', in T. Barker and M. Drake (eds), *Population and Society in Britain, 1850–1980* (1982).

19 Mrs. X.

20 Mrs L. 3. P., p. 44.

21 Mr N. 2. L.

22 Mrs W. 4. L., p. 21.

23 Mrs C. 8. P.

24 These women were widowed before or during this period and were under pensionable age: Mrs B. 3. B's mother*, Mrs S. 3. B.'s mother, Mr N. 2. L.'s mother*, Mr S. 7. L.'s mother, Mrs W. 5. L.'s mother, Mrs Y. 1. L.*. These women were divorced or separated: Mrs P. 5. B*, Mr T. 5. B.'s mother*, Mr F. 1. L.'s mother*, Mrs H. 6. L.'s mother*, Mr H. 7. L.'s mother*, Mrs L. 3. L.'s mother*, Mrs W. 4. L.'s mother*, Mrs L. 3. P.'s mother*. Those marked

with an asterisk went out to work because of financial necessity. The others did not work and appeared to manage either on their own financial resources (which in some cases meant state help) and/or with the help of their children.

25 Hilary Land, 'The Myth of the Male Breadwinner', *New Society*, 9 October 1975.

26 Viola Klein, *Britain's Married Women Workers*, (1965); Alva Myrdal and Viola Klein, *Women's Two Roles: Home and Work* (1956).

27 Myrdal and Klein, *Women's Two Roles*, p. 26.

28 Mrs W. 5. B., p. 80.

29 Jephcott, Seear and Smith, *Married Women Working*, p. 165.

30 Mrs H. 3. P.

31 Mrs T. 2. L., p. 52.

32 Myrdal and Klein, *Women's Two Roles*, p. x.

33 Tilly and Scott, *Women, Work and Family*, p. 221.

34 F. Zweig, *Women's Life and Labour*, (1957), quoted in Myrdal and Klein, *Women's Two Roles*, p. 89.

35 Mrs H. 3. P., p. 84.

36 Mrs M. 3. P. interviewed in 1979 as part of an earlier study.

37 Mr and Mrs C. 8. P., p. 85.

38 Mrs R. 4. B. married in 1959, who continued her teaching and writing while raising her children.

39 Mrs L. 5. B., p. 34.

40 Tilly and Scott, *Women, Work and Family*, p. 196; E. Roberts, *A Woman's Place* (1984), p. 137.

41 Myrdal and Klein, *Women's Two Roles*, p. 23.

42 Mrs A. 3. L., p. 65.

43 Ch. 8: section on 'Fathering'.

44 Lewis, *Women in Britain since 1945*, p. 89.

45 Mr W. 7. B., p. 51.

46 Elizabeth Roberts, *Women' Work, 1840–1940* (1988), pp. 24–5.

47 Roberts, *A Woman's Place*, p. 147.

48 Mr and Mrs K. 2. P., p. 84.

49 Mr T. 5. B., p. 41.

50 Mr and Mrs C. 8. P., p. 123.

51 Mr and Mrs W. 5. L., pp. 96–7.

52 Mrs J. 1. B., p. 27.

53 Mr F. 2. L., p. 70.

54 Mr S. 7. L., p. 95.

55 Richard Brown, 'Women as Employees in Industry', in Barker and Allen, *Dependence and Exploitation in Work and Marriage*, pp. 33 and 42–3, for an examination of the importance of 'life-cycle' changes on the working lives of women.

56 Mrs W. 5. B., p. 18.

57 Mrs O. 1. B., p. 33.
58 Myrdal and Klein, *Women's Two Roles*, p. 116.
59 Mr W. 7. B., see above.
60 Mrs W. 6. B., p. 37.
61 John Bowlby, *Child Care and the Growth of Love* (1965).
62 Jephcott, Seear and Smith, in their study of Bermondsey women workers, wrote, 'Provided that arrangements she made about child care were considered adequate by local standards, the decision to work was socially approved' (*Married Women Working*, p. 116).
63 Jephcott, Seear and Smith found that only 21 of the 98 working mothers they interviewed had pre-school age children (ibid., p. 164).
64 See Mr and Mrs K. 2. P. and Mr R. 1. P.
65 Mrs C. 8. L.
66 Mrs B. 2. B., p. 66.
67 Mr I. 2. L., pp. 52–3.
68 Mrs W. 5. B., p. 79.
69 Richard Hoggart, quoted in Josephine Klein, *Samples from English Culture* (1965), p. 187.
70 M. Young and P. Wilmott, *Family and Kinship in East London* (1957), *passim*.
71 Mrs W. 5. B., p. 79.
72 Mrs E. 2. P., p. 42.
73 Mrs S. 3. B., pp. 26–7.
74 Mr and Mrs G. 7. P., p. 34.
75 Mr M. 13. B., p. 46.
76 Mrs E. 2. P., p. 42.
77 Carol Dyhouse, 'Working-class Mothers and Infant Mortality in England, 1895–1914', *Journal of Social History*, vol. 12, no. 2 (1978); and Roberts, *A Woman's Place*, pp. 166–8.
78 The 1951 Census, table 24, enumerates for each country borough and urban area the persons in full-time attendance at an educational establishment in five-year age groups up to 25. Unfortunately, the 1971 Census, which might have shown the increases in pupils and students in post-compulsory education, does not contain data which are comparable to that in table 24 in the 1951 Census. The office of Population Censuses and Surveys is unable to provide these figures, and local authority figures are unable to give a full picture of those in higher education in the post-18 age groups.
79 Preston police records show an inexorable rise in juvenile crime. In 1949 there were 168 crimes committed by juveniles; the figure for 1962 was 628.
80 Jephcott, Seear and Smith, *Married Women Working*, p. 166.

Chapter 8. Changing Attitudes to Childcare

1 Jane Lewis, *Women in Britain since 1945* (1992), pp. 16–26; J. C. Spence, 'The Purpose of the Family': Convocation Lecture for the National Children's Home (1946); D. Winnicott, *The Child and the Family: First Relationships*, ed. J. Hardenberg (1957); J. Bowlby, *Child Care and the Growth of Love* (1953).

2 The reasons why couples planned their families have been widely examined; see for example: Royal Commission on Population, *Report*, Cmd 7695 (1949), pp. 37–44; Diana Gittins, *Fair Sex, Family Size and Structure 1900–39* (1982), *passim*; Elizabeth Roberts, *A Woman's Place: An Oral History, 1890–1940* (1984), pp. 83–93.

3 Christina Hardyment, *Dream Babies: Child Care from Locke to Spock* (1983), p. 226.

4 Mrs B. 4. L., p. 66.

5 Hardyment, *Dream Babies*, p. 226.

6 Elizabeth Roberts, 'The Family' in J. Benson (ed.), *The Working Class in England, 1875–1914* (1985), pp. 1–35.

7 A. Myrdal and V. Klein, *Women's Two Roles: Home and Work* (1956), p. 117.

8 Quoted in Josephine Klein, *Samples of English Culture* (1965), p. 217.

9 Mrs O. 1. B., pp. 40, 58.

10 Ibid., p. 93.

11 Mrs M. 11. B., pp. 8, 9.

12 Mr M. 10. L., p. 66.

13 Barrow Medical Officer of Health, *Annual Report for 1956*.

14 Barrow Medical Officer of Health, *Annual Report for 1965*.

15 Mrs S. 3. B., p. 75.

16 Mrs J. 1. B., p. 64.

17 Mr and Mrs G. 7. P., p. 93.

18 Mrs P. 5. B., p. 42.

19 Bowlby, *Child Care and the Growth of Love*.

20 See note 1.

21 Mr G. 3. L., p. 43.

22 Mr and Mrs K. 2. P., p. 115.

23 Mrs M. 12. B., p. 63.

24 Mrs B. 11. P., p. 66.

25 Mrs H. 6. L., p. 79.

26 Mrs W. 5. B., p. 31.

27 Mrs H. 3. P., pp. 46, 44, 50, 55.

28 N. Dennis, F. Henriques and C. Slaughter, *Coal Is Our Life* (1956), quoted in Klein, *Samples from English Culture*, p. 181.

29 See, for example, Klein, *Samples from English Culture*, pp. 300–2 and 557–61.

30 M. Young and P. Wilmott, *Family and Kinship in East London* (1957), p. 24.

31 Mr N. 3. L., p. 112.

32 Mrs N. 3. L., p. 18.

33 J. Goldthorpe, D. Lockwood, F. Bechofer and J. Platt, *The Affluent Worker: Industrial Attitudes and Behaviour* (1968), p. 155.

34 Mr and Mrs K. 2. P., p. 13.

35 Mr N. 2. L., pp. 41–2.

36 Mr S. 9. P., pp. 35, 38.

Chapter 9.   *Attitudes to Social Conditioning and Education*

1   Elizabeth Roberts, *A Woman's Place* (1984), pp. 12–3.

2   Mrs P. 6. B., pp. 81–2.

3   Mrs B. 2. B., p. 81.

4   Mr N. 2. L., pp. 41–2.

5   Mrs L. 3. L., p. 18.

6   Mr and Mrs W. 6. L., p. 36.

7   Mr and Mrs L. 3. P., p. 76.

8   Mrs P. 6. B., p. 81.

9   Mr B. 4. B., p. 35.

10 Mr M. 12. B., p. 18.

11 Mr and Mrs T. 4. B., p. 69.

12 Mr T. 5. B., p. 53.

13 Mrs H. 5. L., pp. 124–5.

14 Josephine Klein, *Samples from English Culture* (1965), p. 298.

15 H. Perkin, *The Rise of Professional Society: England since 1880* (1989), p. 423.

16 A. H. Halsey *Changes in British Society* (1978), p. 133.

17 Mr H. 7. L., pp. 35, 39.

18 Mr M. 10. L., p. 88.

19 Mrs T. 2. L., p. 67.

20 Mrs B. 11. P., p. 65.

21 Mr S. 9. P., p. 37.

22 Mrs B. 2. B., pp. 24–5.

23 Ibid., p. 80.

24 Mrs L. 3. B., p. 49.

25 Mrs C. 7. L., p. 59.

26 This comment was noted but not recorded on tape.

27 Mrs J. 1. B., p. 33.

28 Mr and Mrs L. 3. P., p. 141.

29 Mrs X, see section on 'Biographical Notes of Respondents' in the appendix 'About the Respondents'.

30 A. H. Halsey, *Changes in British Society* (1978), p. 128.

31 F. Bedarida, *A Social History of England, 1851–1975* (1976), p. 239, on the tendency of grammar schools to isolate working-class children from their backgrounds.

32 F. Zweig, quoted in Klein, *Samples from English Culture*, p. 300.

33 M. Young and P. Wilmott, *Family and Kinship in East London* (1957), p. 28.

34 R. Fletcher, *The Family and Marriage* (1962), p. 149.

35 Dr. Spock, quoted in C. Hardyment, *Dream Babies: Child Care from Locke to Spock* (1983), p. 227.

Chapter 10.   *The Extended Family*

1 R. Firth, J. Hubert and A. Forge, *Families and Their Relatives* (1970), p. 3. This is an exhaustive study of the meanings and definitions of, and attitudes to, kinship, based on field work in a middle-class area of London. Whilst it examines a group different in both social composition and geographical location to that in this study, it is a useful study of some of the attitudes to kinship which were current at the end of the period covered in this book.

2 M. Anderson, 'The Emergence of a Modern Life-cycle in Britain', *Social History*, vol. 10, no. 1 (1985), p. 75.

3 J. Lewis and B. Meredith, *Daughters who Care* (1988); Lynn Hayes, 'Young People, the Family, and Obligation', unpublished Ph.D. thesis, Lancaster University (1991).

4 J. Klein, *Samples from English culture* (1965), p. 186.

5 Mrs M. 11. B.

6 Mrs F. 1. L.

7 Mrs R. 1. P.

8 Mrs C. 8. P.

9 Firth et al., *Families and Their Relatives*, p. 344.

10 Mrs W. 6. B., pp. 2–3.

11 Mrs R. 1. P., pp. 4, 25.

12 See above, note 1.

13 G. Gorer, *Exploring English Character* (1955), pp. 45–6.

14 J. Cornwell, *Hard-earned Lives* (1984), p. 112.

15 Firth et al., *Families and Their Relatives*, ch. 12, 'The Quality of Kin Relations', details examples of resentments in middle-class families.

16 Mrs B. 4. L., pp. 7, 2, 18.

17 Mr I. 2. L., pp. 75, 76.

18 Mr W. 4. B., pp. 13, 14, 28–9.

19 Mr P. 5. B., p. 9.

20 Mr W. 7. B., p. 11.

21 Mr A. 4. L., pp. 12, 19.

22 Mrs Y. 1. L., pp. 45, 46.

23 Mrs W. 5. B., pp. 27, 37.

24 Mr S. 7. L., p. 90.

25 Mr I. 2. L., pp. 75, 76.

26 J. Finch, *Family obligations and Social Change* (1989), pp. 180–1.

27 Mrs H. 3. P., p. 38.

28 Mrs W. 6. B., pp. 39, 42.

29 Mrs L. 3. P., pp. 45, 46.

30 Mr H. 7. L., pp. 22, 31.

31 Mrs L. 2. L., p. 43.

32 Mrs F. 1. L., pp. 74, 55.

33 Mr K. 1. B.

34 P. Townsend, *The Family Life of Old People: An Enquiry in East London* (1957), p. 25.

35 Mrs B. 10. P., p. 10.

36 M. Young and P. Wilmott, *Family and Kinship in East London* (1957), p. 61.

37 Mr and Mrs K. 2. P., p. 194.

38 Mrs T. 2. L., p. 93.

39 M. Grieco, *Keeping It in the Family: Social Networks and Employment Change* (1987), p. 2.

40 Mr and Mrs G. 7. P., pp. 69–70.

41 Young and Wilmott, *Family and Kinship*, ch. 3, for the importance of links between mothers and daughters.

42 Mr and Mrs W. 6. L., p. 86.

43 Mr and Mrs W. 5. L., p. 62.

44 Mrs O. 1. B., pp. 26–7.

45 Mr and Mrs G. 7. P., pp. 68–9.

46 Mrs Y. 2. P., pp. 8–9.

47 See, for example, Mr G. 6. P.

48 Mr and Mrs W. 5. L., pp. 76, 77, 78.

49 M. Anderson, 'The Impact on the Family Relationships of the Elderly of Changes since Victorian Times in Governmental Income', in E. Shanas and M. B. Sussman (eds), *Family, Bureaucracy and the Elderly* (1977), pp. 36–59.

50 Finch, *Family Obligations and Social Change* (1987), p. 178.

Chapter 11.   Neighbours and Neighbourhoods

1 Josephine Klein, *Samples from English Culture* (1965).

2 Elizabeth Roberts, *A Woman's Place* (1984).

3 G. Gorer, *Exploring English Character* (1955), p. 52.

4 Klein, *Samples from English Culture*, p. 142.

5   Ibid., p. 130.
6   Mrs B. 11. P., p. 47
7   Mrs B. 11. P., pp. 50, 51.
8   Mr W. 7. P., p. 13.
9   Klein, *Samples from English Culture*, p. 276.
10 Mrs B. 11. P., p. 54.
11 Ibid., p. 56.
12 Mr W. 7. P., pp. 51–2.
13 M. Broady, 'The Organisation of Coronation Street Parties', *Sociological Review*, new series, vol. IV (1956).
14 Mr W. 7. P., pp. 45–6.
15 Ibid., pp. 51–2.
16 Mrs M. 12. B., p. 48.
17 Mr and Mrs G. 7. P., p. 45.
18 Mr and Mrs K. 2. P., p. 60.
19 Ibid., p. 61.
20 Mr W. 7. P., p. 12.
21 Klein, *Samples from English Culture*, p. 128.
22 Mr M. 10. L., p. 69.
23 Mr and Mrs G. 7. P., p. 36.
24 Mr S. 9. P., p. 50.
25 Mr M. 10. L., p. 41.
26 Mr N. 2. L., p. 23.
27 It was estimated that in the period 1955–65, 4,142 unfit dwellings were demolished in Preston (*Lancashire Evening Post*, 16 November 1966).
28 Mrs W. 6. B., p. 4.
29 Mr and Mrs K. 2. P., p. 53.
30 Mrs L. 3. B., p. 66.
31 Mrs W. 2. L., p. 47.
32 Mrs S. 3. B., pp. 45–6.
33 Mrs L. 3. B., pp. 34, 64, 47.
34 Mrs A. 4. L., pp. 38, 49, 66.
35 Klein, *Samples from English Culture*, pp. 236–7.
36 Mrs A. 4. L., p. 48.
37 Mr T. 5. B., p. 4.
38 Mr. T. 5. B., pp. 4–5.
39 Mr T. 5. B., p. 65.
40 Ibid., pp. 33–4.
41 Mrs H. 3. P., p. 47.
42 Mrs B. 4. L., p. 15.
43 Klein, *Samples from English Culture*, pp. 210–11.
44 Mrs O. 1. B., see 'About the Respondents'.

45 Mr K. 1. B., p. 26. There were no clear examples in the study of what had been described as 'suburban neurosis' but there was unhappiness and loneliness; cf. Jane Lewis, *Women in England, 1870–1950*, p. 116; and Stephen Taylor, 'The Suburban Neurosis', *The Lancet*, 26 March 1938.
46 Mrs L. 2. L., p. 55.
47 Mrs J. 1. B., p. 55.
48 See ch. 9.
49 Mrs T. 2. L., p. 49.
50 Mr and Mrs G. 7. P., p. 21.
51 Mr S. 9. P., p. 49.
52 Mr and Mrs W. 5. L., p. 130.
53 Mrs B. 11. P., p. 51.
54 Mrs B. 2. B., pp. 46–7.
55 Mr T. 5. B., pp. 84–5.
56 Mr H. 7. L., p. 11.
57 Mr L. 1. L., p. 13.
58 Mrs H. 5. L., p. 123.
59 Mrs H. 6. L., p. 3.
60 Mr and Mrs W. 5. L., p. 6.
61 Ibid.
62 J. M. Mogey, *Family and Neighbourhood: Two Studies in Oxford* (1956), p. 156.

Chapter 12.   Conclusion

1 See chs 4, 5 and 6.
2 *Guardian*, 22 June 1990.
3 As late as the early 1980s the great majority of women reported that they saw marriage and motherhood as their main career (J. Martin and C. Roberts, *Women and Employment* (1984)).

Select Bibliography

Abrams, Mark, *Teenage Consumer Spending in 1959* (London, 1961).

Anderson, Michael, 'The Emergence of the Modern Life-cycle in Britain', *Social History*, vol. 10, no. 1 (1985).

Anderson, Michael, 'The Impact, on the Family Relationships of the Elderly, of Changes since Victorian Times in Governmental Income-maintenance Provision', in E. Shanas and M. B. Sussman (eds), *Family, Bureaucracy and the Elderly* (Durham, N. C., 1977).

Anderson Michael (ed.), *Sociology of the Family* (Harmondsworth, Middx, 1971).

Ballaster, Ros, Margaret Beetham, Elizabeth Frazer and Sandra Helson, *Women's Worlds: Ideology, Femininity, and the Woman's Magazine* (London, 1991).

Barker, Diana Leonard and Sheila Allen, *Dependance and Exploitation in Work and Marriage* (London, 1976).

Bedarida, François, *A Social History of England, 1851–1975* (London, 1976).

Benson, John, *The Working Class in Britain, 1850–1939* (London, 1989).

Benson, John (ed.), *The Working Class in England, 1875–1914* (London, 1985).

Benson, Leonard, *Fatherhood: A Sociological Perspective* (London, 1968).

Bosanquet, Helen, *The Family* (London, 1906).

Bott, Elizabeth, *Family and Social Networks* (London, 1971).

Bowlby, John, *Child Care and the Growth of Love* (Harmondsworth, Middx, 1953).

British Family Research Committee, *Families in Britain* (London, 1982).

Broady, M., 'The Organisation of Coronation Street Parties', *Sociological Review*, new series, vol. IV (1956).

Brookes, Barbara, *Abortion in England, 1900–1967* (London, 1988).

Browne, G., *Patterns of British Life: A Study of Certain Aspects of British People at Home, at Work, at Play, and a Compilation of Some Relevant Statistics* (London, 1950).

Bruce, M., *The Coming of the Welfare State*, 4th edn (London, 1968).

Burnett, John, *A Social History of Housing*, 2nd edn (London, 1988).

Calder, Angus, *The People's War: Britain 1939–45* (London, 1969).

Central Advisory Council for Education (England), *Early Leaving: A Report* (London, 1954).

Chinn, Carl, *They Worked All their Lives: Women of the Urban Poor in England, 1880–1939* (Manchester, 1988).

Cornwell, Jocelyn, *Hard-earned Lives* (London, 1984).

Davidoff, Leonora and Catherine Hall, *Family Fortunes: Men and Women of the English Middle Class, 1780–1850* (London, 1987).

Davidson, Caroline, *A Woman's Work is Never Done: A History of Housework in the British Isles, 1650–1950* (London, 1982).

Dennis, N., F. Henriques and C. Slaughter, *Coal is Our Life* (London, 1956).

Durkheim, Emile, *Division of Labour* (English trans., London, 1947).

Durkheim, Emile, *Suicide* (English trans., London, 1951).

Dyhouse, Carol, 'Good Wives and Little Mothers: Social Anxieties and the School-girl's Curriculum, 1890–1920', *Oxford Review of Education*, vol. 3, no. 1 (1977).

Dyhouse, Carol, 'Working-class Mothers and Infant Mortality in England, 1895–1914', *Journal of Social History*, vol. 12, no. 2 (1978).

Figes, Eva, *Patriarchal Attitudes* (London, 1970).

Finch, Janet, *Family Obligations and Social Change* (Oxford, 1989).

Finch, Janet and Penny Summerfield, 'Social Reconstruction and the Emergence of Companionate Marriage, 1945–59', in David Clark (ed.), *Marriage, Domestic Life and Social Change: Writings for Jacqueline Burgoyne* (London, 1991).

Firth, R., J. Hubert and A. Forge, *Families and Their Relatives* (London, 1970).

Fletcher, Ronald, *The Family and Marriage: Britain in the Sixties* (Harmondsworth, Middx, 1962).

Frankenberg, R., *Communities in Britain* (Harmondsworth, Middx, 1966).

Gillis, John, *For Better, for Worse: British Marriages 1600 to the Present* (Oxford, 1985).

Gittins, Diana, *Fair Sex: Family Size and Structure, 1900–39* (London, 1982).

Goldthorpe, J. and D. Lockwood, 'Affluence and the British Class Structure', *Sociological Review*, vol. 11, no. 2 (1963).

Goldthorpe, J., D. Lockwood, F. Bechofer and J. Platt, *The Affluent Worker: Industrial Attitudes and Behaviour* (Cambridge, 1968).

Goldthorpe, J., D. Lockwood, F. Bechofer and J. Platt, *The Affluent Worker in the Class Structure* (Cambridge, 1969).

Gorer, G., *Exploring English Character* (London, 1955).

Gorer, G., *Sex and Marriage in England Today* (London, 1971).

Graham, Hilary, *Women, Health and Family* (Brighton, 1984).

Grieco, M., *Keeping It in the Family: Social Networks and Employment Change* (London, 1987).

Hakim, Catherine, *Occupational Segregation*, Department of Employment, Research Paper no. 9 (London, 1979).

Hajnal, J., 'Age at Marriage and Proportion Marrying', *Population Studies*, vol. 7 (1953).

Halsey, A. H., *Changes in British Society* (Oxford, 1978).

Hardyment, Christina, *Dream Babies: Child Care from Locke to Spock* (London, 1983).

Hardyment, Christina, *From Mangle to Microwave: The Mechanisation of Household Work* (Oxford, 1988).

Harris C. C., *The Family and Industrial Society* (London, 1983).

Harris, C. C. (ed.), *Readings in Kinship in Urban Society* (Oxford, 1970).

Hayes, Lynn, 'Young People, the Family and Obligation', unpublished Ph.D. thesis, Lancaster University (1991).

Hoggart, Richard, *The Uses of Literacy* (Harmondsworth, Middx, 1959).

Holdsworth, Angela, *Out of the Doll's House: The Story of Women in the Twentieth Century* (London, 1988).

Humphries, Stephen, *The Handbook of Oral History: Recording Life Stories* (London, 1984).

Jephcott, P., N. Seear and J. Smith, *Married Women Working* (London, 1962).

Joshi, Heather, 'The Changing Form of Women's Economic Dependency', in H. Joshi (ed.), *The Changing Population of Britain* (Oxford, 1989).

Kerr, M., *The People of Ship Street* (London, 1958).

Klein, Josephine, *Samples from English Culture* (London, 1965).

Klein, Viola, *Britain's Married Women Workers* (London, 1965).

Land, Hilary, 'The Myth of the Male Breadwinner', *New Society*, 9 October 1975.

Last, Nella, *Nella Last's War* (Bristol, 1981).

Leonard, Diana, *Sex and Generations: A Study of Courtship and Weddings* (London, 1980).

Lewis, Jane, *Women in Britain since 1945* (Oxford, 1992).

Lewis, Jane, *Women in England, 1870–1950* (Brighton, 1984).

Lewis, Jane and B. Meredith, *Daughters Who Care* (London, 1988).

Lewis-Faning, E., *Report of an Enquiry into Family Limitation and its Influence on Human Fertility during the Past 50 Years*, Papers in the Royal Commission on Population (London, 1949).

Lofgren, Orvar, 'The Sweetness of Home: Class Culture and Family Life in Sweden', *Ethnologia Europaea*, vol. XIV (1984).

Lummis, T., *Listening to History* (London, 1987).

MacGregor, O., *Divorce in England* (London, 1957).

Martin, Jean and Ceridwen Roberts, *Women and Employment: A Lifetime Perspective* (London, 1984).

Mogey, J. M., *Family and Neighbourhood: Two Studies in Oxford* (Oxford, 1956).

Morgan, D. H. J., *The Family, Politics and Social Theory* (London, 1985).

Myrdal, Alva and Viola Klein, *Women's Two Roles: Home and Work* (London, 1956).

Needleman, L., 'The Demand for Domestic Appliances', *National Institute Economic Review* (1960).

Oakley, Ann, *The Sociology of Housework* (New York, 1974).

Perkin, Harold, *The Rise of Professional Society: England since 1880* (London, 1989).

Pollard, S., *The Development of the British Economy, 1914–80*, 3rd edn (London, 1983).

Phillips, Roderick, *Putting Asunder: A History of Divorce in Western Society* (Cambridge, 1988).

Roberts, Elizabeth, 'Working Wives and Their Families', in T. Barker and M. Drake (eds), *Population and Society in Britain, 1850–1980* (London, 1982).

Roberts, Elizabeth, *A Woman's Place: An Oral History of Working-class Women, 1890–1940* (Oxford, 1984).

Roberts, Elizabeth, 'The Family', in J. Benson (ed.), *The Working Class in England, 1875–1914* (London, 1985).

Roberts, Elizabeth, *Womens' Work, 1840–1940* (London, 1988).

Robinson, Olive, 'The Changing Labour Market: Growth of Part-time Employment and Labour Market Segregation in Britain', in S. Walby (ed.), *Gender Segregation at Work* (Milton Keynes, 1988).

Ross, Ellen, 'Labour and Love: Rediscovering London's Working-class Mothers, 1870–1918', in J. Lewis (ed.), *Labour and Love: Women's Experience of Home and Family, 1850–1940* (Oxford, 1986).

Rosser, C. and C. Harris, *The Family and Social Change: A Study of Family and Kinship in a South Wales Town* (London, 1965).

Rowntree, B. S. and G. R. Lavers, *Poverty and the Welfare State* (London, 1951).

Royal Commission on Population, *Report*, Cmd 7695 (London, 1949).

Sarsby, Jacqueline, *Romantic Love and Society: Its Place in the Modern World* (Harmondsworth, Middx, 1983).

Singleton, John, *Lancashire on the Scrapheap: The Cotton Industry, 1945–70* (Oxford, 1991).

Slater, Philip, *The Pursuit of Loneliness: American Culture at Breaking Point* (Boston, Mass., 1970).

Social Trends (London, 1971, 1976, 1988).

Spence, J. C., 'The Purpose of the Family', Convocation Lecture for the National Children's Home, 1946.

Stone, Lawrence, *The Family, Sex and Marriage in England, 1500–1800* (London, 1977).

Summerfield, Penny, *Women Workers in the Second World War: Production and Patriarchy in Conflict* (London, 1984).

Taylor, Stephen, 'The Suburban Neurosis', in *The Lancet*, 26 March 1938.

Thane, Pat, *The Foundations of the Welfare State* (London, 1980).

Thompson, Paul, *The Voice of the Past: Oral History* (Oxford, 1978; rev. edn, 1988).

Tilly, Louise and Joan Scott, *Women, Work and Family* (New York, 1978; 2nd edn, 1987).

Titmuss, R. M., 'The Position of Women', in *Essays on the Welfare State* (London, 1958).

Townsend, Peter, *The Family Life of Old People: An Inquiry in East London* (London, 1957).

Weeks, Jeffrey, *Sex, Politics and Society* (London, 1981).

White, Cynthia, *The Women's Periodical Press in Britain, 1946–77* (London, 1977).

Williams, Raymond, *Culture and Society, 1780–1950* (London, 1958).

Wilson, Elizabeth, *Only Half-way to Paradise: Women in Post-war Britain, 1945–68* (London, 1980).

Wimbush, E. and M. Talbot, *Relative Freedoms: Women and Leisure* (Milton Keynes, 1988).

Winnicott, D., *The Child and the Family: First Relationships*, ed. J. Hardenberg (London, 1957).

Woodward, D. and E. Green, 'Not Tonight Dear: the Social Control of Women's Leisure', in R. Wimbush and M. Talbot (eds), *Relative Freedoms: Women and Leisure* (Milton, Keynes, 1988).

Young, M. and P. Wilmott, *Family and Kinship in East London* (London, 1957).

Young, M. and P. Wilmott, *The Symmetrical Family: A Study of Work and Leisure in the London Region* (London, 1973).

Zweig F., *Womens' Life and Labour in Lancashire* (London, 1952).

Index